PUTTING A ROOF ON WINTER

Hockey's Rise from Sport to Spectacle

PUTTING
A ROOF ON
WINTER

MICHAEL McKINLEY

GREYSTONE BOOKS

Douglas & McIntyre Publishing Group
Vancouver/Toronto/New York

Greystone Books
A division of Douglas & McIntyre Ltd.
2323 Quebec Street, Suite 201
Vancouver, British Columbia V5T 4S7

CANADIAN CATALOGUING IN PUBLICATION DATA
McKinley, Michael, 1961–
    Putting a roof on winter

    Includes index.
    ISBN 1-55054-798-4

    1. Hockey—History. 2. National Hockey League—History. I. Title.
GV846.5.M252 2000   796.962'09   C00-910555-7

Editing by Brian Scrivener
Text design and typesetting by Tanya Lloyd/Spotlight Designs
Jacket design by Peter Cocking
Jacket photograph courtesy of Notman Photographic Archives,
    McCord Museum of Canadian History, Montreal
Printed and bound in Canada by Friesens
Printed on acid-free paper

We gratefully acknowledge the financial support of the Canada Council for
the Arts, the British Columbia Ministry of Tourism, Small Business and
Culture, and the Government of Canada through the Book Publishing
Industry Development Program (BPIDP) for our publishing activities.

ACKNOWLEDGMENTS

This book has had many helpers, and my debt of gratitude owes them all. As a complete list would run pages, those named below took regular shifts as the story herein played itself out. So, thanks to Nancy Merritt Bell, muse; Rob Sanders, publisher; Brian Scrivener, editor; Peter Cocking, designer; Tanya Lloyd, typesetter; Phil Pritchard, Jane Rodney, Craig Campbell, Jeff Davis, and Andrew Bergant, both current and ex of the Hockey Hall of Fame; the staff at the National Archives of Canada, as well as those at the Metro Toronto Reference Library, the Provincial Archives of Ontario, Cambridge University, McGill University, Public Archives of Nova Scotia, the New York Public Library, Columbia University, the University of British Columbia, and the Vancouver Public Library; Bill Fitsell, Charles Coleman, Eric Whitehead, Dick Beddoes, Roy MacSkimming, Russ Conway, William Houston, Roy MacGregor, Douglas Hunter, Alison Griffiths and David Cruise, Michel Vigneault, and all those hockey writers whose own works have so much helped this one. Lastly, I would like to thank James Creighton for having a great idea, and for not keeping it to himself.

In memory of the Rocket,
who blew the roof off.

CONTENTS

1

"THE MAN WHO INVENTED HOCKEY"

It was St. Patrick's Day, that late-winter carousal when French Montrealers pinned shamrocks over their fleurs-de-lis and joined their Irish brethren to celebrate the fifth-century missionary who freed Ireland from its snakes. But on this St. Patrick's Day, the people of Montreal were not in a festive mood. When NHL referee Red Storey woke up that March 17, 1955 morning and turned on the radio, the announcer posed a menacing question. "Is this St. Patrick's Day," he asked, "or blow up the Sun-Life Building Day?"

The Sun-Life Building, the largest edifice in the British Empire, was the headquarters of the National Hockey League. And the president of the NHL was one Clarence S. Campbell, an Anglo-Scottish Canadian who was a Rhodes Scholar, a lawyer, a Second World War veteran, and a prosecutor at the Nuremberg War Crimes trial. The people of Montreal didn't care about Campbell's impeccable establishment credentials. To them, he had turned the meaning of St. Patrick's Day upside-down: here the cold-blooded snake had committed the outrage by banishing the saint, a.k.a. the Canadiens' Maurice "Rocket" Richard, from hockey for the rest of the season, and all of the playoffs.

Rocket Richard was not just a hockey player, he was the human battle-standard who led French Canada to glory every week. While francophones might be treated as second-class citizens in the streets of

Montreal and elsewhere, Rocket Richard redeemed them with his heroic exploits on ice.

Throughout the unforgiving rinks of the NHL, the man wearing Number 9 on the back of his Montreal Canadiens' *tricouleur* was the toughest, best player in the toughest, best league. His triumphs were the triumphs of francophones from Rue St. Denis to Chicoutimi, and in this 1955 season he was going to go even higher: after winning his first league scoring-title, he would then avenge the Canadiens' loss to Detroit in last season's Stanley Cup Final. But now all that was ruined, for Richard had been betrayed and humiliated by Campbell, just another in a long line of English bastards.

That St. Patrick's Day night, Rocket Richard, wearing the uniform of a civilian, sat behind the place he usually saw from the other side, the Montreal goal. The people in the Montreal Forum, a building that had barely contained the roof-lifting magic of hockey gods like Vezina and Joliat and Morenz, sat like they were in a mausoleum, taking their cue from the Rocket. Despite being in a battle for first place with Detroit, the Canadiens played as if the Rocket really had died, and the Red Wings were all over them, scoring two quick goals. It was going to be a dreadful night.

Clarence Campbell had no such gloom about him as he escorted his secretary — and fiancée — Phyllis King and two of her female friends into his usual seating block at the Forum. The fastidiously punctual Campbell was late, and everyone noticed. Now, that old electricity — those jolts that would crackle through this building more temple than ice rink — sparked. President Campbell was no longer a coward in his absence, he was a provocateur with his presence. Showing up late in the company of three young women was insult added to injury. Did he understand nothing?

The blithely unaware Campbell and his guests had been dining at the Montreal Amateur Athletic Association and had been delayed. Still, such was his confidence that nothing was amiss that, without any security escort, he put three young women into the line of fire. At first, the ammunition was just boos and catcalls, but soon it was eggs and tomatoes hurled from the seats near the Stanley Cup banners in the rafters, missiles landing on and near the president and his party. He would soon be "Campbell soup," as one fan promised.

Then the unthinkable happened. A fan, his hand outstretched in feigned friendship, slapped the president of the NHL in the face. Nothing like this had ever happened before. This was a hockey rink, where the wars were fought within the confines of the ice, and respect for authority ruled everywhere. This was like smacking the governor general upside the head. Now anything could happen.

When the game was only nine minutes old, it did. Clarence Campbell was saved from the emboldened mob when, suddenly, an explosion belched smoke into the stands. Campbell had been in the army; he knew tear gas when he smelled it.

And just as suddenly, the game was over, forfeited to Detroit, and the fans in the Forum were pushing and shouting and cursing their way onto St. Catherine Street, where they collided with the mob protesting Richard's suspension. The friction soon generated flame, leaping into the St. Patrick's night skies of Montreal as the mob rampaged along three miles of central Montreal, smashing, looting, and baying for blood. This would be the price that the snake Campbell would pay for muzzling their liberator, Maurice Richard. The country that had given the world hockey would now see just how powerful a social force that game had become, for it had just busted out of its icy arena and caught fire. But how did a game born on frozen ponds move the otherwise chilly hearts of a cold climate to this?

That story also begins in Montreal, when, almost 75 years to the day earlier, the very group that francophone Quebeckers raged against on the night of the Richard Riot convened in a fancy ice rink to create something new, something that would move people so much that it would become the meaning of life, and maybe even death, in winter.

———

March 3, 1875 was a cold day. In New York, trains coming from Montreal and the Atlantic were delayed by snow, while they weren't arriving at all in Toronto, which had been blasted by a winter storm wreaking havoc across the northeast. In Boston, news came that the *U.S.S. Gallatin* ice-cutter was steaming north to free nine schooners trapped in the Atlantic ice, and the chill had reached as far London, England, where ice and snow attacked the Home Counties at a time of year when daffodils were usually popping up amid afternoon tea in the garden.

All of this bad weather was good news for James George Aylwin Creighton. On the morning of Wednesday, March 3, 1875, the 25-year-old Dalhousie honours engineering graduate woke up to a cold, foggy Montreal, with the McGill Observatory's thermometer struggling to break 9 degrees Fahrenheit. It would be a chilly day, and an even colder night. As far as James Creighton was concerned, this was very good indeed, for he had a plan. And though his plan was revolutionary, it still depended upon the weather.

With his slender build, thinning hair, and walrus mustache, James Creighton didn't seem the kind of glamorous impresario one might see in the city's salons, conjuring up revolution. After working on the Maritimes' Intercolonial Railway, Creighton was lured to Canada's largest city by the engineering opportunities of the Lachine Canal project, and by the possibilities for a clever young man with quiet ambition.

James Creighton had grown up with hockey surrounding him. Born in Halifax on June 12, 1850, to William Hudson Creighton and Sarah Albro, Creighton and his family lived at 45 Hollis Street, close to Halifax Harbour, whose Northwest Arm was a carnival of winter sports come the freeze. Speed skaters practised their quick, choppy starts; figure skaters carved their artistry into the ice; lovers spooned with languorous, self-absorbed glides; and children like James Creighton, having mastered walking on earth, would try to fly on frozen water.

As a boy, James Creighton would have been first exposed to proto-hockey through the hurley players, and it is from their "ball and stick" sport that hockey comes. Though hurley had existed in Nova Scotia for decades, the arrival in the 1830s of Irish immigrants to work on the Shebunecadie Canal near Dartmouth, Nova Scotia, created a kind of hurley boom.

By the time young James was a toddler, hurley was so popular that it was inflaming the sensibilities of editorial writers in the local newspaper. The January 22, 1853 edition of the *Acadian Recorder* feared that "hurley" or "rickets" and boisterous players wielding their hockey sticks or "hurlies" on Sundays were creating moral and physical dangers to the good citizens of Halifax.

Six years later, hurley had survived the prohibitionists, and a reporter from the *Boston Evening Gazette* ventured into town to find out more about this exciting northern game called "hurley," since Nova Scotia was seen by New Englanders as being the sport's Mecca. The editor added a note to his piece saying he had sent for Nova Scotia "hockey" sticks so that Bostonians could see if they had any hockey talents themselves.

It was this sense of experimentation that Creighton brought with him to Montreal, although he did not begin with hockey. Creighton had grown up playing rugby football, ice hockey, and field hockey, and he had also judged figure skating, following in the tradition of his father, who was one of the sport's most respected arbiters. Once in Montreal, he became a stalwart of the city's rugby football scene and a figure-skating judge at the city's tony Victoria Rink. To the athletic young Anglo men of Montreal, James Creighton was a sportsman of note and clearly a man to be followed. And so they did, under the roof of the Victoria Rink, to make history.

As far as we know, James Creighton simply wanted to help a group of rugby football mates stay in shape during the long winter, and this moved him to bring them indoors to play hockey. Since the art of hockey writing had not yet been invented, there were no reporters in the media room to ask Creighton "Why?" afterward.

Details from other sources are scant, too, and any reconstruction risks imposing Now upon Then, with the result being a kind of "Hockey Night in Ancient Canada." It also makes us realize how much we owe the electronic media for forming and preserving our memory of games, for more often than not, it's that great game we saw on TV (or on the highlight reel on the late-night sports round-up) that fixes in the mind and defines all others. So James Creighton's singular act, one which would come to resonate through the centuries, was not exactly performed in the dark, but in the dusk.

Or rather, under the gaslight of Montreal's Victoria Skating Rink, built in 1862, just below St. Catherine Street between Stanley and Drummond. The 10,000-square-foot rink was the city's biggest and swankest, with filigreed iron beams supporting a vaulted 52-foot-high roof. At night, gas jets cast a soft glow over the ice, while a band played skater's waltzes. The band did not serenade any hockey players, however, for the Victoria (and other rinks like it) was a place only for skating: public skaters, speed skaters, and masquerade-ball skaters were all protected from the snow and the wind by its roof.

It was this roof that appealed to Creighton, too. He and some fellow Montreal athletes had already practised hockey under it, despite the fact that hockey was a resolutely outdoor game. Creighton's role as figure-skating judge held sway with the Victoria Rink's caretaker, who agreed to allow Creighton and his friends inside the forbidden place when it was closed to the public. On Sundays, the players greased the rink keeper's palm, for people still risked the wrath of their neighbours if they defiled the Sabbath with anything looking like fun.

So the indoor game that Creighton and his mates staged on March 3, 1875 was not an act of mad spontaneity, but a revolution that they had been rehearsing — with every intention of showing it off.

Montreal's *Gazette* newspaper took note, announcing in that day's edition that "A game of hockey will be played at the Victoria Skating Rink this evening between two nines chosen from among the members. Good fun may be expected, as some of the players are reported to be exceedingly expert at the game ..."

The significant detail in the *Gazette's* advertisement is that "two nines"— or two teams of nine players — would take to the ice. Men and women had played freewheeling games of shinny, or "pond" hockey, for decades. Shinny was a wild affair, with as many as 50 or 100 players on skates chasing balls, tin cans, wooden blocks, and even discs of frozen horse manure called "horse apples" in free-flowing improvisation. But James Creighton was going to change that.

Even though the Victoria Rink was huge, its ice surface was relatively small, only 85 feet wide by 200 feet long, so Creighton and his colleagues had to limit the size of their teams to avoid the undignified chaos of too many players and too little ice. Not incidentally, the surface dimensions of this first indoor hockey rink set the precedent for North American rinks, one that stands to this day.

With size and space accounted for, the next order of business was rules. Creighton had taught the game to his Montreal friends using a code of play from his boyhood on Halifax harbour. These rules would later come to be known later as the "Halifax Rules," and they regulated a type of game that seems repressive when compared to the hockey of today.

As Creighton and his friends knew it, hockey was played with a block of wood, a kind of proto-puck that they were not allowed to raise off the ice. Players couldn't raise their sticks above their shoulders, and to score, a player had to send the "puck" through a "goal" marked with stones or rocks on the ice. In Nova Scotia, these goal-markers were placed parallel to the sides of the rink, so players couldn't easily score on a long shot.

When the "pucks" were shot through the rocks, umpires standing in the goalmouth rang their hand bells to acknowledge a fair goal, and the teams would change ends. Since there was no goal net to bulge and trap the puck when it went in, the umpires had to have keen eyes. Then as now, there were frequent disputes between players and referee.

Early hockey's offensive strategy was similar to that of rugby. There were no coloured lines painted on the ice, but players had to keep "on-side," which meant that they couldn't skate ahead of the puck carrier, and they couldn't get behind the opposing defense. The forward pass was allowed in Halifax, but not in that first indoor game in Montreal, so passing was like rugby, too — lateral. It would remain so for nearly another 40 years.

Replacement players were not allowed, so the team that started the game was the one that finished, staying on the ice for the entire 60 minutes, thankful for a 10-minute break halfway through. Goal-tenders were especially challenged, having to stand for the whole game. And, as a further indignity, goalies had to use the same type of stick as the rest of the players.

The hockey sticks used on March 3, 1875 were also courtesy of James Creighton. One of the players in that match, Henry Joseph, recalled that he had never seen a hockey stick until James Creighton imported sticks from back home and used them to teach his protégés the game. The aboriginal Mi'kmaq craftsmen of Nova Scotia had per-fected their art of stick-building courtesy of the hornbeam tree, a tree so strong it was nicknamed "ironwood." Indeed, the popularity of the Mi'kmaq's sticks was such that the province's forest of old-growth hornbeams was nearly wiped out.

On the night of Creighton's historic match, "a very large audience" of 40 people came to the Victoria Rink to watch this exhibition of indoor hockey under gaslight, which, seen from the vista of today's blazing TV lights and thumping rock'n'roll, seems quaintly romantic. Since the two teams came from the Montreal Football Club and the Victoria Rink, it's likely that the spectators were friends and sweethearts, along with those Montrealers of sufficient social standing to be a rink "subscriber."

They would also have been cold. Though the Victoria Rink had a roof, its ice was natural, and there was no heating system to interfere with nature's work. There were no luxury boxes for the spectators either, not even padded rinkside seats. The spectators on March 3, 1875 had to stand, on an eight-inch-high platform that ringed the arena. They probably thumped their feet during the match to keep circulation going, or drew heat from a hip flask.

They might also have ducked a few times, too, for there were no boards or glass between the spectators and the players. The *Gazette* had played upon this danger as being part of the thrill, noting that "Some fears have been expressed on the part of intending spectators that accidents were likely to occur through the ball flying about in too lively a manner, to the imminent danger of lookers on, but we understand that the game will be played with a flat, circular piece of wood, thus preventing all danger of its leaving the ice ..."

Though it was common to play outdoor hockey with a ball, Creighton's use of the flat wooden disc was a legacy of his Nova Scotian boyhood, where such pucks had been used for some time, though "puck" would not yet enter the lexicon until 1876 as far as hockey was concerned. The expressions "puck in, puck out, and pucked" certainly were, referring to situations for putting the ball into play in hurley, which is also one of hockey's direct ancestors.

Creighton and his teammates showed their audience other innovations as well. Instead of marking the goal with rocks or stones, they drove two six-foot-tall metal posts into the ice eight feet apart at each end of the rink and topped them with pennants.

Compared to today's players in their layers of armour (which all too frequently fails to protect them), the men in Montreal on March 3, 1875 were seriously underdressed. Wearing rugby club jerseys, shorts, and long woolen stockings, the players took to the ice without benefit of protective padding, and despite the rule against slashing, anyone who has ever taken up a hockey stick in competition knows that the collision of wood and flesh is unavoidable.

The players' skates were state of the art, as far as Nova Scotia's famed Starr Manufacturing Company was concerned. Ten years earlier, Starr had introduced its revolutionary "spring skate," which allowed the skate blade to be firmly clamped to a skater's boots and fastened easily with a metal lever.

Before this innovation, skaters relied on rope or leather to tighten the blades to their boots — a far-from-perfect method. Since the friction between foot and boot is violent during hard skating, the straps had to be pulled especially tight to keep the blade in place. This must have been painful on cold feet.

For insurance, the blades were sometimes screwed into the boot heel and then strapped on. With the spring skate, players didn't have to worry about the skate falling off or coming loose, and so it allowed them greater control, making their speed and precision all the more intense.

Shortly after 8 P.M. the game began, and the next day's *Gazette* featured the world's first post-game hockey report:

"The game is like lacrosse in one sense — the block [of wood] having to go through flags placed about eight feet apart in the same manner as the rubber ball — but in the main the old country game of shinty gives the best idea of hockey. The players last night ... were as follows: Mssrs Torrance (captain), Meagher, Potter, Goff, Barnston, Gardner, Giffin, Jarvis, and Whiting. Creighton (captain), Campbell, Campbell, Esdaile, Joseph, Henshaw, Chapman, Powell, and Clouston. The match was an interesting and well-contested affair, the efforts of the players exciting much merriment as they wheeled and dodged each other, and notwithstanding the brilliant play of Captain Torrance's team, Captain Creighton's men carried the day, winning two games [goals] to the single of the Torrance nine. The game was concluded about half-past nine, and the spectators then adjourned well-satisfied with the evening's entertainment."

While the dramatic standard set by this account would not bring sweat to the brows of future hockey scribes trying to beat its sense of excitement, the anonymous witness from the *Gazette* is on an anthropological mission to explain this novelty to the masses. Significantly, he fails to note that all of the players in the "Paris of North America" had English or Scottish surnames, a fact that wouldn't have been lost on the city's French or Irish communities, who were excluded from English athletic society.

Two days after the game, on March 5, 1875, the Kingston, Ontario, *Whig-Standard* newspaper published another detail of the night, one as deep in its irony as in its echo, resonating to this day throughout rinks, bar rooms, and NHL board rooms: "A disgraceful sight took place at Montreal at the Victoria Skating Rink after a game of hockey. Shins and heads were battered, benches smashed, and the lady spectators fled in confusion."

Somehow the *Gazette* reporter missed this brouhaha, or perhaps by the time the news had reached Kingston, it had become somewhat embellished. Nevertheless, it hints at the passion the cold game would generate now that it had been moved inside, constrained by space, and so amplified in its speed and force. Even if benches were not quite pulverized, and the lady spectators not chased into the icy streets (which had only been tarmacked five years earlier), indoor hockey would release a Mediterranean heat in both its players and its fans.

With much less room to work, players had to think faster and pass with more precision. On the river, players could outskate an opponent by just heading for the riverbank 100 yards away and cutting into a wide arc around their pursuers. Or they could just whack the ball or wooden block as far as strength would permit to set off a stampede of skaters in chase. Now, under these constraints of space and rules, skill would become paramount, and a hierarchy of excellence would soon develop. So would leagues, and trophies, and then, hockey would become both a business and a profession.

But on that night in Montreal in 1875, there were no such bold predictions. After it was over, the world went about its business none the wiser that something extraordinary had happened in Montreal, something that would alter the social landscape of Canada, and then the world's northern countries, in just a matter of decades. There were probably no shouts of "Encore!" and "Bravo!" and "Maestro!" and champagne receptions at the end of Creighton's experiment. No, there was only the humble fact that a young Nova Scotia engineer had seen a possibility, and, in exploiting it, had given the world its first indoor hockey game.

———

In the cold light of the following day, March 4, 1875, Montreal's *Gazette* made a shocking admission. Reviewing James Creighton's feat, the newspaper reminded readers that "the game of hockey, though much in vogue on the ice in New England and other parts of the United States, is not much known here."

Could a defining clause in the Canadian experience really be a child of the United States? The *Gazette* doesn't say anything more, but its silence raises questions. Were there American James Creightons then staging indoor matches in Boston or New York? Indeed, historian Bill Fitsell points out that references to hockey appeared in the United States in 1802, with the Norfolk, Virginia, *Herald* revealing that boys in the middle and northern colonies were playing "bandy on ice" and calling it "shinny." If Montreal, generally considered "hockey's shrine," is freely admitting in 1875 that hockey is more at home across the border, then whose game is it and where did it come from?

The hunger for some hibernal genius who was responsible for hockey's grand design, some Michelangelo or Bach or Shakespeare of the ice, seems not only natural, but necessary. James Creighton, however, was not hockey's Prime Mover, nor through some icy alchemy did he distill hockey from thin air in 1875. In the absence of hockey's equivalent of the Book of Genesis, though, with the patriarchs helpfully listed in descending order, James Creighton assumes a kingly place, for in being the first person to organize and mount an indoor hockey game, his singular act set in motion a glorious world to come.

The anthropologist Johan Huizinga, in *Homo Ludens,* his classic study of mankind at play, argued that there was something both sacred and theatrical in humankind's sporting instinct, and it is this world James Creighton discovered on March 3, 1875. "Just as there is no formal difference between play and ritual," wrote Huizinga, "the 'consecrated spot' cannot formally be distinguished from the playground. The arena, the card-table, the magic circle, the temple, the stage, the screen, the tennis court, the court of justice, etc., are all in form and function playgrounds, i.e., forbidden spots, isolated, hedged round, hallowed, within which special rules obtain. All are temporary worlds within the ordinary world, dedicated to the performance of an act apart."

James Creighton didn't invent hockey on that winter's night under the roof of that Montreal rink, but rather, he had found its temple. If baseball has its "field of dreams" in W. P. Kinsella's aphorism "If you build it they will come," then hockey's guiding animus could well be "If you move it inside, it will become." Creighton's genius in putting hockey under a roof was to allow it to grow in a kind of sporting hothouse, protected from the harsher elements on which it grew up, yet still fed by them under "controlled conditions." Hockey still needed natural ice (though artificial ice would debut in London in 1876); it just didn't need heavy snow and howling wind banging down on that ice.

It would be indoors where hockey became a sport, gaining definition and character by the very fact of its physical confinement. The "temporary world" of each game in each arena spilled over into the next game, and into the next generation. Hockey would become refined in its structure and rules, it would develop standards to surpass, and it would populate the ice with heroes and their exploits to fire our hearts and minds in the coldest, deadest season.

Ironically, hockey has its origins in summer. Its ancestors are the "ball and stick" games that people have played ever since someone made the inspired discovery that a tree branch could be used to knock a rock back and forth for amusement. In Athens, 400 years before the birth of Christ, the artists sculpting the marble friezes on the Parthenon — the temple dedicated to the wise virgins — depicted a ball-and-stick game, where the two players hunch down over the ball in a proto–face-off position. It is an image Aristotle himself might have noticed while mulling over revisions to his *Poetics,* and one he might have thought of when working out his famous dictum that drama — like hockey — is about conflict.

Eventually, people realized that ball-and-stick games could be played on winter ice, just as they realized there were faster ways to get across frozen lakes and rivers than on leather sandals or moccasins. So the bone skate came to be, which was more a crude pontoon that strapped on to feet to give traction and speed on ice.

In time, the bone refined into metal, and the sandal into a boot; the tree branches and stuffed animals skins that served as "stick and ball" were replaced by carved sticks, and the balls were now expertly made of hard-packed leather. The Dutch, with their frozen canals, perfected the metal ice skate, and by the middle of the sixteenth century, Dutchman Pieter Brueghel had cast his keen artistic eye on winter society to paint *Hunters in the Snow,* which depicts people playing a ball-and-stick game on skates. One man even has his stick raised as if to take a slapshot — 400 years before Boom-Boom Geoffrion thundered the puck off the rink boards of the NHL to win credit as the slapshot's inventor.

This artistic example, though, probably depicts a variation of *kol-ven,* a medieval Dutch antecedent to golf. Its existence is yet again a reminder that though hockey might be "Canada's Game," it had a lot of help in getting its passport.

When the Europeans settled North America in the seventeenth and eighteenth centuries, metal skates and ball-and-stick games came with them. The Irish ball-and-stick game of "hurling/hurley," along with the English game of "bandy" or "wicket," and the Scots "shinty" or "shinny," survived the passage across the Atlantic. However, these games, too, had been played on ice before their players ever set sail for North America.

The *Dublin Evening Post* reports on January 29 and February 2 of 1740 that two teams of gentlemen played "a match of hurling" on the frozen River Shannon. It's quite likely that the game was not confined to the ice of Ireland but also played in any of the northern European countries whose waterways froze in winter.

The European immigrants discovered something even more astonishing than the rigours of a New World winter when they arrived: they discovered that the people already living in North America had these ball-and-stick games, too. The Iroquois of Quebec played *baggataway,* a game popularly known as lacrosse. The Mi'kmaqs of Nova Scotia played a ball-and-stick game called *oochamkunutk,* after the bat or stick with which it was played, and when the Mi'kmaq joined the settlers for games of hurley on ice, they called this different game by a different name: *alchamadijik.*

Warren Lowes reveals in his book *Indian Giver* that George Becket, a white frontiersman exploring the central prairie territory of the Blackfoot tribe in 1745, came upon a field about 100 yards long with four-foot goals at each end. On it, teams of as many as 15 young aboriginals hit a ball made of leather with their curved cherrywood sticks. The Teton-Sioux played a similar game on ice, using two sharp pieces of carved buffalo shoulder bone attached to flat birchwood runners as skates.

The word "hockey" itself is thought to derive either from the French *hoquet* — a shepherd's crook — or more likely from the Iroquois word *hoghee,* meaning a tree branch, which was often used as a stick.

Hockey historian Gary Ronberg, writing in *The Hockey Encyclopedia*, reveals that French explorers traversing the St. Lawrence valley in 1740 encountered a group of Iroquois shooting a hard ball with sticks, shouting out "Hoghee" as they played (and which is said to mean "it hurts").

There is also evidence that in the mid-eighteenth-century New York Dutch communities and settlers in New England played ball-and-stick games on ice, and there had long been an affinity between hockey-mad Nova Scotia and the "Boston States," which helps explain the remark made by Montreal's *Gazette* the day after James Creighton's historic indoor match, the one suggesting that hockey was much better known in New England than in Montreal. In 1783, a British Army colonel based in New York City reported a group of skaters "bearing down in a body in pursuit of the ball driven before them by their hurlies."

The prototypical game that the world knows as hockey, however, was born somewhere in Canada, and probably due to the migration of the Irish and their game of hurley. In Ireland, hurley was a two-tiered game: in the south, it was played by the gentry in summer; in the north, it was played by humbler folk in winter.

The winter game was different, too, more like field hockey or shinty in that players couldn't lift the hard wooden ball up in the air on their sticks nor handle it, as they could do with the soft animal-skin ball in the southern version. The northern game was also played with a narrow crooked stick, rather than the flat round-headed one in the south.

The Clash of the Ash in Foreign Fields: Hurling Abroad reveals that Irish immigrants to Newfoundland (who were not gentrified southern Irish) not only played hurley on ice in the 1780s, they also started hurley riots in Ferryland, Newfoundland, in the same decade. Despite this late-eighteenth-century brouhaha courtesy of the Irish in Newfoundland, it was neither a Newfie nor an Irishman who brought the game to Montreal, but rather an Anglo Nova Scotian.

Hockey's anthropologists and dreamers searching for the game's defining origins look to Montreal, Kingston, and Windsor, Nova Scotia, places that have all — with passionate energy — claimed to have sired Canada's real national sport. Much has been written over the past century advancing one claim over another, but now a kind of grudging consensus has been reached. Early hockey probably achieved its greatest degree of sophistication in Nova Scotia, then was housed, regulated, and established in Montreal, with Kingston being an important hockey centre through the years, but probably not where the game first took root. The real question then is what made Montreal the perfect place for a Halifax engineer to bring his manna called hockey?

—◌◠◌—

In 1873, James Creighton set out for Montreal to work on the Lachine Canal. With a population of 150,000, Montreal was Canada's largest city and the tenth largest in North America, a place that presented a cornucopia of opportunities for an ambitious young engineer.

As Canada's centre of commerce and culture, however, it had also suffered most from the "Great Panic," an economic crisis that then swept the country and the world. Prime Minister John A. Macdonald's government had gone down to defeat in 1873 over the "Pacific Scandal"—corruption charges associated with the building of the transcontinental railway. Canada's new prime minister, Alexander Mackenzie, called a halt to railway funding as the depression deepened. The fact that the company most associated with the Pacific Scandal corruption was headquartered in Montreal was symbolic.

In 1873, public soup kitchens first appeared in the city; by 1875, two of its banks — the Mechanics and the Jacques Cartier—had collapsed in the wake of the failing national economy. Montreal's factories weren't producing because no one was buying. The streets teemed with workers and immigrants who had nothing to do, and no social safety net to catch them when they fell, for the welfare state did not yet exist.

Montreal was also one of the dirtiest cities on the continent, with an open sewer snaking along what is now Rue Sainte-Antoine, which cuts today — as it did then — through downtown Montreal. In 1875, Montreal's new mayor made the construction of an underground sewer a priority, and three years later, at a cost of $259,000, the new system lessened the immediacy of the city's pollution. Even so, sewage still emptied into the great river, which must have preserved some rather unpleasant sights when frozen.

So it was into a depressed, smelly, and frequently desperate city that James Creighton came to make his way. With his engineering degree from a fine university, and with his railway experience, he had employ-ment. With his well-established Nova Scotia athletic pedigree, he had society. Still, there is a mystery.

If Montreal was such a worldly thoroughfare, why didn't the citi-zens of the British Empire's most cosmopolitan redoubt already have the game perfected? How did hockey manage to escape the attention of the people who would turn it into a religion? Why did Montreal *need* James Creighton?

Montreal was certainly a centre of winter life. Like Halifax, Quebec City, and other frigid Canadian centres, Montreal made a virtue out of the winter by staging carnivals. Skating waltzes and snowshoeing par-ties along the St. Lawrence were hugely popular, and in 1870, Montreal inaugurated its lavish winter carnival tradition, staging a massive winter celebration to honour Queen Victoria's son, Prince Arthur, who was stationed in Canada to take officer's training with the Royal Artillery.

There were skating parties and snowshoe exhibitions and fancy-dress ice balls at the Victoria Rink, with Montrealers decked out as powdered ladies of the Court of Louis XIV; foppish Renaissance courtiers; kilted Scottish chieftains; and an exotic mix of *bohèmes* from Greece, Turkey, and the Far East. Yet, until James Creighton moved into the rink in 1875, there was no hockey.

There is, however, a wonderful story that suggests hockey had been in Montreal long before James Creighton. In February 1941, the *Montreal Star* ran a two-part series featuring the reminiscences of the 84-year-old John Knox, whose father was allegedly a Montreal hockey pioneer. In an accompanying photo, John Knox holds up a modern ice skate and hockey glove, a symbolic link to his father, Michael, who played in a hockey match in Montreal in 1837— the year bloody upris-ings stained both Upper and Lower Canada.

One Saturday in February of that year, the "Uptowns" and the "Dorchesters" faced each other on an open air rink above the corner of today's Boulevard Rene Lévesque and Rue Bleury. Knox's father played for the mainly anglophone Dorchester team, who won this first match, and who then challenged a mainly francophone team called "The Canadians" to the title.

John Knox even supplied the *Star* with a roster of the two eight-man teams, left to him in his father's papers. The Canadians were manned by Jev Charlebois, Dollard Roy, Emile Guilbeault, Josh Devlin, Dick Duchesneau, Alex L'Esperance, and Pat Hogan; the Dorchesters featured Jim McLure, Jim Stapleton, J. Perreault, Pete Glennon, Mort Gleason, Paul Joyal, Joseph Dixon, and Michael Knox.

The players' names reveal that the two sides were mainly French and Irish. This reflects the historical truth that the French of Quebec learned hockey from the Irish, as both groups were Catholic, and both were largely excluded from the English cultural and power elite.

Knox's recollection of his father's remembrance of that game's climax is a mixture of anachronism — calling the puck the "rubber" when Charles Goodyear didn't invent vulcanized rubber until 1839; naming positions each man played with terms that did not enter hockey's lexicon until the 1880s — and memories perhaps coloured by 104 years' worth of Saturdays between then and his account. Even so, the game's élan is vivid in the old man's mind:

"Josh Devlin tore out of the centre of the scrimmage ... He went around the goal gathering speed, and at the exact second the rubber passed out to him. He caught it like the expert he was and cut into the centre and went past Dion and Perreault like a shot ... He went right in on Paul Joyal and let fly with a shot of terrific velocity from about 12 feet out. Paul had no chance."

The newspapers at the time made no mention of this significant series, even though they did report on boxing and horse-racing events and were clearly attuned to sporting culture. If that 1837 game really *had* been hockey, then the *Gazette* probably wouldn't have professed such ignorance of it when Creighton staged his indoor game nearly 40 years later. These 1837 matches were not the introduction of "ice hockey" to the world, but almost certainly Irish ice hurley, and just another immigrant pastime on a Saturday afternoon, so not newsworthy at all.

What Mr. Knox's account serves to do is remind us that hurley was in Montreal, too, just as it was in Halifax, but the crucial distinction is that it was an *ethnic* game. Though Montreal was ostensibly a bicultural place where English and French could feel at home, the English had ruled Quebec ever since British general Wolfe defeated French general Montcalm outside Quebec City in 1759. (In fitting cultural symbolism, both generals died from wounds incurred in the battle.)

Then as now, the ethnicity factor in Quebec made the game James Creighton so enjoyed in Halifax largely foreign to the Anglos who ran the ship of state in Montreal. If the game was good enough for the French and Irish, then it wasn't good enough for the English elite.

Until James Creighton came along with *his* game. He was English, educated, a sportsman, and an organizer. He arrived in Montreal three years before the Intercolonial Railway that would link the city with Halifax was completed, and while other Maritimers had doubtless trod streets of the city before him, he possessed the right combination of timing and ability, and he joined the right social circles. This gave him the chance to teach his game to the Anglo rugby players who wanted a winter challenge, and it was the kind of game that they probably saw as superior to that being played by the city's ethnics on frozen ponds.

After taking a first-class honours law degree at McGill University, Creighton played hockey in Montreal for a few more years, helping to develop the organized game, then moved to Ottawa to become an esteemed law clerk and Master in Chancery to the Canadian Senate, helping to revise the country's laws. He married Eleanor Platt, he wrote articles for *Scribners* magazine, and he played on an amateur hockey team in Ottawa called the Rideau Rebels, with two sons of Canada's then governor general, Lord Stanley. The governor general was subsequently moved by this exciting colonial sport to endow it with its greatest trophy, so it's not a stretch to say that James Creighton had a hand in the creation of the Stanley Cup as well.

Though a holder of the prestigious King's Counsel for his legal talents, and the venerated Order of St. Michael and St. George for his service to the state, James Creighton remained modest about his profound contribution to hockey. Had the young engineer not been ambitious, though, and not traveled to Montreal in search of opportunity, had he not possessed a brilliant, provocative mind that loved both order and innovation, then who knows how the fate of hockey might have changed?

It's possible that the Irish and French of Montreal might have combined to bring the game to life, but they lacked the distinct advantage Creighton possessed: he was a member of Anglo society. And as such, had a subscription to the culture of power. He had access to the Victoria Skating Rink, he had the command of 17 English

Montrealers who wanted to learn, and he had the ear and the eye of the "media."

This by no means undermines his achievement, but rather it points up the nature of any enterprise that becomes "history." James Creighton succeeded because his endeavour was worthy of recording, and then imitating. How different things might have been for John Knox's father and his fellow players had a reporter take interest in them. Creighton took a wild outdoor game played by immigrants and aboriginals and elevated it to one played by gentlemen indoors, which gave it order, respectability, and a social structure.

Creighton never dreamed of calling himself the "man who invented hockey," and indeed, it would be wrong in the purely technical sense to do so. Yet in finding hockey's temple, he transformed it so profoundly that it was as good as an invention, for everything that came after came because Creighton had put the first roof on winter by moving hockey indoors. His vision gave hockey the chance to evolve from a rough-hewn pond game into the world's greatest winter sport, and to those who love it, the greatest sport, period.

Despite the magnitude of Creighton's achievement, what was on his mind that night can only be guessed at. His aim was probably no more than that of any sporting spectacle of his time: to play fairly and well, for the honour of the side, and so that those who came out to watch would want to do so again, and the spectacle could soon be repeated.

James Creighton is not known much beyond serious hockey circles, and he has yet to win a place in the game's official shrine, the Hockey Hall of Fame. Part of that is due to hockey's curious institutional memory, one that can compile a Bible's worth of statistics but lose the men who made them. And part of the mystery is due to James Creighton himself, who, near the end of his 80-years'-long life, modestly allowed that he had once been captain of the first regular hockey team in Montreal. Anything he might have thought about the why and how of his indoor spectacle was etched in the ice with his blades on the night of March 3, 1875, when he and some friends skated out to change the world.

2

THE NATIONAL DREAM

It has had quite a life. Indeed, the fact that it's in the second century of its existence is somewhat of a miracle. It has been drop kicked into a frozen Rideau Canal by drunken Ottawa Senators — the hockey team, not the politicians. It has been stolen from a Montreal photographer's studio, and when no ransom was forthcoming, served as a flower pot until its owners came by to collect it.

It has been abandoned by a champagne-fueled crew of Montreal Canadiens on a Côtes des Neiges hill, after they'd stopped to change a flat tire. Onward they motored to a party at their owner's house, only to realize, at the party celebrating their winning of it, that *it* was missing.

It has also been seriously abused. Detroit Red Wing Gordon Pettinger dropped his shorts and used it as outhouse, earning himself a swift banishment to Boston. Colonel John Reed Hammond of the New York Rangers used it as an incinerator, burning the paid-up mortgage to Madison Square Garden in its bowl, earning a 54-year-long "curse" for the Rangers, one mercifully ended in 1994 thanks to the cursed-from-birth Vancouver Canucks.

It has been smooched with, waltzed with, slept with, and met with other intimacies that might make those who believe it the greatest chalice yet devised think twice before they sip champagne from its bowl. It is coveted by huge multinational corporations and little Russian boys; by hip young TV marketing people who love what it can do for ad revenues; and by those hockey fans of a great age, who pray that "next year" will be this year, because it might be their last chance to see their favourites claim the Cup for their own.

Outside of yachting's America's Cup, established in 1851 in the heady globe-conquering days of the first World's Fair in London, England, the Stanley Cup is the oldest professional sports trophy in North America. Its influence, though, reaches across oceans and continents, for each season men advance from the northern hemisphere's various frozen redoubts in their quest to engrave their family name forever on its silver bands. To anyone who has ever set a cold eye on the Stanley Cup and promised to make it theirs, the silver bowl with the long, thick trunk is the whole point of enduring one more brutal winter. Once you come out on the other side, and see the Cup glinting in the spring sunlight, it's a symbol not just of championship, but of survival. And the Stanley Cup's origins are built upon survival, too, for its very existence was proof that James Creighton's roofed hockey experiment had *not* caved in under the winter snows but had achieved such success that it now needed a crown.

Fittingly, the Stanley Cup's life began with a regal celebration. On March 12, 1892, just 17 years after James Creighton staged his revolutionary hockey game in Montreal, there was a feast in Ottawa. Across the street from Parliament at the posh Rideau Club, Ottawa sportsmen and their friends clinked the crystal to celebrate the "Ottawas" hockey club, champions of the two-year-old Ontario Hockey Association.

Though the team was the favourite of Sir Frederick Arthur Stanley (a.k.a. Baron Stanley of Preston, Canada's sixth governor general), he was otherwise engaged. So one of his aides, Lord Kilcoursie, known to his "Rideau Rebels" hockey teammates as Frederic Rudolph Lambert, rose with a message from the Queen's man in Canada.

It was a letter, and no ordinary one at that, not least of which because Stanley hated writing letters. No, its power came in its promise, one that would ring off the chandeliers of the Rideau Club and echo into all the winters to come.

"I have for some time been thinking if there were a challenge cup which could be held from year to year by the leading hockey club in Canada," wrote Lord Stanley. "There doesn't appear to be any outward or visible sign of the championship at present. Considering the interest that hockey matches now elicit and the importance of having the games played under generally recognized rule, I am willing to give a cup that shall be annually held by the winning club."

And so the Stanley Cup was born. It wasn't called the "Stanley Cup" to begin with, as Lord Stanley wasn't a megalomaniac. Rather, the "Dominion Challenge Trophy" would reflect Canada's dutiful membership as a "dominion," or self-governing territory in the British Commonwealth.

Later in that year of 1892, Charles Colville, a captain in the Coldstream Guards and Lord Stanley's aide-de-camp, went back to the mother country to fetch the outward and visible sign of Stanley's promise. Captain Colville visited G. H. Collis, Silversmith, in London's stylish Regent Street, and picked up the trophy that Stanley had commissioned.

About the size of a football and sitting on a cherrywood base, the trophy's bowl was made from a combination of silver and nickel alloy. This simple little trophy cost 10 guineas — about 30 weeks' pay for the average working man in London at the time. Why Stanley didn't commission the trophy in Ottawa or Montreal, where silversmiths were also known to operate, remains a nice colonial irony.

Ever since humanity first started clubbing itself over the head in war, society has valued trophies as a tangible proof of its victories. The word "trophy" is descended from the Greek *trope*, which means "a rout." Appropriately, hockey's greatest trophy came from the battlefield, too, though a moment of military cunning one summer morning in the fifteenth century took about 400 years to morph into the Stanley Cup.

The Wars of the Roses were bleeding into their third decade, and King Richard III was fighting for his crown on Bosworth Field. Though Lord Thomas Stanley's younger brother William had sided with Henry, the Tudor Pretender to the Throne, the cagey Thomas held back his troops on the morning of August 22, 1485, to see which way the battle went. When Thomas's stepson Henry began to take the day, he wisely threw his men into battle on the winning side. A grateful King Henry VII rewarded him with estates and titles, eventually making him Earl of Derby. With the exception of that of Shrewsbury, the Stanley family earldom is the oldest and most esteemed in England — and proof that being late sometimes has its advantages.

The Stanley Cup's father was no stranger to political machinations himself. Frederick Stanley's own father had been a Conservative prime minister of Britain, and both Stanley and his brother sat in the House of Commons, with Canada's future governor general rising up into Cabinet. Stanley served variously as Secretary of State for War, as Secretary to the Treasury, as Privy Councilor in various governments, and, by 1885, as the Colonial Secretary for the British Empire, which was then painting the world red.

Stanley was more than a one-dimensional imperialist, moving the hopes and dreams of the world's peoples like chess pieces around some map in Whitehall. He was, by all accounts, madly in love with his wife, Constance, herself the eldest daughter of the Earl of Clarendon, and theirs was a marriage that created a happy household. As a visitor remarked, Lord and Lady Stanley "seem more like brother and sister to their children, and they evidently get on perfectly."

There were 10 Stanley children in all, but two of them — a boy and girl — died in infancy. Despite his title, his old Etonian background, his service in the Household Guards, and his high government rank, Stanley was a jovial, relaxed father who was full of bad jokes and always game to take the family sailing, or hunting with his pack of beagles, or to the races. On inclement days, he loved to play chess.

He probably thought he'd be seeing much of the chessboard in cold and rough Canada, even though he took up his vice-regal position with enthusiasm. As an imperialist, Stanley saw himself as an important cog in the expanding machine of empire. Queen Victoria thought so, too, and appointed him a Knight Grand Cross of the Order of the Bath in 1880. The Queen also had a soft spot for "Freddy Stanley," finding him more attractive than his stolid elder brother.

But by 1890, Victoria's ardour had waned. Stanley had been in Canada two years and had taken to dodging the Queen's letters, not out of malice, but because he felt his time could be better spent than in writing and answering the damned things. The fact that the Queen of England had a hard time getting a letter out of Stanley makes his "challenge trophy" missive to a bunch of Ottawa athletes all the more remarkable.

Stanley's trophy was not hockey's first. The Montreal Winter Carnival's Cup dated from 1883; the Montreal-based Amateur Hockey Association already had its own Senior Amateur Trophy; and the Ontario Hockey Association, formed in 1890, had the Cosby Cup, which Stanley's beloved "Ottawas" won in 1891.

Lord Stanley's trophy was unique in that it would not be "owned" by any one amateur hockey association or fall prey to the petty wranglings of regional identity. Stanley's suggestion that teams should play for the "Dominion Challenge Trophy" in each other's rinks ensured that regional rivalries would develop. By virtue of making the teams travel, Stanley made Canadians go with them, or at least go along in their hearts. For hockey had won the hearts of Canada, leading the country's *Dominion Illustrated Monthly* magazine, in 1893, to boldly anoint hockey "the National Winter Game."

Stanley didn't encounter ice hockey until the late winter of 1889, when he walked in on the middle of a game at the Montreal Winter Carnival. As governor general, Stanley was following a tradition begun six years earlier, one in which the British Crown's Canadian representative would grace Montreal's winter social season with a little royalty-by-proxy. Since it had long been a royal protocol that the monarch waits for no one, Stanley couldn't be seen lolling in the stands with the hoi polloi.

So he, Constance, eldest son Edward, and 14-year-old daughter Isobel, along with their entourage, arrived in the middle of a hockey match between Montreal's Victorias and Amateur Athletic Association in the bunting-draped Victoria Rink. The Stanley arrival stopped the action dead. The band kicked in with "God Save the Queen," the Queen's loyal subjects applauded, then the match resumed, and Stanley fell under hockey's spell.

So much so that he built an outdoor rink on the grounds of Rideau Hall, his official residence, so he could watch his own private hockey matches. Stanley even tried the game himself, stickhandling the puck through the winter shadows one Sunday afternoon. A few days later, word of the governor general's outing had reached republican New York, where a newspaper huffed that the Queen's representative had stained the Lord's Day with blasphemy — just as the Halifax newspapers of James Creighton's boyhood had railed against similar transgressions nearly four decades earlier. Hockey was competing against nothing less than Christianity for the souls of Canadians on the Sabbath.

Stanley's family followed their father's lead. Isobel played on a Government House team against the Rideau ladies in 1889. When she returned to England in 1893, her contemporary, Miss Emily Lytton, sniffed that the 18-year-old Isobel was "too much inclined to be like a boy and has in consequence lost much of her charm."

Stanley's sons Arthur and Algernon played on a five-aside team at Rideau Hall, and the governor general's "house" team became jocularly known as the Rideau Rebels, featuring Stanley's sons, as well as four members of the Coldstream guards, all kitted out in bright red jerseys. When the Rebels played road games in Kingston or Toronto, they did so in luxury, traveling in the plush comfort in Lord Stanley's private rail car.

By 1893 the City of Ottawa could proudly claim a four-team hockey league and Lord Stanley as a full-fledged hockey fan. Stanley watched Ottawa games from his own vice-regal box at ice level in Dey's Skating Rink, which E. P. Dey had built in 1884 after buying a few lots on the edge of what is now downtown Ottawa. The other 2,500 spectators who could fill the rink to capacity had to make do with cold wooden benches until 1889, when the Ottawa Hockey Club moved across the street and down a bit to display their winning ways at the new Rideau Rink, located on what is now Laurier Avenue East, which also had wooden benches, and was just as cold.

The Ottawa cold was a trifle now there was the possibility of crowning all with the governor general's prize. As champions of the 1892 – 93 season, Ottawa had an aggressively proprietary interest in Stanley's trophy — they thought it should be shipped directly to them. Still, Lord Stanley had foreseen such hubris, and so, anticipating NHL events more than a century later, he created the two-referee system by nominating two trustees for the Cup, whose job was to prevent it from being hijacked by any one team, and so defeat its purpose.

The Cup's first custodians, Ottawa sportsmen Sheriff John Sweetland and publisher Phillip D. Ross, thought the Cup's debut would not be enhanced by handing it over without first seeing the very thing it was intended to encourage: regional competition. So, in the late winter of 1893, trustees Sweetland and Ross decreed that the Ottawas should play Toronto's Osgoode Hall for the championship — in Toronto, no less. Livid, and claiming the champions' right of home venue, Ottawa refused. There was no series — and no winner of the first Dominion Challenge Trophy.

In February of 1893, Ottawa had calmed down. Now part of a five-team league, with themselves, three teams in Montreal, and one in Quebec City, Ottawa was a titan at home. The boys in Ottawa's red-and-black sweaters swept all four visiting Quebec teams from January to March, but the ice in Quebec was not so smooth. When Ottawa lost to their nemesis, the Montreal Hockey Club, they saw their Dominion Challenge Trophy hopes fade. Montreal, as champions of the Amateur Hockey Association of Canada, would finish with a better overall record for the season, and so win the Cup. But there was another problem.

When Sheriff Sweetland traveled to Montreal to present the trophy to the team, the chairman of the Montreal Hockey Club was out of town. Conveniently, the gentlemen of the Montreal Amateur Athletic Association gave Sweetland a warm Montreal welcome and happily accepted the trophy on behalf of their absent colleague.

That sporting gesture made the Montreal Hockey Club furious. Not only had the Cup's trustees done a tawdry end-run by not contacting them directly, but also they had given the trophy to impostors. So the Montreal Hockey Club told the MAAA that they would not accept the trophy under any circumstances, and to send it packing to his Lordship at once.

The Montreal Hockey Club had always practised at the city's Crystal or Victoria Rinks but had no voice in the official affairs of the Montreal Amateur Athletic Association, with whom it had "connected" status. The team felt that they had achieved success on their own initiative and resented the Athletic Association accepting Lord Stanley's trophy on their behalf.

The brahmins of the MAAA, a bastion of Anglo culture in Montreal, would rather walk naked, *en masse*, into the freezing St. Lawrence River than return the governor general's trophy as if it were flawed goods. A special meeting of the directors was called, and, as the MAAA's official history records, "In order not to offend the former governor general of Canada and not to seem ungreatful [sic] in the public's eye, the directors decided to retain possession of The Stanley Cup." Just to be doubly sure of avoiding the wrath of the people, "The public was never informed of the dispute." In superbly Canadian fashion, the first Stanley Cup was won by a committee, in secret.

The first publicly resolved Stanley Cup series came to pass on March 22, 1894, two years after Stanley first announced his prize. Five thousand people crammed into Montreal's Victoria Rink, the largest crowd it had ever hosted, to watch Montreal, in their blue jerseys crested by a twin-winged wheel, face Ottawa.

The crush of fans stood on a platform 12 inches above the ice, or hung with the bunting from the balconies of the rink. Though Ottawa scored the first goal, Montreal went on to win 3–1 in a match coloured by end-to-end play, intense periods of pressure by both teams, and tribal decoration among the female fans. "Every lady almost in the rink wore the favours of their particular club," said the *Gazette*, and "never did belted knight in joust or tourney fight harder than the hockey men."

At the time, newspapers rarely identified their reporters, and the *Gazette*'s anonymous scribe was not shy with his opinion of the match's lesser moments, often sounding like he'd stepped from today's "sports personality" columns. "The referee was not nearly strict enough," the reporter complained, while the ice "conditions could be much improved upon if these great deciding games could be held earlier in the season." There was also the all-too-familiar issue of violence. "Nobody was ruled off, but James and Pulford ought to have been. Hockey is not necessarily synonymous with homicide."

The surviving victors were carried off the rink on the shoulders of their delighted companions, though whether they held the bowl aloft and took a victory lap of their rink is not recorded. And neither are their names on the Cup.

Players names were first engraved on the Stanley Cup in 1907, with those of the Montreal Wanderers etched inside the bowl itself. Though the Montreal Hockey Club would later have its team name added to the trophy, the names of the "first" Stanley Cup champions—Tom Paton, James Stewart, Allan Cameron, Alex Irving, Haviland Routh, Archie Hodgson, Joe Lowe, Bill Barlow, and A. B. Kingan—do not grace the Stanley Cup itself. At the time, it probably didn't even occur to those players to so immortalize themselves, but now it would be unthinkable not to.

Indeed, so cherished has the Cup become that people have tried to get their names on it any way they can. Former Edmonton Oiler owner Peter Pocklington's father, who had no connection other than blood with the Cup-winning Oilers, saw his name added by the team, and then removed in indignation by the NHL, the evidence visible as a series of x's on the thing that's known affectionately today as "The Jug."

The Jug has become the symbol of excellence for grown men who strap on their skates to play the game of hockey. It is an object of desire for women and children, too, and for those other grown men who will never get closer to it than at the Hockey Hall of Fame in Toronto, or when it's on tour to the rinks and malls of North America.

Over the next century, there would be many who would try to make it theirs — not permanently, as Lord Stanley forbade — but just for one shimmering moment, when the whole hockey world could look on with envy or pride and know that for this year, the Jug was yours.

—◊—

By the time the first Stanley Cup was won, accepted, and engraved, hockey had taken hold of the Canadian imagination in the Maritime provinces, Quebec, Ontario, and even Manitoba. In less than two decades after James Creighton's historic match, the game had reached a level of sophistication in which a trophy like Stanley's could mean something.

The game had changed a good deal since James Creighton staged his 18-man match in 1875. Now comprising seven skaters aside, teams played two 30-minute periods, with a 10-minute intermission. Behind the front line of three forwards and a "rover" stood the two defensemen, lining up one behind the other as "point" and "cover-point." The last line of defense, as always, was the goalie, who still had no protective equipment, and could neither fall nor smother the puck to make his saves. Goaltenders had to remain standing in front of their goalposts, now four feet high and six feet wide, a dimension still known to goalies today.

Hockey sticks could now be any length a player wished, though they couldn't be more than three inches wide (a hurley legacy, or possibly to prevent them from becoming clubs). The heel of the blade lay flat while the blade curved upward at the toe, useful for lofting the puck down the ice — an effective method of advancing it before forward passing, and one that remains so in today's dump-and-chase game. Yet "lofting" was not thought sporting in some circles and, though practised in the Maritimes, was banned in Montreal.

The stick's upward blade curvature would have made backhand passing tricky and backhand shots a challenge. Consequently, spectacular displays of individual stickhandling and rebounding were the order of the day, along with bruised shins when the opposing team tried to take the puck from the rusher — and missed.

The puck, now a standardized one-inch-thick-by-three-inches-diameter disc, could be played when it went behind the two metal goal posts. Before 1886, the referee stopped the game each time the puck went behind the goal, an interruption that did nothing to improve the humour of the players.

Despite its eminence today as a Stanley Cup town, Toronto didn't see hockey make a serious visit until 1887, when the Montreal Amateur Athletic Association goalkeeper T. L. Paton went to Toronto to visit his friend Massey. Paton regaled Massey with exciting tales of this game on ice, and the Torontonian was so enthused that he cabled Montreal with an order for 18 hockey sticks, a puck, and — most importantly — a set of rules. Just like ordering the game from the Eaton's catalogue.

Hockey caught on fast in Hogtown. The winter following Massey's initiative, the *Toronto Globe* was reminding the city's residents that hockey "holds the same place in the hearts of [Montrealers] as lacrosse does in the summer," and reported that two teams had been formed by crack athletes to show the game to the Queen City.

Hockey was also gaining a broadly participatory audience, one that further defined the skill — and social milieu — needed to challenge for the Stanley Cup. In the last decade of the nineteenth century, working men's clubs iced teams, as would Nova Scotia miners and barristers. Manufacturing and mercantile leagues had sprung up in Montreal, Toronto, Ottawa, and Winnipeg, while "bank leagues" in St. John, Winnipeg, Ottawa, and Toronto promoted both friendly sporting competition and business.

Women also played hockey in leagues, with the first recorded women's ice hockey match staged at the Rideau Rink in Ottawa on February 10, 1891. As the game evolved, women's hockey teams would come to boast wonderful names such as the "Civil Service Snowflakes" and the "Dundurn Amazons," but at the first recorded women's match, no such tribal identification was in place, with the *Ottawa Citizen* simply announcing that Number Two team defeated Number One team 2–0.

Though women had played the game on the pond for as long as men, they still faced social obstacles when they tried to organize. In

1894, a Queen's University women's team drew the ire of the local archbishop after they challenged the men's team to a scrimmage. The cleric felt the women's desire to play hockey at all was the first blast of the apocalyptic trumpet. The women, suitably chastened, wittily called themselves the "Love-Me-Littles" and continued to play anyway.

In deference to delicate public sensitivities, which could withstand bloody mayhem in the male league but might swoon if a female leg were glimpsed, the women played in long skirts, which they used to tactical advantage. Goalies would spread out their skirts along the goal line to stop the puck, while forwards would take advantage of their billowing modesty to conceal the puck when they stickhandled.

By the turn of the twentieth century, women's hockey matches coloured the whole country. They were even in Vancouver, where winter ice is a rarity, and in Dawson City, where it is not. In 1900, the first women's league was established, stocked by three teams from Montreal, Trois-Rivières, and Quebec City. In that same year, the first-money-making women's matches were staged in Montreal, when the Quebec Society charged admission to a women's game to aid wives of Canadian soldiers fighting the Boer War.

While the rest of the country was creating the social and professional structure by which a game becomes a sport, Nova Scotia was continuing its pioneering of what was now an industry. In 1886, the Starr Company's skate department alone kept one hundred Nova Scotian men in jobs, working 14-hour shifts to meet the company's world sales of 11-million skates between 1877 and 1907. At the turn of the century, a Starr skate would part a player from $2.40 — the 40 cents being the cost of the blade, the boots making up the rest.

Nova Scotia was also home to a potent example of hockey's social division, despite the game's widespread popularity. While the racial segregation that so stained baseball is well known, most Canadians would probably be surprised to learn that Nova Scotia's large black population — largely descended from "Americans" who migrated north during the War of Independence or to escape slavery — also had its own "Coloured League," which iced teams against other black Maritime squads.

In February of 1902, 1,200 Haligonians crowded into Halifax's Empire Rink to see the West End Rangers, "the coloured champions of P. E. Island" skate out in gorgeous gold-and-black jerseys to take on the Seasides, who were the "coloured champions" of Nova Scotia.

It would take more than a half century before a black man would play in the NHL, when on the night of January 18, 1958, New Brunswick's Willie O'Ree pulled on the brown and gold of the Boston Bruins in a game against Montreal. No Montreal headlines announced this pioneering event, and *Hockey Night in Canada,* which broadcast the game, ignored it as well.

By the turn of the twentieth century, hockey had won the hearts of a large segment of the country, and a hierarchy of excellence was rapidly establishing itself. Of course, some places were more excellent than others, and the early years of Stanley Cup play are coloured with epic battles, and one or two mismatches of staggering proportions.

It would take just over a decade from its inauguration for the Stanley Cup to reach the point where it was less democratic than its patron had hoped, and the conditions for winning it would have to be changed. But in between, there were some wild rides.

More than anything else, the creation of a transcontinental railway popularized hockey, opening up the harsh landscape so that Lord Stanley's dream could be realized under a series of roofed rinks that popped up to mark this westward progress.

In 1881, the Government of Canada, after a decade of political skullduggery, payola, and no small amount of bull-headed vision, began construction of what Liberal Opposition leader Alexander Mackenzie had called "an act of insane recklessness."

Yet Prime Minister John A. Macdonald persisted. Aided by the seemingly endless cash of the megalomaniac industrialist Sir Hugh Allan, the national railway would be built. Or rather drilled through the primordial rock of the Canadian Shield and shouldered into the howling Prairie winds, then insinuating itself past the near-impenetrable Rockies, and onward through the canyons of British Columbia to the luxuriant coast. The Canadian Pacific Railway would bring British Columbia into Confederation, get trade flowing east and west — as opposed to north and south — and settle the vast open spaces of the Prairie. And along with the railway would come ice hockey.

On November 3, 1890 — 15 years after James Creighton's indoor match in Montreal — a group of Winnipeg sportsmen convened to form the first hockey club in Manitoba. In honour of their sovereign Queen (and following the example of eastern clubs), they christened themselves the Victoria Hockey Club, and shortly afterward, the "Winnipegs" obliged them by becoming their only opposition.

All matches during that inaugural season of 1890–91 were played on an outdoor rink, and the comfort of standing on a wooden platform under a wooden roof to watch this exciting new game was still a couple of years away. More competition was not, however, and the following season a team of soldiers from Fort Osborne entered the fray, their barracks' rink proving a popular venue for matches.

On November 11, 1892, the Manitoba Hockey Association was born, and that 1892–93 season was called by those who were there "the best hockey the West has ever seen." The Victorias, then barely three years old, had become champions of Manitoba and, with their sights on higher targets, the transcontinental railway opened up a world of possibility.

Allying themselves with their rival "Winnipegs," they made an immodest proposal: a combined squad of Manitoba All-Stars would hop an eastbound CPR train and take on all comers in Canada's patriotic headquarters of Ontario.

The Ontario Hockey Association had been formed the same year as that of Manitoba, but the success of the game in Ottawa, Kingston, and, more recently, Toronto, combined with the Ontarians' "divine right of hockey" to lead them to believe that they would give the westerners a pasting. They couldn't have been more wrong.

The Winnipeggers' tour began with a flameout: fire destroyed the rink that housed their equipment and uniforms. Merchants who had funded the tour dug deeper. With new skates and sticks, and improvised uniforms of black trousers and white jerseys featuring crossed hockey sticks forming a "W," the Winnipeg All-Stars rode the rails eastward.

Led by "The Winnipeg Wonder," Jack McCulloch, a speed-skating champion and dazzling goalscorer, the Manitobans announced their presence in Hogtown on February 8, 1893, handing Toronto's Victoria team an 8-2 lesson in hockey. Two nights later, they sent Osgoode Hall into the frigid night to think about their 11–5 loss.

For their encore, the Winnipeggers marched into uppity Kingston and beat the Queen's University team 4–3. As a reporter for Kingston's *Daily British Whig* newspaper sneered, "What would you expect from fellows who have ice to practise upon the whole year?"

Yet the Winnipeggers were not content simply to beat their eastern hosts; they were also showed them exciting innovations. Montreal crowds were captivated by the Manitobans' new style of "facing" the puck. Instead of hitting sticks together three times before drawing for the puck in what was called a "bully," the Winnipeggers placed the puck between the two players facing off, and after the referee checked that both were ready, called "Draw!" and the puck was up for grabs.

The Manitoba All-Stars also introduced the eastern clubs to the idea of protective gear, wearing shin pads outside their trousers, with their goalie's legs shielded by a pair of cricket pads. They also drew praise for their shooting, masterfully peppering goalies with both forehand and backhand shots.

By the time the series was over, the Winnipeg All-Stars had won eight of their 11 games, losing to teams in Montreal and Ottawa, which *Athletic Life* characterized as two cities where hockey had become "too firmly established to permit its exponents being routed by the plucky westerners, with their comparatively brief experience at the game."

Winnipeg also lost their final match to a combined Toronto team, but they were at the end of a great and grueling road trip, and had also been generously watered and fed by their Toronto hosts the night before the match. Even so, the Winnipeg All-Stars had bested their eastern betters by a combined score of 63 goals to 40.

The Winnipeg All-Stars came home to jubilation, their stomachs filled with feasts, and their heads with possibility. The coming of the railway to the West not only had helped to popularize the game, but also had opened up the idea of a country. Now East-West competition meant something far broader than a game between Ottawa and Montreal, or Kingston and Quebec. Three years later, the western upstarts were ready to take up Lord Stanley's challenge.

On February 8, 1896, the Winnipeg hockey community — now boasting 30 hockey clubs — was ecstatic. As the *Daily Tribune* proudly announced, the Winnipeg Vics were off to Montreal "for the honour [sic] of the Stanley Cup and the Championship of Canada."

In true Stanley Cup spirit, though, there was an argument over refereeing, with Montreal objecting to the Cup trustees' appointment of a Toronto man. The trustees replied that Montreal could forfeit the Cup, so the cagey Montrealers then claimed they needed a postponement to heal three of their "disabled" players. The answer was no: the Winnipeg team was already on the rails, and the show would go on.

Two thousand Montrealers — and 25 noisy fans from Winnipeg — crammed into the Victoria Rink on a cold night to see Winnipeg skate out in bright scarlet jerseys splashed with a yellow Manitoba Bison crest. Their goalie, Cecil "Whitey" Merritt, accented his uniform with his highly practical white cricket pads and a luxuriant walrus mustache.

Montreal boasted a swank mustache of its own on the lip of muscular Mike Grant, whose family's blacksmith business boasted 120 years' existence in Montreal. Despite this civic pedigree, when the horse-cobbling Grant, a three-time Montreal speed-skating champion, was first asked to pull on the elegant V-crested maroon jersey of the Victorias, some Montrealers were scandalized.

The Montreal team was composed — like others competing at the highest levels in Canada — of the sons of the upper classes, and Grant wasn't one of them. The early game was the province of amateur athletic clubs and sporting associations, high above the lower-class rabble knocking each other around on a frozen pond. In the end, Mike Grant's fine, clean defensive play at cover-point, and his teammates' high regard, earned him the captaincy of the club. As even greater testament to his worth, he was asked to referee matches — in his own league — on his days off.

Grant was also one of hockey's pioneer rushing defensemen, defying the convention of the time, where defensive players would often lift the puck high in the air with a powerful flick of the wrists, then give chase. Grant would take the puck behind his net, then gather speed as he shouldered his way down the ice, pulling adrenaline-pumped spectators to their feet along with him.

The Winnipeggers had star qualities all their own, and, though coming from the polyglot west, their players still represented the cream of the amateur ideal. The team's captain, J. C. Armytage, was a 25-year-old ex-Ontarian of multiple sporting talents, as well as a trainer of unparalleled skill. When not heading up the forward line, Armytage put his men through rigorous drills, guaranteed to have them on the ice, said the papers, in the "fittest possible condition."

"Whitey" Merritt, he of "the quick and reliable eye" and the lavish mustache, was a Goderich, Ontario, native who first played hockey in 1873 as an 11 year old. In front of him stood "The Remarkably Steady" Fred Higginbotham at point, and at cover-point, Roddy Flett, a 23-year-old Manitoba native who excelled at football, rugby, lacrosse, curling, and baseball, and who would represent Manitoba in rowing at the Henley regatta come the summer.

Donald H. "Danny" Bain, a fast, clean skater and premier stickhandler, had also packed many sporting honours into his 23 years. Having triumphed as Manitoba's roller-skating and cycling champion, he was also Winnipeg's top gymnast and Canada's trapshooting title holder. When he was 56 years old, Bain won championships in pairs figure skating, and over the course of his life, he added to his silver collection with medals in snowshoeing, lacrosse, and golf. Indeed, such were Bain's athletic gifts that he would be named Canada's All-Round Athlete of the nineteenth century. "I kept at a sport just long enough to nab a championship, then I'd try something else," he said, not entirely kidding, though he managed to stick with the Vics for seven years, three of them as captain.

Rounding out the Vics were Attie Howard, another native Manitoban, and at 25, "the truest shot in the Dominion," while "Toate" Campbell was a gifted bank shooter, sending the puck in on goal off the boards curbing the rink, a common method of eluding hard-charging defensemen like Mike Grant.

Yet on this historic Stanley Cup night, mighty Mike Grant and his teammates were under siege from the opening face-off. After 10 relentless minutes, Winnipeg's captain Armytage put the puck through Montreal's posts, and the Winnipeg fans burst into huddled cheering all over the rink.

One of the boons of the national railway was a companion national telegraph service, allowing the rudiments of hockey broadcasting to connect the imagination of the country with the game on cold winter nights. Hundreds of Winnipeg hockey fans crowded into the Manitoba, Queens, and Clarendon hotels to hear a staggered play-by-play coming down the Canadian Pacific Railway telegraph wires. "Superintendent Jenkins and Mr. Thos. Masters of the C. P.

Telegraphs manipulated the keyboard," reported the *Free Press*, "while Manager Tait, in clarion tones, but with a distinct Scotch accent, sang out the bulletins."

At 9:50 P.M., Mr. Tait was positively operatic as he sang out news of a Winnipeg victory. Cheering rocked the city as "everybody wanted to shake hands with everybody else and for several minutes old enmities were forgotten in the magnificent victory."

Back in Montreal, the vanquished Victorias nobly hosted the West's first Stanley Cup champions to a banquet at the Windsor Hotel. It was a nice gesture, but Winnipeg's supporters could have easily picked up the tab, having won "enough money to start a private bank" betting on the result, crowed the *Winnipeg Free Press*. "No less than two thousand cold plunkers were passed over the Windsor hotel counter after the match to-night, and went down into the jeans of the Winnipeg supporters."

In the wee hours of the morning, after the bets had been paid off and the victory meal digested, a more primal form of worship took place when "the winning of the Stanley Cup was celebrated in a worthy manner. It holds some two gallons of drink, but the Winnipeg crowd were a big, dry crowd, and the cup had to be filled more than once to clear their throats efficiently."

As Lord Stanley had hoped when he bestowed it, the Montreal Victorias were not going to be content to lose their trophy to the wilds of the West, where all sorts of rough frontier indignities might befall it. So, 10 months after their loss, the Montrealers took the train across the snows of December to Winnipeg, to try to get the damn Cup back.

The men from Canada's biggest and most sophisticated city were surprised by Winnipeg's new McIntyre Rink. No frozen pond this, the rink's side boards rose much higher than Montreal's 18 inches, creating all sorts of opportunities for strategically bouncing the puck — and the opponent. Unlike the square Montreal rink, the McIntyre was slightly rounded, its goal posts far enough out from the end-boards to allow the puck to rebound. The Montrealers spent a morning trying to perfect their rebounding under the curious eyes of 700 Winnipeggers — as many people as would sometimes show up for a match in Montreal.

Winnipeg newspapers called the Stanley Cup championship game "the greatest sporting event in the history of Winnipeg," and tickets sold for as much as $12 — enough money to take two dozen people out for a sumptuous meal. Fifteen hundred Winnipeggers jammed into the McIntyre Rink on the night before New Year's Eve to watch a hard-slogging game.

Back in Montreal, telegraph dispatches were boomed out through a megaphone to a huge crowd gathered outside the CPR offices. The messenger was hoarse when the game was done, for the two sides had put the puck through the posts 11 times. In the end, the Montreal Vics had scored one more goal than the home team, and the Stanley Cup's brief first visit to the West was over.

Winnipeg would play for the "Jug" again in 1900, losing to the powerhouse Montreal Shamrocks, but winning it in 1901. The Halifax Crescents came west to take the Cup from Montreal in that same year, and were rewarded with an 11–0 pasting. The Haligonians, however, gave hockey another gift, for their practice of draping fishing nets over their goal posts became adopted by the rest of the hockey world in 1900, and so the "goal net" was born (although indoor roller-polo matches on both sides of the border had seen wire-mesh nets since the mid-1880s).

In less than a decade, the Stanley Cup had gone from being a vice-regal sports trophy to a national dream because the dream could come true for any team good enough to lay down the challenge and get to a train station. The railway had made the big country so accessible that a traveler could go from Montreal to Vancouver in a comfortable 85 hours. If James Creighton had put a roof on Canada's dominant winter sport, the railway made the roof portable.

—⁓—

Hockey's evolution into a controlled indoor "institution" from a loosely organized outdoor game lies largely with the economic, technological, and social development of North America in the mid-to-late nineteenth century. Immigration, industry, and the making of land into a commodity to manage the growth of the city all helped move the folk tradition of the local pond into a secular, urban, marketable product.

The game was lucrative for these "amateur" athletic clubs in cities. From 1893 to 1903, the Montreal Amateur Athletic Association showed a hearty average annual net profit of $2,000, with rink-user fees and admission charges its greatest source of revenue. Gambling also helped shore up the roof, for the chance to win big money on a hockey match attracted a high-rolling element that further defined the game. You could put "2,000 plunkers" and more in your jeans from wagering on Stanley Cup games. Indeed, one of the surest signs that hockey had caught the spirit of the country at the turn of the twentieth century was that the elite clubs of Eastern Canada were arguing about money.

In December of 1901, officials from the Canadian Amateur Hockey League convened in Montreal to sort out what had become a business. As the governing body for three Montreal teams, and for one each from Quebec and Ottawa, the CAHL was keen to establish regulations more suited to the world of commerce: if your team wasn't ready to do battle 15 minutes after the advertised time of the start of the game, then your club would be $10 poorer. Any team defaulting on a game — unless they put it in writing five days in advance — would pay their opponents $100.

Yet the real source of friction lay, as it often still does, in the land of gate receipts. The hockey teams demanded an increase on their share of the gate, from one-third to 40 percent, for after all, it was their toil and talent that kept the punters coming to watch. And they also wanted two season tickets for each of their nine players.

The Montreal Arena Corporation balked in an all-too-familiar way: *they* were the ones taking the financial risk, building and maintaining rinks in order to give the players a venue to showcase their talents. Indeed, the MAC had been formed exclusively in 1898 to build what would become known as the Westmount Arena, at the corner of St. Catherine and Wood Avenue. The Westmount boasted at least 5,000 seats and several thousand standing-room spaces, and, as MAC director William Northey later recalled, the distinction of being "the first rink built exclusively for hockey in the world." In the end, the players buckled under the Montreal Arena Corporation's iron-fisted logic and won only their season-ticket demand. It would be the type of hollow victory characterizing almost all of player-league relations for more than six decades.

On the ice in March of 1902, though, the Montreal Amateur Athletic Association squad was on the edge of more important victory: the Stanley Cup. Even though money now swirled around hockey, and winning the Jug could mean much more of it for the winning club, the Stanley Cup was about being the best.

The gentlemen wearing the MAAA's double-winged wheel on their chests had been the best in the CAHL and had won the right to challenge the Winnipeg Victorias. The Jug match had now become a three-game series, as the Cup's trustees had realized the lucrative possibilities for regional rivalry and extended the challenge to create "competitive interest," with increased gate revenue being a tolerable consequence.

The Montrealers and their supporters rode the rails the 1,500 miles out to Winnipeg, with the MAAA taking advantage of whistle-stops to wind-sprint up and down the station platforms before astonished fellow passengers. The city of Winnipeg was once again hot with Stanley Cup fever, and good tickets were nearly impossible to get, even for the outrageous sum of $20. That price would rise to $25 before the game began — double the cost of the best men's silk-lapeled wool overcoats, newly stocked in the shops in time for spring.

And spring it seemed to be. Nearly 5,000 hockey fans turned out for the first game in the middle of a thaw, one that the *Montreal Star* claimed had turned the arena into a "miniature lake." Two thousand of the faithful waited outside the rink, hoping the waters would part to release one of the 50-cent standing-room tickets into their hands to let them witness the impending Winnipeg rout.

The Winnipeg team was big, and the newspapers loved to point out that the Montrealers were small. Montreal's speediest — and smallest — player was Dickie Boon, a 118-pound dynamo whose slaughter was widely predicted when he first entered the league two years earlier at the defensive position of cover-point. Using his small size and punishing speed to advantage, Boon instead crippled his opponents — not with bodychecks, but by stealing the puck and racing away with it.

Team speed was helped by Jack Marshall, a robust forward for the Winged Wheelmen, who had worked in Winnipeg the previous year. Marshall had discovered the speedy tube skates Winnipeg speedskater Jack McCulloch had helped to perfect, and he had imported the skates to Montreal. His small, fast teammates took to them at once.

In that first game in Winnipeg, however, Montreal's speed was hampered by the slushy ice, and no sooner would Dickie Boon be off to the races than the puck would be hydroplaning off out of control. The unseasonable conditions were frustrating to both sides, but Winnipeg managed to endure, winning the first match.

After the false spring, a blizzard returned things to normal for the second match. Even so, the rink was packed with another 5,000 Winnipeggers, who were such devoted fans of hockey that they even cheered Montreal's panache, the spectators' "applause ... so spontaneous and prolonged that one could almost imagine they resided in Montreal."

The change in weather helped the slight, speedy Montrealers by making the ice fast. Jack Marshall and Art Hooper scored twice and Charles Liffiton added another as Montreal took it to Winnipeg with a vengeance. The *Montreal Star*'s sports editor, Peter Spanjaardt, sat at rinkside, filing telegraph reports back to Montreal.

It was Spanjaardt who, in the hot emotion of the second game, while a blizzard howled outside, coined one of the most romantic terms in Canadian sports history. "The heavy bodying of the Winnipegs was a waste of energy," he wrote, "for if the little men of iron from the east were thrown off their feet against the fence they were down only a second ... When the puck whizzed into the Winnipeg net for the fifth time the immense crowd that filled the rink became almost awe-stricken, and whispered 'What manner of men are these Montrealers?'"

The next day's edition of the *Montreal Star* led with Spanjaardt's heroic epithet: "Montreal's Little Men of Iron Won," and so one of hockey's great nicknames was born, despite the fact that goalie Billy Nicholson provided 300 pounds of ballast in the net.

In response to the massive Stanley Cup interest in Montreal, the *Star* announced it would "broadcast" the third and deciding St. Patrick's Day match via telegraph to its offices at St. Catherine and Peel and in Point St. Charles, as well as to the Montreal Amateur Athletic Association gymnasium. At each venue, Montrealers would crowd together to await word on whether these Little Men were truly made of iron, or of ice.

With the temperature at 10 degrees below zero and the ice hard and fast, the conditions for the last match — and the betting money — favoured the speedy Montrealers. Little Dickie Boon was the "brightest star" in Montreal's firmament, though Winnipeger Fred Scanlan's sturdy Irish noggin — bandaged though it was — held up long enough for him to be classed in the same league, along with his matinee idol left winger, Tony Gingras.

The fast ice made the game even rougher, with players colliding at full steam, and "nearly all suffered injuries." With only a minute left, and Montreal hanging on to a 2–1 lead, the Winnipeggers launched a furious assault, but they simply ran out of time. "Well, the Cup is Going Back East," the *Winnipeg Tribune* sanguinely announced the next day, and so it did, in style.

After feasts in Winnipeg and Toronto, the Little Men of Iron disembarked to a delirious crowd at Montreal's Windsor Station. The horses set to pull the champions' sleighs were let loose, with people now clamouring for the honour so that they could one day tell their grandchildren they had pulled the men who had won the Stanley Cup through the snows of Montreal back to their clubhouse.

The adulation was all the more remarkable in that Montreal was not unused to winning the Stanley Cup, now having won 10 of them in less than a decade. The Winged Wheelmen were given three civic receptions and diamond rings, the beginning of a tradition that continues to this day when players value their Cup rings as much as having their names engraved upon the trophy. The names "Boon, Marshall, Bellingham, Hooper, Gardner, Nicholson, Liffiton," and the two substitutes "Hodge and Elliot" chimed through countless family dinner conversations, and were claimed in re-enactments of the match by schoolboys and girls at outdoor rinks. The Little Men of Iron had captured that elusive and unpredictable thing — the imagination of the public. And they couldn't have done it had the Stanley Cup not captured it, too.

———*◊◊◊*———

The Stanley Cup champions are those around whom the legends have been forged, and the players who shine brightest are those who won the ultimate prize, or have come close enough to reflect a bit of their own glory upon it. Ottawa knew all about coming close, having suffered double humiliation in their 1897 attempt to become Champions of the World, losing the first game 15–2 to the Montreal Vics, and having their management cancel the second, understating that "it would not be in the interest of hockey generally to continue the present contest."

The Ottawa Hockey Club of 1903, however, were a confident and game bunch. With a season-record six wins and two losses, they were on top of the Canadian Amateur Hockey League. Yet so, too, were the current Stanley-Cup–holding Montreal AAAs, and with an identical record. When the Vics successfully defended the Cup against Winnipeg, they turned their attention to the team from Ottawa, one nicknamed the "Senators."

One player on that magnificent Ottawa squad came by the senatorial nickname honestly. Frank McGee, the Senators' centre and rover, was a 24-year-old Ottawan from a large Irish Catholic family with an impeccable Canadian pedigree. His uncle, Thomas D'Arcy McGee, was one of Canada's Fathers of Confederation, and also the country's first victim of political assassination when he was shot dead by a Fenian gunman in 1868.

McGee's father, John Joseph, was Clerk of the Privy Council, and McGee had grown up in a life of Ottawa privilege, yet one that had in no way softened him as a hockey player. At five-foot-six and 160 pounds — average for the time — and with the strong, lithe muscles of the natural athlete, McGee could not only speed the puck with style and skill into the other team's goal, he could also throw bodychecks so punishing that his mere reputation for them cleared opponents from his path.

What made McGee even more remarkable was his vision — or lack of it. In the winter of 1900, while playing for a Canadian Pacific Railway team in an exhibition fund-raiser for Canada's campaign in the Boer War, McGee took a nasty blow to his eye from an opponent's stick. The papers reported he had only been cut, but McGee's left eye was gone. And so was he.

The one-eyed McGee retired from hockey, and, in an irony not lost on any fan, spent the next two seasons as a referee. Out of his good right eye, though, McGee saw his beloved game in the hands of others, and he wanted it back for himself. Despite the risk of losing his remaining eye, the competitive flame was luring him to once more don the red, white, and black of the Ottawa Senators.

And so he did, on the night of January 17, 1903. The Senators' opponents that night were the glorious Winged Wheelmen of Montreal's AAA, themselves in possession of the Stanley Cup. Frank McGee responded to this sudden elevation in pressure by scoring two goals in Ottawa's 7–1 win. A month later, McGee entertained the governor general, Lord Minto, with a five-goal display to lead the Senators to a 7–6 win over the Montreal Victorias. And a month later — or two months after returning to play hockey — one-eyed Frank McGee joined his mates to play for the Stanley Cup.

The Senators were all Ottawa natives, their hockey sense honed and fortified on freezing days out on the Rideau Canal. Point man Harvey Pulford, like so many hockey players of the day, was a superlatively versatile sportsman, winning national championships in football and lacrosse, as well as the amateur heavyweight boxing championship of Eastern Canada from 1896 to 1898.

Goalie "Bouse" Hutton had also won titles in lacrosse and football and had tied as league-leading goalie the year before with a 1.7 goals-against average over eight games. Cover-point Art Moore had won national championships in lacrosse and football; rover Harry "Rat" Westwick was a lacrosse star; and wingers Billy and "Suddie" Gilmour — with the third Gilmour, Davie, serving as a substitute — were good, hard-charging skaters who could adjust their level of skill according to the temper of the match.

The Senators were lavished with first-class service befitting their nickname on the Canada Atlantic train down to Montreal. With two parlour cars to themselves, Frank McGee and his teammates would have done well to enjoy the luxury, for the first match, March 7, 1903, was the kind best seen through a window.

With rain and sleet pelting down, and the temperature creeping up, the ice was dreadful, and the game, bloody. Ottawa's Harry Westwick, after being whacked on the shins for a third time by Montreal's Bert Strachan, had to leave due to a "bone protruding through [his] skin."

Frank McGee's exalted reputation was no protection either. With the crowd repeatedly calling out "Watch McGee, watch McGee," Montreal's stickmaster Strachan decided this would be easier if McGee were unconscious, and whacked McGee "twice on the head with malice aforethought." The savagery only served to make McGee play harder, though he couldn't put the puck in the net.

Montreal tied the game in the second half, when suddenly, with 90 seconds to go, the referee called time. Two months earlier, Westmount's mayor had pulled the plug in that very arena on a tie game, in case it spilled over into Sunday morning and desecrate the

Sabbath. Thus, the first match of Frank McGee's first Stanley Cup game ended in 1–1 tie at one minute to midnight — to keep the pious burghers of Westmount happy.

The second match was played at the second incarnation of Ottawa's Dey's Skating Rink, the first having been demolished in 1895 to make room for the Canada Atlantic Railway. With 3,000 partisans hollering for the Cup, Lord Minto officiated at the ceremonial "face," while the ladies in his vice-regal party sported Ottawa's colours — conveniently, for their sense of fashion propriety, still red, white, and black.

The warm weather had touched Ottawa, too, and the ice was woeful, with water three inches deep in spots. Even so, the Senators were out to prove to their fans that the ice was *theirs,* and so was the Stanley Cup.

The Senators pummeled the Cup-holding Montrealers 8–0, with the Gilmour brothers accounting for five of the Ottawa tallies, and Frank McGee adding the other three. Though the two-game series was tied, Ottawa had won it on a 9–1 goal differential. Ten years after its birth, Ottawa finally had possession of the prize Lord Stanley had always wanted them to have.

After such a tough series, the Senators hoped to apply a little leisurely champagne to their wounds, but the early Stanley Cup "challenge" years were not for the faint-hearted. No sooner had the Senators laundered their uniforms than the Cup's trustees accepted a challenge from the Rat Portage Thistles, a club formed in 1894 in the logging and mining town of northwestern Ontario that became Kenora in 1905. So two days after their Cup triumph, the Senators were called to defend it.

Ottawa agreed to the challenge because neither they nor the league wanted to disrupt the start of the following season. Still, the Senators wanted to finish the whole affair as quickly as the confines of two 60-minute matches would allow.

Most of Rat Portage's seven-man squad had played together since 1896, when they were still schoolboys. Even so, the men in the white sweaters crested with the green thistles — the prickly national emblem of Scotland — confessed to the *Ottawa Citizen* that their first game was marred by a bad case of "stage fright."

Rat Portage's speedy and handsome winger Billy McGimsie had shown great assurance in his daring rushes, scoring twice, but

Ottawa's Frank McGee and Davie and Billy Gilmour topped him with six goals. The Thistles came out scrapping in the second game, but the ice was bad, and the hockey-fatigued crowd even smaller than the last time, barely cresting 1,000.

Yet while the Rat Portagers were speedy and gritty, Billy and Davie Gilmour combined with a pair by Frank McGee to lead Ottawa to a 4–2 victory. The Thistles had been outscored 10 goals to 4, and even worse, had lost $800 on their Cup adventure, when the low box-office reduced their recoupment share of the gate receipts to nothing. The Senators, on the other hand, had won their second Stanley Cup championship within the week.

The Senators had braved all kinds of hardship in their double championship, but nothing had prepared them for dinner with Lord Minto at Rideau Hall. So they turned to the patrician nephew of a Father of Confederation for advice, and McGee, ever the practical joker said, "Just do what I do."

As the governor general looked on in astonishment, Ottawa's first Stanley Cup champions followed McGee's lead and tucked into the food with their hands. When the finger bowls were set for another course, McGee drank his, and so did the team. Lord Minto, whose own *noblesse oblige* had by now kicked in, followed what was clearly a secret hockey ritual to which he was being admitted. He drank from his finger bowl, too.

The Ottawa club's directors showed their gratitude for a glorious season by giving each player a silver nugget. While actual payment for play might still be forbidden, a little donated precious metal was not. And so was born the sobriquet of the team, who in 1950 would be voted Canada's finest of the half century. From now and forever, they would be called the "Ottawa Silver Seven."

—◆◆◆—

In January 1905, the Ottawa Senators must have figured that fabulous Frank McGee was up to an especially inspired practical joke. After successfully defending their Stanley Cup four times in the previous year, the mighty Silver Seven would find themselves on the receiving end of a most unusual challenge: Yukon gold wanted the Stanley Cup.

Many suggested the gold was of the fool's variety, for the Dawson City Nuggets were a team composed of civil servants, aging ex-players, and one teenager. Yet to understand the story of the Nuggets' grand adventure is to first understand the animus of Joseph Whiteside Boyle, one of Canada's most flamboyant and original characters.

Swashbuckling and prudent, romantic and practical, Boyle was the grandson of an Irish immigrant who had fled the Emerald Isle 20 years before during the Great Famine, a "second son" in search of a little space in which to live his own life. Joe Boyle, on the other hand, wanted to unleash his life to fit all the space the world had to offer. It was only natural that gold should glitter brightest to him.

Within a year of George Carmack's 1896 discovery of the world's most precious metal in the Klondike's Rabbit Creek, prospectors headed north to mine the veins and pan the rivers, dreaming of El Dorado. Tales of a huge gold strike were leaked to the press from a report filed by North-West Mounted Police Inspector Charles Constantine. Indeed, Constantine's estimate that $2.5 million in gold would be mined from the Yukon earth in 1897 was goosed even higher by sensation-hungry news editors to the astonishing figure of $20 million.

By the late spring of 1897, the docks of Seattle and San Francisco were groaning under the weight of Yukon miners disembarking with their plunder — gold squeezed into suitcases, crockery, empty whisky bottles, bodily crevices, and anything else that wouldn't leak. Joe Boyle was in San Francisco then, too, trying to win a grubstake to fund his mission to riches and glory in the Yukon. He would find both, though not in the manner he first might have expected.

Joe Boyle was an adventurer born. Despite his mother's touchingly naive plans for him to be a Baptist minister, Joe collected his graduation papers from Woodstock (Ontario) College in 1884 and hightailed it to New York, to work with his father and two brothers in the horse-racing game. Yet the sport of kings wasn't enough, and one day, when his brothers returned to the rooms they shared with Joe on Lower Broadway, they found a note: "I've gone to sea. Don't worry about me. Joe."

And so, just going on 17 years old, Joe Boyle had set sail for adventure on a barque called the *Wallace*. And adventure he got, in an Errol Flynn Hollywood film come true. In his three years before the mast, Boyle survived a perilous tropical storm en route to India, where he inspired his fellow sailors to pump water from the bilge for days to save their very lives. He even leaped into the sea to rescue a fellow sailor by fighting off an attacking shark with a knife.

It was primal mortality that defined Boyle's life back on land. At six feet and 200 pounds, Joe Boyle was a natural at boxing, but his real brawn was his brain, for his talent lay in making the grand plan — and money off promotion and gambling. It was because of boxing that Joe Boyle found himself in San Francisco in 1897, though at 29, he must have felt himself a distinctly unheroic character: two children dead in infancy, two living with his parents, and two more — one yet unborn — living with his estranged wife, Millie, in New York. He had stolen Millie from his brother, and now he was giving her two-thirds of his liquidated assets as the cost of their failed marriage.

Any thoughts of failure were buried deep in Boyle's complicated soul, for opportunity now called in the person of Frank P. Slavin. A 36-year-old Australian who had once lit up the boxing world as "The Sydney Slasher," Slavin was going to finance Boyle's ticket to Klondike bullion. Unfortunately, the flabby "Slasher" was no match for his opponent, and Boyle's anticipated $1,000 purse vanished like a palooka after the bout. So, too, had Boyle, and while a battered Slavin cussed out his partner, Joe Boyle was off buying steamboat tickets for them to head north. He had taken the precaution of having money wired from Ontario — just in case Slavin should lose.

Dawson City was a circus, filled with all the dreamers, scoundrels, and attendant service industry of whores, hucksters, and saloonkeepers that humanity could serve up. So profitable was the feeding of the 30,000 adventurers swarming Dawson at the height of the gold rush that one restaurant owner retired rich after only a single season. He had made his gold from soup, selling it at the hugely inflated price of a dollar a plate.

Joe Boyle did not immediately strike gold, and over the next eight years, his fortunes would snake like the Yukon River. Boyle's big idea was to consolidate many small mining claims into one large one, and then use the power of water to mine the gold hydraulically, with machines, thus turning the men with pans, sifting in the river, into local colour. Boyle also made money through his timber concessions, for trees grew slowly in the Yukon, and wood had a value almost as great as gold for buildings, mine shafts, railways, and fuel.

Since Boyle was often forced to go to Ottawa to plead his cause to the politicians and financiers, these jaunts provided him with the contacts he needed when called upon by the Klondike Hockey Club in the summer of 1904 to negotiate the arrangements for a very special tour.

Given that winter lasted six months up north, there were some who reckoned that some of the finest hockey in the country was being played in Dawson City. By 1904, there were four men's clubs in the Dawson Hockey League: the North-West Mounted Police, the Civil Service, the Amateur Athletic Association, and one from the general population, called the "Eagles." Dawson's women could play, too, on the "Dawsons" or the "Victorias."

Dawson also boasted a two-year-old, state-of-the-art covered arena, which had its own electric power plant, and whose builders had cleverly overcome the problem of making ice in the Yukon. The pipes for flooding the rink were laid above ground in a box covering, with manure insulating all to prevent freezing. Hot water was pumped in to make ice, for cold water would have frozen as soon as it hit the frigid air, thus making the rink lumpy and unplayable.

The rink had an attached clubhouse, training and dressing rooms, showers, lounges, a dining room, and all the amenities one would expect to find in civilization — unless you wanted to smoke. Joe Boyle had given up smoking and drinking a decade earlier after a particularly riotous bender, and while the Irish in him didn't mind others drinking, he hated smoking. Anyone who wanted a puff would do so in a segregated area at the top of one of the arena's distinctive three-storey towers, so the pollution would ventilate into the Yukon chill and not into the lungs of the Nuggets, training below.

Selected from the Dawson City hockey clubs, the Nuggets were an all-star elite. Weldy Young, a civil servant who had actually patrolled the point for Ottawa from 1893 to 1899, would be captain and coach. Norman Watt, George "Sureshot" Kennedy, and Hec Smith, who had all come in search of their fortunes in 1898, would now try again respectively as left winger, right winger, and centre of the hockey prospectors.

Dr. D. R. McLennan, a "hard man" on the staff of the territorial administration, had played in an 1895 Stanley Cup challenge for Queen's University against the Montreal Victorias, and now would play rover. J. K. Johnstone, a former Mountie who worked in the post office, would play point; cover-point Lorne Hannay had gone home to

Brandon and would be collected when the Nuggets' train passed through Winnipeg. Archie Martin, who worked in Boyle's timber operation, would be the spare man and trainer, while Quebec native Albert Forrest, all of 17 years old, would stand up for the Yukoners in goal.

Ottawa's ice was 25 feet longer than Dawson City's rink, and Joe Boyle knew that superior conditioning would help his squad conquer the larger surface. Though in Ottawa on business, he monitored the players' conditioning drills from afar, with Weldy Young posting the daily results to him.

Training would not end when the Klondikers hit the rails, either, for Boyle was determined the team didn't go to flab on its two-week ship-and-train odyssey. He commanded the railway to turn its smoking car into a fitness room, where the Nuggets could sweat over weights and "pulling machines" while the Rockies and Prairie rolled by.

Many whistle-stop clubs wanted to take on the Dawson City crew as they rode the rails east, but Ottawa insisted the challenge would be rendered void if Boyle's squad played anyone before they met the Silver Seven. This proviso hampered Boyle's ability to recoup the $10,000 the Stanley Cup quest would cost, but he figured he'd be raking it in after the match, when the new Stanley Cup champions staged their victory tour.

The first game of the best-of-three series was scheduled inauspiciously for Friday, January 13, and the world-traveler Joe Boyle had studied the timetables of ships and trains to best lay out an itinerary that would have his squad in Ottawa four days ahead of their match. These four days would be precious, allowing the team to retrieve their land legs and break in the new equipment they would pick up on arrival.

Mother Nature, however, was not proving to be a fan of the Dawson City expedition. Indeed, so temperate was the weather right up until mid-November that the team didn't have any ice to practise on, and people blamed the artillery barrages from the war between China and Russia as the culprit perverting nature. There was another wrinkle as well: federal elections were scheduled for the end of December, and Captain Weldy Young, in charge of the electoral lists, would have to follow afterward by coach.

And still there was no snow. Boyle's old boxing partner Frank Slavin had made the 330-mile walk from Whitehorse to Dawson City (a fairly routine trek in those days) and had reported that the roads were frozen solid. So, on Sunday, December 18, 1904, Martin, Kennedy, and Smith departed by dogsled, while the rest of the team set out on bicycles the following day.

With the first game less than four weeks away and thousands of miles to go, the Nuggets hoped to cover at least 50 miles a day. When the road suddenly thawed, the team found themselves trying to ride through mush, and their bicycles broke down. So they would walk.

The weather changed again, and walking was miserable. Laden down with provisions and exercise gear, covering between 30 and 40 miles a day, with the arctic winds beating the temperatures down to 40 below, the players feared that their aching, raw feet would soon be finished off by frostbite. At night they camped in North-West Mounted Police sheds, and they spent Christmas 1904 huddled in such a shed 50 miles outside Whitehorse, warmed by the thought they were off to compete for hockey's greatest prize.

Though exhausted when they finally reached Whitehorse, the Nuggets, astonishingly, were still on Joe Boyle's schedule and had two days to make their ship in Skagway. They would arrive in Ottawa as planned, with four days to spare. Yet after filling their bellies with a belated Christmas feast and falling into their first real beds in nine nights, they couldn't have rejoiced at the snow now falling outside their hotel windows.

The Nuggets' two-day window to make their ship collapsed with the blizzard and heavy snow drifts that blocked the railway line to Skagway. The team cabled the ship to wait, and when the railway line opened on the third day, the Nuggets still hoped. The *S.S. Amur* had indeed postponed its departure a full 24 hours, but it was not long enough. When the players rushed to the Skagway dock, they were devastated to learn the ship had pulled out two hours earlier. And with the temperature nearly 50 below zero, the Nuggets' next ship, the *S.S. Dolphin*, had to wait three days before it could crack the ice to dock.

Things got worse. The seas between Skagway and Vancouver were so rough that the team was now merely trying to survive the passage, all thoughts of exercising on the pulling machines canceled by heaving swells and stomachs. When the *Dolphin* arrived on the south coast of British Columbia, both Vancouver and Victoria were blinded by fog, and the ship could not dock. So the Nuggets sailed to Seattle, then made their way back to Vancouver to catch the transcontinental to Ottawa on January 6, 1905. Seasick, battered by the elements, and probably more than a little dispirited, Joe Boyle's crew were now five days behind schedule.

Late in the afternoon of January 11, 1905 — 25 days since the first crew left for Whitehorse — the Dawson City Nuggets arrived in Ottawa. A huge crowd turned out to welcome them, displaying the hospitality Ottawa was famous for bestowing upon visitors — but only up to a point. The desperate Nuggets had cabled the Ottawa Senators *en route*, supplicating for mercy, but the Senators were unmoved: Governor General Earl Grey would "face" the puck as scheduled at 8:30 P.M. On Friday the 13th.

Before the first match, the Nuggets were feted by Frank McGee and his Senators at the Ottawa Amateur Athletic Club. The visitors were given honorary membership, and freedom of the club's rooms for as long as they were in town. It was about all the Senators would give away.

On Friday the 13th, Ottawa's Dey's Skating Rink was filled with more than 2,200 curious fans as the Dawson City crew skated out in their black sweaters trimmed with gold. The Silver Seven, in their red, black, and white, felt confident that these matches were theirs to win, for after all, the Stanley Cup was on display in an Ottawa shop window. The symbolism was apt: what the Silver Seven owned, the men from the land of gold couldn't buy.

Even so, Joe Boyle was satisfied with events so far. Earl and Lady Grey settled into their seats, a few of his mining associates had turned up to cheer for the Dawson crew, and Boyle had managed to replace the Ottawa-based referee with a man from Brockville, Ontario — an impartial 50 miles away.

The road-weary Dawson City Nuggets acquitted themselves well for the first 10 minutes, and were only down 3–1 when half time was called. The match had been rough, though, and in the second half, it got rougher. Dawson City started a fight, after Norman Watt had tripped Ottawa's Alf Moore, who whacked Watt in the mouth with his stick. Watt retaliated by smashing his stick over Moore's head and knocking him out for 10 minutes.

Despite the fact that the mighty Frank McGee only put one puck past the Klondikers' teenage goalie Albert Forrest, and despite

Forrest's complaints that at least six Ottawa goals were off-side, the Silver Seven took the first game by the unflattering score of 9–2.

Frank McGee had heard that someone in the Dawson City camp had sneered at his paltry one goal, and in the second game, he became a dervish. McGee scored four Ottawa goals in the first half, and then 10 more in the second. In Ottawa's 23–2 pasting of the Klondikers, one-eyed Frank McGee would score 14 goals — eight of them in an eight-minute-and-20-second onslaught. "Dawson never had the chance of a bun in the hands of a hungry small boy," eulogized the *Citizen*.

Sportingly, the Ottawa papers made special mention of goalie Albert Forrest's heroic performance, with the beleaguered teenager standing on his head to keep the rout from being even more obscene. "The only man on the Dawson team who played a really fine game of hockey was Forrest," said the *Citizen*, "who in goal gave as fine an exhibition as the most exacting could desire. But for him Ottawa's figures might have been doubled."

The Silver Seven had retained the Stanley Cup and were in a festive and generous mood. They celebrated their massacre by hosting the losers to a banquet, and then, well fed and watered, took their glittering prize and drop kicked it into the Rideau Canal, which was fortunately frozen solid at the time.

The Nuggets were scheduled to go on tour, but Boyle knew he needed help to recoup his investors' money. With the Nuggets nursing both wounds and pride, Boyle worked the phones to try to woo Fred Taylor, a rising hockey star in Ontario, to come play for his team on their eastern swing. The canny Taylor declined, his hockey eye looking on better prospects to the south.

When Captain Weldy Young finally caught up to the team, the Nuggets went down to the Maritimes and worked their way back home, playing — and actually winning — matches from Cape Breton, through Halifax, Moncton, Fredericton, Trois-Rivières, Montreal, Kingston, Toronto, Pittsburgh, the Lakehead, Winnipeg, and Brandon.

It was now spring, and the thaw had canceled planned Nuggets matches in Regina, Calgary, and Nelson and Rossland in the Kootenays of B.C. Many Nuggets, having family and friends in the Prairies, decided to linger, but young Albert Forrest continued back to Dawson City, the first Nugget to return. He was especially proud of the fact he had walked in from Whitehorse in only seven days.

The Stanley Cup's trustees tightened up the rules after Dawson City's remarkable challenge, and now any team that wished to take on the reigning Cup champs would have to prove their right to do so against other teams of established ability. No more would an unknown and untested hockey crew step off a train after an epic transcontinental journey to face the best in the country.

The Ottawa Silver Seven were eventually stopped, too, when the Montreal Wanderers ended their remarkable dynasty in 1906, preventing the Senators from taking their eleventh Cup since 1903. Frank McGee retired in the early winter of 1906, aged 25, and took a job in the Interior Department of the federal government. He retired as a legend, the man who set the extraordinary record of 63 goals in 22 Stanley Cup games — a record that still stands for Cup play.

—◦◦◦—

Freddy Stanley had returned to England in the early spring of 1893 upon the death of his brother to assume his title as the 16th Earl of Derby. Even so, he and his family took the spirit of the Canadian winter home with them. The five Stanley brothers even organized a hockey game on the frozen ponds of Buckingham Palace in the winter of 1895.

Playing on the opposing "Palace" team were none other than the hedonistic Bertie, Prince of Wales, who would become King Edward VII, and his brother, the Duke of York. Doubtless unamused, Queen Victoria looked on from the safety of a balcony, mulling the grim future that would befall the monarchy should this rough and fast colonial game claim her sons. All things considered, she need not have worried about hockey.

After returning to England, Stanley became a member of the prestigious Jockey Club, and a horse-racing enthusiast of considerable skill (or luck), his stable winning 33,000 pounds sterling in 1906, topping all other British owners. In June 1908, he returned from an evening stroll around his estate at Holwood, Kent, settled into his chair to have a chat with his beloved Constance, and died with his boots on. He was 67, and he had lived a remarkably rich life, but for the thing for which he is most remembered. In the grandest irony of all, the man who made possible Stanley Cup glory for the young country of Canada never saw a contest for the cup that bore his name.

3

THE PROFESSIONALS

In the winter of 1903, 19-year-old Frederick Wellington Taylor was an angry young man. Taylor, whose calculated stubbornness would soon become legendary, had just butted heads with the powerful amateur hockey establishment. And he had lost.

Fred Taylor was not used to losing. As one of the finest young hockey players in Ontario, the keen-eyed, dimple-chinned Taylor dominated every rink that felt the touch of his swift blades. Ever since he joined the Listowel, Ontario, Mintos in 1887, Taylor had confounded opponents with his skill and speed at centre, winning him the first of his many nicknames, the "Listowel Whirlwind."

With its new arena and hockey-mad crowds of 1,200, little Listowel, about 20 miles northwest of Kitchener-Waterloo, became a force on the local hockey circuit. By the 1900–01 season, the Mintos had moved into the tough Northern League of the elite Ontario Hockey Association. On Taylor's strength as a goalscorer, they won the league championship that inaugural season, repeating the following year.

Not only did the Mintos (named after Canada's governor general) prove themselves worthy of their elevation into the big leagues, they introduced some important innovations. The Nova Scotians had long used fishermen's net to cover the goal posts, and the Mintos followed suit, introducing the goal net to league play. They would even cart their own nets to the rinks of deprived teams, boasting as they went "Have nets, will travel."

Fred Taylor also introduced padded uniforms, for as the lightest and fastest man on the ice, he was often the target of clumsy attempts to stop him. Taylor had his mother sew layers of felt into the shoulders and lower back of his undershirt. Then he dismantled a lady's corset and fitted its bone stays into his canvas pants to protect his thigh muscles. After Taylor's innovation, the ladies of Listowel couldn't find an unmolested corset anywhere.

In the early winter of 1902–03, the young hockey star accepted an invitation from former Listowel teammates to cross the border into Michigan. Taylor's friends, studying dentistry in the United States, wanted him to play against a team from Houghton, in the copper-rich mining country of the northwestern corner of the state. Taylor so out-classed everyone else on ice that the newspaper reports of his skill, ironically, finally filtered into Toronto. So began Taylor's problem, along with his salvation.

When Fred Taylor's phone rang in October of 1903, William "Billy" Hewitt, the formidable secretary of the Ontario Hockey Association (and father of Foster Hewitt, *Hockey Night in Canada*'s "voice" for more than half a century) was on the other end of the line. Hewitt had read the newspaper reports of Taylor's brilliance, and invited him to come to the Big Smoke to play for the Toronto Marlboros, the most glamorous team in the senior league.

As Taylor recalled in Eric Whitehead's splendid biography, *Cyclone Taylor: A Hockey Legend*, "I was flattered and I wanted to go. After all, it was my chance to move up into big-time hockey, but then I had second thoughts."

Suddenly, Taylor's small-town soul feared the bright lights of big, unforgiving Toronto. He also didn't want to leave his job in the local piano factory, since this would create hardship for his parents and four siblings. Taylor's father made just $75 a month, and the additional $10 a month that Taylor added to the family's coffers from his weekly wage of $5 made a big difference. So Taylor told Billy Hewitt thanks, but no thanks.

Hewitt was stunned. Didn't Taylor know whom he was rejecting: the mighty Toronto Marlies, and the mighty Billy Hewitt? As he would come to do throughout his hockey life, Taylor refused to back down, so Hewitt blurted out just what kind of fight Taylor had picked for himself. "If you won't play for the Marlies," said one of hockey's celebrated builders to the young and sensitive player, "then you won't play anywhere."

As secretary of the OHA, Hewitt was in a position to make good on his threat and had the ingrate Taylor blacklisted. Taylor tried to test the ban by accepting an invitation to play in Thessalon, a town just southeast of Sault Ste. Marie and, though far from Listowel, still in Ontario. Thessalon badly wanted Taylor's services, but word was swift from the OHA's headquarters. Taylor was banned on every square inch of Ontario ice, and any team that tried to hoodwink the OHA would not be a team for long. Fred Taylor was finished in Ontario hockey.

It was a banishment that launched Taylor into hockey stardom. After sitting out for a season and not liking it at all, Taylor decamped in the winter of 1905 to the foreign wilds of Portage la Prairie, Manitoba, where the OHA couldn't touch him. Though young Taylor had been wary of leaving home, Billy Hewitt's sentence had now forced his talent onto a larger stage.

With a population of 3,000, Portage la Prairie wasn't much bigger than Listowel, but there were players who were big indeed. It was a wild time for the young game of hockey, as competing amateur leagues such as the Manitoba, the Federal, and the Canadian Amateur Hockey Association all sought the services of pioneer hockey's stars. Winnipeg's Victorias boasted Russell Bowie, whom some thought the best centreman of his day; Montreal had Ernie "Moose" Johnson; Ottawa's Nationals featured the feisty "Newsy" Lalonde; Westmount had Art Ross and geniuses-in-waiting Frank and Lester Patrick; and the speedy Rat Portage Thistles had Si Griffis and Tom Phillips. They were future Hall of Famers all.

In his first game out for Portage la Prairie, Taylor quickly established his pedigree, scoring two goals against Winnipeg, which sent the question "Who is this guy?" rippling through the crowd. The Rat Portage Thistles, touted the fastest team in hockey, asked themselves the same thing after Taylor had breezily scored a trio of goals against them.

When the game was done, Thistles stars Griffis and Phillips were waiting for Taylor outside his dressing room. Instead of laying a beating on the man who had beaten them with the goals, they took Taylor to a local cafe and laid on ham and eggs and an extraordinary invitation. To the Stanley Cup.

The Thistles were going to take a run at the Jug, and they wanted Taylor on their side. Their reasoning was sound: his Portage la Prairie team was not going to finish at the top of the standings, and Portage could afford to loan Taylor to the Thistles for a couple of weeks to make the small-town Ontario squad indisputably the fastest team in hockey.

The offer caught Taylor's fancy. Banished not so long ago from Ontario, he could now play for an Ontario team competing for the biggest prize of all. So Taylor convinced Portage to let him join the Thistles in Montreal for the big series against the Wanderers. Yet the day before Taylor was to catch his train to Montreal, the phone rang for Fred Taylor again. His past had caught up with him.

On the other end of the line was John McNamara, sheriff of Houghton County, Michigan. Taylor was a wanted man — not by the law, but by the Portage Lake team in Houghton, Michigan, the place where Taylor had starred in an exhibition series three years earlier. Houghton was in tough against Pittsburgh for the league championship, and they needed help. Some Canadians on the Portage Lake squad told their manager McNamara that the man who could give them that help, and much more, was Fred Taylor.

McNamara's offer came with a sweetener: money. Taylor, who had been grateful for the $20 a month at his piano factory job would receive $400 and expenses for the rest of the season for joining Portage Lake. It was an offer he couldn't refuse.

—⁓—

Canada's amateur athletic clubs were forged in the smithy of British Victorian idealism, in which gentlemen engaged in sport for the honour of competition, for the chance to do one's best for one's club or society, and for the love of the game. While this might be a fine notion in the privileged clubs of Mayfair or Chelsea (and it wasn't always thus there either, since professional gaming has a long history in Britain), it had a distinctly different resonance in the human experiment unfolding in North America.

Workers increasingly lived in growing cities, and their leisure time was now a commodity — something they could choose to spend. You could join an organized athletic league befitting your social station, such as the bank workers' and mine workers' hockey leagues. Or you could spend some of your take-home pay on entertainment, which increasingly meant watching hockey.

With the invention of the International Hockey League in Michigan, players could be paid for providing that entertainment. To be sure, they had collected bits and pieces of tour revenues up in Canada, but it was an ad hoc proposition, with the overwhelming share going to the owners and the players picking over the scraps. The IHL was a radical change. Now players were given a market in which to negotiate their price. And the market was a powerful place.

Just as Fred Taylor had found his way to the IHL by being banished from the OHA, one of the founding members of the world's first pro league had run afoul of Canadian amateurism himself. When 18-year-old John Liddell MacDonald Gibson had set out in 1898 from Berlin, Ontario (renamed Kitchener during the First World War), for the Detroit College of Medicine in 1898, the would-be dentist departed hot with the memory of his own banishment.

Another multitalented athlete who had won championships at rowing, skating, and swimming, and who had starred at football, lacrosse, and soccer, Gibson ruled the ice at "point," delivering body checks of thundering — and clean — force. His disgrace came not on the ice, but after his Berlin team won an 1898 match against their archrivals, Waterloo. In his joy at their 3–0 victory, Berlin's mayor rewarded Gibson and each of his mates, including the sons of the Seagram distillery family, with gold pieces. The Ontario Hockey Association, still aflame with the zeal of amateurism, was harsh in their response, suspending the entire Berlin team for the rest of the season — for playing for money.

The experience embittered Gibson. A citizen could pay to watch games and he could even wager large amounts of money on them, but if a player accepted an honour that had potential monetary value, it stank of corruption. So Gibson headed south.

The handsome, powerful six-footer, who would become known as the "Father of Hockey" in Upper Michigan, hung out his dentistry shingle in 1901 in Houghton. Like Fred Taylor, he, too, had once played an exhibition game in the town, tucked up in the southern edge of the odd Keweenaw Peninsula — itself divided in two by Lake Superior. The peninsula's howling arctic winds and deep snow had defeated the first rugged souls who attempted to take the copper from the earth in the mid-nineteenth century, and the region was so cold it was called "The Canada of the United States."

Upper Michigan had another similarity to Canada: it was crazy about hockey. The rudimentary game had been played in the United States for as long as it had been played in Canada, but in the latter half of the nineteenth century, ice polo became more popular in the United States than hockey.

Ice polo had grown out of roller polo, which had developed in the posh resort community of Newport, Rhode Island, by horse-polo players, after James Plimpton introduced the roller skate there in 1866. By 1878, roller polo was a club sport, and teams of five or six aside played indoors, on a 40-by-80-foot surface, using four-foot sticks and a ball.

Given its blue-blooded origins, roller polo spread through the Ivy League towns and cities, who all had special roller-polo rinks, and then into Eastern Canada. According to hockey historian, Bill Fitsell, the first ice polo match debuted in New Brunswick, at a winter carnival in 1885, and spread west and south. Ice polo also used the thin, curved polo sticks and a ball, and its popularity rose quickly. A decade after its debut, Canadian teams were touring the northeastern United States for exhibition games of both ice hockey and ice polo, although with the altruistic mission of teaching their ice polo mad American cousins how to play hockey.

By the turn of the twentieth century, the geographically blessed United States had made up for its natural deficiencies by building artificial ice arenas in Baltimore, Philadelphia, Pittsburgh, and Boston. Houghton, however, had no need for the fake stuff. Houghton was cold, and on a Saturday night, the miners would fuel themselves with all kind of liquid fire to ignite their boisterous enthusiasm for the game on ice.

By the winter of 1902–03, they had much to cheer. "Doc" Gibson had organized the Portage Lakes Hockey Club. Gibson, now well connected as a member of several fraternal lodges, had befriended James Dee, a local businessman, who had only a vague notion of what hockey was until Gibson came along. After seeing his dentist pal's skill on ice, Dee was hooked. He formed the Houghton Amphidrome Company to build the 3,000-seat Amphidrome Rink, which held almost as many people as there were in town.

Gibson's Portage Lake team was a worthy tenant and regularly sold out the rink. In their green-and-white turtleneck sweaters, emblazoned with a winged "PL" on the chest, Doc Gibson led his Canadian-born Portage Lakers into battle in the same colours he had led his Berlin team. It was a glorious season, with the Portage Lakers a juggernaut riding 14 straight wins, defeating Pittsburgh for "the championship of the country."

Team president James Dee donated $100 for a victory party, and while the players feasted, their imaginations were hungry. They knew they were good, but they wanted to be the best in the world. They wanted the Stanley Cup.

The Stanley Cup, however, did not want them. Portage Lake's challenges to the champion Montreal AAA "Little Men of Iron" and to Frank McGee and his glittering Ottawa Silver Seven were both turned down. Rather than give up, the Portage Lakers chose a path familiar to anyone who follows contemporary sports: they would buy themselves a championship team.

Michigan's Copper Country was no stranger to venture capital. The region's mining companies had encouraged free enterprise, scorning the "company store" policy that existed in other industrial regions, where workers gave their wages right back to the company through purchase of the food and supplies in the firm's provisions shop.

Houghton's free-enterprise attitude and the Americans' deep belief in "success through hard work" fit beautifully with the Portage Lake hockey team's desire. And Canadian players on other clubs liked it, too. William Hodgson "Hod" Stuart, the star of the Pittsburgh Bankers, accepted an offer from Portage Lake, and in Stuart, the team had the kind of player who is today called "the franchise."

A strapping Gary Cooper-esque defenseman of great skill and tough checking, Stuart debuted with his hometown Ottawa Senators during the 1898–99 season, along with little brother Bruce, a forward. The Stuart brothers moved on to play for Quebec shortly before the Senators' rise to dynastic glory, then headed south. Pittsburgh boasted its fancy "Casino" rink, with luxurious tiered boxes, a huge 275-foot-by-125-foot ice surface, and thousands of incandescent lights which bathed the rink in gold. Yet gold was a dominant motif in Pittsburgh, and the team was stocked with Canadian imports who were handsomely paid. Indeed, Hod Stuart could make $15 to $20 a week, while topping up his income with a day job supplied by the team. With what is a rich irony in today's world of multimillionaire players, Pittsburgh's nickname was the "Bankers" because player Arthur Sixsmith was the secretary to banker Andrew Mellon, later to become U.S. Secretary of the Treasury.

Gibson's Portage Lakers offered Stuart even more, and once Hod had signed on with them, brother Bruce followed for the start of the 1903–04 season. So, too, did Milton "Riley" Hern, an Ontario native who had been backstopping the Pittsburgh Keystones. In a 1903 *Toronto Globe and Mail* report, Hern freely admitted that he signed with Portage Lake because they offered him more money. Portage Lake's business plan paid off, and the Lakers racked up 23 wins in 25 games.

Late in 1904, James Dee went to Chicago to meet with other American rink operators and team presidents, and the six-team International Hockey League was born. There would be one Canadian team; two in Pittsburgh; and three in Michigan — Portage Lake, Calumet, which was farther north up the Keweenaw Peninsula, and the "American Soo" team from Sault Ste. Marie, thus known to distinguish it from the "Canadian Soo" squad in Sault Ste. Marie, Ontario.

When Fred Taylor stepped off the train in Houghton on the morning of January 30, 1906, he was lonely and full of trepidation looking out on the cold, desolate landscape. He later said it made him feel like an "astronaut" looking at "the moon for the first time."

The 21-year-old hockey whiz wasn't lonely long, as Portage's captain Bruce Stuart and goalie Riley Hern were waiting for him. The duo tipped the railway porter 25 cents on the dazed Taylor's behalf, then took their new teammate straight to a hotel, so he could get sorted out before practice — just two hours away.

With new friends and the prospect of getting on the ice so soon, Taylor's sense of doom melted, except for the fact that he forgot to bring his skates. Five dollars was pried out of the club kitty to buy him new ones, double the cost of the first pair of skates he ever had.

After his playing coach Grindy Forrester gave him a quick, terse lesson about not getting ahead of his forward line and putting them off-side, Taylor prospered, scoring 11 goals in only six games. The fans loved his scintillating touch and gentlemanly manner, and his first newspaper notice in Houghton — on the day he arrived — gushed that he was "one of the fastest and most effective if not the very best player that Western Canada has ever produced." One that Billy Hewitt and Ontario had lost.

In Houghton, Taylor played the position of "rover," who, in the old seven-man-aside game was free to criss-cross the ice to make things happen. And make things happen Taylor did, winning the league scoring-title and the number one spot on the All-Star Team while leading Portage Lake to its first IHL championship.

While Taylor was lifting fans to their feet with his creative, virtuoso play, his teammate "Bad" Joe Hall was putting opponents in their place. A Staffordshire, England, native, Hall grew up in Manitoba and migrated to the Portage Lake squad the same season that Taylor did. Notorious for his flame-thrower temper, which could ignite at provocations real and imagined and caused him huge regret afterward, Hall could also play a skilled game, like many of today's "enforcers." In 20 matches with the Portage Lakers, Hall scored 33 goals from his position at right forward, leading the team in goals and earning himself an all-star selection.

He also was what today's sports world calls a free spirit. When Hall heard that Canadian Tommy Burns — whom Fred Taylor knew from back home — had just won the world heavyweight boxing title in Los Angeles, he saw a unique opportunity. Commandeering the reins of the hansom cab carrying himself, Fred Taylor, Stuart, and Hern, Hall took the cream of the Lakers on a rollicking ride through the streets of Pittsburgh. When he finally reined the horses in at the door of the team's hotel, some expensive and unique hockey talent was shaken, but otherwise fine. The usurped cab driver was furious, but Hall slipped the man a dollar, and all was forgiven.

A man to rival Fred Taylor in his ability to romance more than one hockey team at once was Didier Pitre, just a 20-year-old Montreal Nationals star in the 1904–05 season when he got wind of Michigan gold. Pitre's friend Jean Baptiste "Jack" Laviolette swanned into Montreal with tales of the glorious riches to be had in the IHL, where stars like Fred Taylor and Hod Stuart were pulling in $100 a week, or quadruple what a man could live well on for a month.

Laviolette, a spirited, glamorous 26-year-old Belleville, Ontario, native, had just come off his first all-star season for the IHL's Michigan Soo team. The Montreal Nationals' management rightly feared that

Laviolette would try to lure young Pitre away to the filthy lucre of the United States. So they took the huge Pitre, who weighed 200 pounds (at a time when the average playing weight was about 40 pounds less), and tried to hide him.

Through the fraternal network of news and rumour that hockey players still rely on to see through managerial subterfuge, Jack Laviolette found Pitre and convinced him to show up at Montreal's Windsor station just in time to catch the train south. As Laviolette walked into the station, his heart thumped at the sight of the manager and directors of the Montreal Nationals heading straight for him. Was Laviolette by any chance stealing Didier Pitre for a life of woe in the pros? Laviolette said that yes, he was, but since there was no sign of the disputed party, and the train was about to leave, it appeared as if he had lost.

Under the mocking laughter of the Montreal officials, Laviolette hopped aboard the train alone, then hopped off from the other side once it started to roll. Retreating back into the city, Laviolette tracked Pitre down and this time got his signature on a contract. Then he, too, hid Pitre, close to home in the basement of Windsor station until the next train was ready to depart. Once safely aboard, Laviolette kept the curious at bay by suggesting his friend in the sleeper car was sick with influenza — then a frequently fatal illness — and that he best be left undisturbed. He was.

Pitre and Laviolette made it safely to Michigan, where Pitre became an IHL star, with his fast, elegant skating making him an all-star in each of this three seasons, and his accurate "cannonball" shot putting him third of the league's top three goalscorers and winning him his lifelong nickname.

By 1907, however, the IHL was having trouble attracting players, since Canadian teams had quickly realized they were losing their best to the United States, and with them, significant revenue. Even though "amateur" clubs had begun to pay their players competitive wages, Edouard "Newsy" Lalonde — a genius at both lacrosse and hockey — was happy to escape the *Cornwall* (Ont.) *Free Press* where he worked as a printer's devil to take up a $35-a-week offer from the Canadian Soo.

The feisty rover received his offer by telegram, along with $16 for a one-way train ticket. Showing a reckless spirit, the 19-year-old Lalonde withdrew his life savings from the bank—also $16—and without any surplus money for food or equipment, climbed aboard the train taking him to his well-paid future. Newsy expected to watch the first game from the stands, but when Soo star Marty Walsh broke his leg 20 minutes into the match, there was a scramble to find Lalonde a pair of skates. On he jumped into the play, and as he was rushing up ice, he was thumped hard into a rink fence.

With no substitutes left on the bench, and Lalonde writhing on the ice, a local boxer came to the rescue. Jack Hammond handed the gasping Lalonde a hip flask, and Lalonde gratefully swigged. As bad luck would have it, Hammond was carrying two flasks that day: one filled with whisky, the other, with ammonia. He had given Lalonde the wrong flask, and as Newsy later recalled, "It burned my mouth and my gums and my throat. I thought I was a goner."

Lalonde survived, scored two goals in the game, and was given a raise to $50 a week. He would add 24 more goals over 18 games that season before accepting an offer with Toronto of the Ontario Professional Hockey League the following year.

Now that the Canadians were coughing up cash, Hod Stuart wanted to go home, too. He was tantalized by an offer from Dickie Boon to play for the Montreal Wanderers at a salary that would make Stuart the richest player in the game. In December 1906, Stuart's Pittsburgh team refused to play a game against the Michigan Soo because of the choice of the referee — an increasingly common complaint as the IHL entered its final season. The Pittsburgh management accused Stuart of rabble-rousing and released him from the team. A free man, he joined the Wanderers, where he attracted 6,000 fans for his first appearance in a Montreal uniform.

Doc Gibson, who had retired before the IHL began, had to lace on his skates to play his two and only games for the league at the start of the 1906–07 season, as the once-mighty Portage Lake team was now having trouble recruiting players. Fred Taylor was still there, though, and notched another 23 goals in 14 games for Portage Lake, leading the team to its second IHL championship with a victory over Pittsburgh.

The delirious *Houghton Gazette* crowed that the IHL pennant would be hammered with so many "ten penny spikes" in the Amphidrome that "it will now be impossible to remove it." A U.S. Army artillery battery kept their cannon fixed on the track by which

Lord Stanley of Preston served as Canada's governor general from 1888 to 1893 and in his tenure became an avid hockey fan. His legacy to the game is the "Dominion Challenge Trophy," which the hockey world reveres as "The Stanley Cup."
HOCKEY HALL OF FAME

above: James Creighton (fourth from left), the man who staged the world's first indoor hockey match in Montreal in 1875, poses with members of Ottawa's "Rideau Rebels" circa 1889. The Rebels included two sons of Canada's governor general, Lord Stanley, who would soon give hockey its most coveted trophy. HOCKEY HALL OF FAME

facing page, top: The Kenora Thistles pose proudly with the Stanley Cup, which they won in January 1907, and lost two months later to Montreal's Wanderers. Nevertheless, the Thistles' not only had won hockey's great prize, but also had the distinction of representing the smallest town (population 10,000) ever to lay claim to the trophy. HOCKEY HALL OF FAME

facing page, bottom: Though slight in size, the Montreal Hockey Team's speed and pluck helped them win the Stanley Cup in 1902, as well as fame in homes and schoolyards across the country as "The Little Men of Iron." NOTMAN PHOTOGRAPHIC ARCHIVES, MCCORD MUSEUM OF CANADIAN HISTORY, MONTREAL

above: Led by the competitive zeal of Dan Bain (seated, 4th from right) and the crack goal-keeping of Cecil "Whitey" Merritt (seated, 2nd from right), who pioneered the use of cricket pads, the Winnipeg Victorias became the first team west of Montreal to win the Stanley Cup, capturing their first in 1896, and this, their second, in 1901. HOCKEY HALL OF FAME

facing page, top: An outdoor hockey game in Dawson City, Yukon, at the turn of the 20th century. Hockey had spread far in the 25 years since James Creighton's first indoor game, and players in Dawson would soon leave the pond for an indoor rink—with its own power plant, clubhouse, training rooms, showers, lounges, and dining room. HOCKEY HALL OF FAME

facing page, bottom: Hockey's earliest dynasty, the Ottawa Silver Seven, won eleven Stanley Cup challenges from 1903–06. Led by the patrician "One-Eyed" Frank McGee (top left), whose record of 63 goals in 22 Stanley Cup games between 1893 and 1918 still stands, the Silver Seven were voted Canada's finest sports team of the half-century in 1950. HOCKEY HALL OF FAME

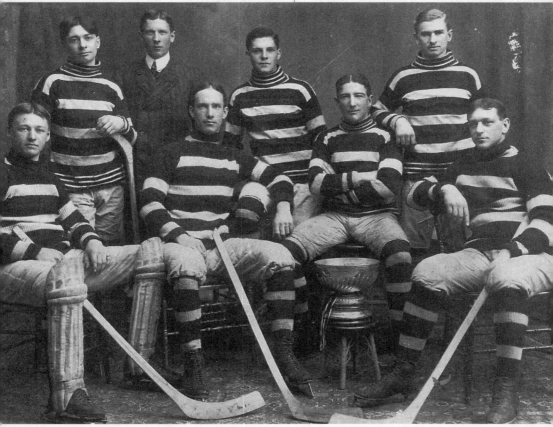

above: The Dawson City Nuggets pose with their creator, Joe Boyle, outside Ottawa's Dey's Rink in 1905. The Nuggets made one of the most epic—and unlikely—trips in Stanley Cup history, traveling more than 4,500 miles by foot, bicycle, boat, and train in hostile weather to challenge the powerhouse Ottawa Silver Seven. HOCKEY HALL OF FAME

facing page, top: The 1910 Renfrew Millionaires were the finest team that money could buy, featuring Fred "Cyclone" Taylor, Edouard "Newsy" Lalonde, and Frank and Lester Patrick. The creation of wealthy Senator Michael O'Brien and his son Ambrose, whose freespending ways sent pro salaries skyrocketing, neither the O'Briens nor the Millionaires could buy themselves the Stanley Cup. HOCKEY HALL OF FAME

facing page, bottom: The Vancouver Millionaires pose outside the Vancouver Arena, at the time the world's largest indoor rink with 10,550 seats. The Millionaires were the invention of hockey's pioneering geniuses, Lester and Frank Patrick (seated, wearing a suit), who brought artificial ice and pro hockey to the Pacific Coast in 1911. Led on ice by Fred "Cyclone" Taylor (second left, back row), the Millionaires would reward the Patricks' vision with the Stanley Cup in 1915. HOCKEY HALL OF FAME

following page: Fred "Cyclone" Taylor, poses as 22-year-old "superstar in waiting" in his Portage Lake, Michigan, uniform in 1906. Taylor, like many other Canadian hockey talents, followed the money south to the International Hockey League, the world's first professional hockey league. HOCKEY HALL OF FAME

RENFREW 1909-10 HOCKEY TEAM

the Lakers' train would roll into town, lest any enemy should try something foolish. Once the train was sighted, the town's factories let loose with a victory fanfare of their whistles, and the disembarking players were mobbed by hundreds of Houghton's citizens, who paraded them through the streets that had been decorated in green and white. But the party would be short-lived.

Just a few days later, a recession hit the American economy, and copper prices took a beating. There would be no more gold to pay the now high-priced talent. The world's first pro hockey league was undone by the very thing that had given it life: money.

Through the alchemy of Doc Gibson's hockey talent and social connections and the American genius for self-invention, Fred Taylor had been lured south to participate in hockey's first great business experiment, one that had shaken the hypocrisy from Canadian amateurism. He had competed on the professional stage with some of the greatest talents in the game and had come out on top. He had been well paid and had acquired a taste for money. Though the small-town fear of homesickness had long since left him, Fred Taylor knew that his future was now at home. As far as pro hockey went in Canada, the party was just beginning.

—◊◊◊—

Those Canadian hockey players back home from the American pro league in the spring of 1907 would see around them a society that a contemporary Canadian would find startlingly familiar. Immigrants were coming in the tens of thousands to the promised land, and the term "New Canadians" was coined to distinguish them from the "Old Canadians" who had crossed the pond maybe 20 years earlier. The House of Commons was discussing the elimination of patronage, while the Canadian National League declared itself in Toronto to oppose Prime Minister Wilfrid Laurier's leanings to free up trade with Uncle Sam. Quebec was riled as well, suspicious of their fellow Quebecker Laurier for paying insufficient attention to their demands for linguistic and cultural distinctiveness.

Canadian hockey was plunging into new territory, too, courtesy of the American experiment in professionalism. Hockey would become a business in Central Canada, as well on North America's west coast.

Through it all would skate Fred Taylor, his professional star arching toward its lofty zenith — and attracting the attention of everybody.

When Taylor arrived home in Canada in the spring of 1907, hockey was a fractious world where the amateur frequently collided with the professional. The fleet and precise Thistles from Kenora, Ontario (pop. 10,000), who had tried to woo Taylor two years earlier, could vanquish the mighty Montreal Wanderers for the 1907 Stanley Cup, and the series reflected the struggle between the new, aggressive commercialism, and the remnants of the amateur ideal.

The Montreal Wanderers, who had been formed in late 1903 from disgruntled elements of the Montreal AAA Hockey Club and the Victoria Club, were presented as a model of the new in the *Kenora Miner and News,* sparing "no expense to bolster their championship team." The Thistles, on the other hand, were a bunch of amateurs "fortified by a bulwark of self-confidence." That aplomb was shaken on their roundabout journey to Montreal, for the Thistles missed their connection in St. Paul, Minnesota, and the rail car that would have been theirs was destroyed in a collision near Chicago.

Still, the Thistles considered their escape a lucky omen, and their welcome in Montreal was warm. New recruit Art Ross, who would become one of the guiding spirits of the twentieth-century sport, was a Westmount boy, while Tom Phillips and Si Griffis spent time greeting a parade of friends in the Windsor Hotel lobby. The other new recruit, "Bad" Joe Hall, spent time persuading newsmen that rumours of his brutality were greatly exaggerated. "Please say ... that I have not earned any of the hard things that have been said about me out West," pleaded Hall. "I was accused of breaking Magnus Flett's arm in the Strathcona game, when all Flett got was an accidental crack on the fingers. He was out playing two days later, so his arm could not have been broken, could it?"

Hall, who had been enlisted as a spare forward, would not get into this series, for the Thistles didn't need his help. Led by future Hall of Famers Billy McGimsie, Tom Phillips, Tom Hooper, Si Griffis, and Art Ross (Joe Hall would also make the pantheon for later exploits), the dynamic Thistles dispatched the Wanderers 4–2 in the first match, and then beat them 8–6 in the second. "The term 'poetry in motion' has some meaning when an enthusiast watches the Thistles glide along," the *Montreal Gazette* exclaimed. "There isn't a slow man on the challengers' team, unless it is the goaltender, and he was not asked to do any speedy runs."

The Thistles' 23-year-old Tom Phillips, a left-hander who played right wing, used his devastating shot to score seven of Kenora's 12 goals and was hymned from the stands by the chant "Never a man like Phillips, never another like he." Teammate Art Ross, who would go on to build the Boston Bruins, called him "the greatest hockey player I have ever seen." Fred "Cyclone" Taylor, the man for whom hockey genius Frank Patrick coined the term "superstar," said Kenora had revolutionized hockey with their speed and passing, changing the game from a dump-and-chase to one of precision. "The Thistles, by skating fast, turned the game wide open," said Taylor, "and by 1903, every senior team in the country had changed to that pleasing style."

The victory was doubly sweet for Kenora: not only was it their third attempt to win the Cup, they were now — and remain — the smallest town to ever win hockey's icon. The Kenora Opera House was bedecked with Union Jacks, with the Stanley Cup "a rather squat and somewhat insignificant looking piece of silverware when compared to the splendid western championship trophy sitting to its left." The Thistles sat in the opera boxes, their faces radiating the "barricade of silverware" lining the stage, above which the town's electricians had rigged "an immense thistle worked out with red, white, and blue electric lights."

The ecstatic townspeople gave their triumphant team nine silver loving cups, as well as a silver tea service to their trainer, and a silk hat to the team's manager, F. A. Hudson. There was a speech by the mayor, a piano solo, and a Mr. Herbert Carpenter got the crowd's blood up with a spirited rendition of "Land of Hope and Glory." The team's doctor reminded his audience that the Cup champions were just a schoolboy team five years earlier, and had to fight stronger teams and a good deal of snobbery to get to the top of the hockey world. Ultimately, the good doctor conceded the Thistles' "success was due to the administrations of Kenora's female population." Though other teams had tried to pry the Thistles away, they remained loyal to Kenora for "affection and sympathy will hold a man when dollars will not."

Even so, Captain Tom Phillips's message to the adoring crowd was a mixture of pride and recognition of the inevitable. "Now that we have the cup, I hope the team that takes it from us will have as much trouble as the Thistles had in winning it."

Two months later in March 1907, the Wanderers headed west to try to take the Cup back. There was much acrimony over Kenora ringers Alf Smith and Harry "Rat" Westwick, imported from Ottawa, and Montreal's "professionals" Hod Stuart and Riley Hern. The controversy between amateur and pro went all the way to Parliament and made the front pages of Canada's newspapers.

When the two teams finally worked things out, the disputed men played, and the two-game series took place on the slush of a neutral rink in Winnipeg. Given the publicity, thousands of fans from all over the country turned up, keen to watch the teams play on bad ice, which Montreal won on aggregate goals. The Cup went back to Montreal.

The conflict over pros and ringers was a battle in a larger war. Teams fought over the box office, and the players fought in the rinks. As with Marty McSorley's attack on Donald Brashear nearly a century later, society could not divorce brutality on the ice from that 10 feet away in the stands, and on-ice mayhem wound up in the courts. When Ottawa's "Baldy" Spittal and Alf and Harry Smith viciously attacked Montreal Wanderers players with their sticks during a 1907 match, they were arrested. Alf Smith and Spittal were fined $20 each, while Harry Smith was acquitted of assault.

On March 6, 1907, Owen McCourt, a 23-year-old sniper with the Cornwall Hockey Club who led the Federal League in scoring, became involved in a melee during a match against the Ottawa Victorias. When a stick crashed down on his head, McCourt was mortally wounded, first slipping into a coma, and dead the following morning. A coroner's inquest ruled that McCourt had been killed by the stick of Ottawa's Charles Masson, but Masson escaped a manslaughter conviction when witnesses couldn't testify with any certainty that it had been Masson's blow that had killed McCourt. There had been so many.

Despite his strapping stature and athletic gifts, Hod Stuart had wearied of the constant, violent punishment he received from opponents. He left the game after winning the 1907 Stanley Cup to work on a construction job with his father. The man who had been "the most talked about player in the whole of America" was only 28 years old when he dove into shallow waters in the Bay of Quinte on a June afternoon and accidentally snapped his neck on the rocks.

The shocked hockey world held "The Hod Stuart Memorial Match" the following year, and the Wanderers beat a team of challengers

10–4. Nearly 4,000 people attended hockey's first all-star game, and nearly $2,000 worth of gate receipts would, said the papers, "go to Stuart's widow and two little children without any deduction for the expenses either of the clubs or the rink management."

With Hod Stuart's star extinguished, the Montreal Wanderers needed another bright light in their firmament, and they saw it in Fred Taylor. In August 1907, who should step off the train from Montreal but Taylor's old Portage Lake teammate Riley Hern, armed with instructions to bring Taylor back as a Wanderer. The problem, as was usually the case with Taylor, was that others wanted him, too.

Montreal's Victorias and teams in Quebec City and in the Ottawa Valley's mineral-rich town of Cobalt had sent Taylor wooing letters. The Ottawa Senators, now more grey than silver, coveted the 22-year-old Taylor's swift skates and soft hands. They dangled in front of him an offer of $500 for the Eastern Canada "Amateur" Hockey League's 10-game season, plus a guaranteed $35-a-month job with Canada's Immigration Department.

Taylor, who had received $400 for a shorter season in the IHL, didn't think the money was all that great, but to his poor-boy sensibility, a job for life with the government was hard to ignore. So, though the Wanderers' offer was tempting, Taylor took the sure thing.

The sure thing nearly melted like ice in August when Taylor guilelessly offended Frank Oliver, the Liberal government's minister of the Interior, and the man who would give him his civil service job. When Oliver asked Taylor to produce his letter of job recommendation from his local MP, the hockey player answered that he was sure the local MP was a nice-enough guy, "but unfortunately he's a Liberal." Taylor, ever the Conservative Party diplomat, added "our family wouldn't go anywhere near him."

Things were smoothed over by a hockey-loving deputy minister, and Taylor got both the job and a place on the mighty Ottawa Senators. At the first practice, the team thought Taylor's speed was just showing off, but they soon came to appreciate that "fast" was just Taylor's normal speed. And, two weeks before the start of the 1907–08 season, Fred Taylor was already looking to bolt.

Without warning, Taylor vanished to Renfrew, in the Upper Ottawa Valley, to hear out wealthy Senator Michael O'Brien and his son

Ambrose, who coveted Taylor as the brightest jewel in their rich three-team league. The self-made Senator O'Brien had earned a fortune mining gold, silver, nickel, and cobalt, in logging, in woolen mills, and, eventually, in arms production during the First World War. Like many rich men, he wanted more than money: he wanted his Renfrew hockey team to win the ultimate prize.

The Stanley Cup would put Renfrew on the map the way it had done for Kenora, and O'Brien and his fellow millionaires went after it. Despite the assistance of their local MP, Tom Low — also a self-made titan of industry — Renfrew could not get into a recognized league, which was the only way they could win the Jug.

So they had started their own, offending Upper Canada sensibilities by calling it the "Federal League." The Renfrews were a powerhouse, slaughtering opponents and winning their league championship. If they could snare a player like Fred Taylor — who had yet to play a professional game in Canada — there was no way the bigger, snobbish leagues could ignore them.

The shocked Ottawa Senators dispatched their club secretary to Renfrew, and, after a frantic search, he found the hockey star shaking hands with a big, rich-looking man wearing a coonskin coat and derby hat. The Ottawa sleuth followed Taylor until he was alone and then began his interrogation. Had Taylor signed a contract? Taylor, cleverly, said no, he hadn't, but that he *had* heard the Ottawa club didn't really want him.

The Ottawa man squelched that rumour and reminded Taylor that he had signed a contract with *them*. As if in some silent movie, the man in the coonskin coat and two of his reinforcements suddenly burst into the room to try to stop this counter-hijack. Taylor quickly took the moral high ground, telling the Renfrew men that he was going back to Ottawa, where he was wanted. Renfrew was stunned, for Taylor was walking away from a $2,000 salary — $200 more than anyone was then making to play hockey.

There was shrewd method in Taylor's apparent selflessness, for now he knew his value without even having suited up in Canadian pro hockey. He could only delightedly imagine what he would be worth to the O'Briens after showing the Ottawa hockey world just what a rushing defenseman really meant. And so Fred Taylor's life as a pioneer pro in Canada began.

He was an instant hit. After watching Taylor score four astonishing goals for Ottawa on January 11, 1908, the Earl Grey, Canada's governor general, enthused within earshot of a reporter that Fred Taylor was "a cyclone if ever I saw one." The next day the *Ottawa Free Press* announced "in Portage la Prairie they called him a tornado, in Houghton, Michigan, he was known as a whirlwind. From now on he'll be known as Cyclone Taylor."

The Cyclone had two splendid seasons in Ottawa, rousing the capital with his rushing virtuosity. The Eastern Canada Hockey Association decided that the Stanley Cup would be awarded to the league champion at the end of the 1909 season, which came down to a duel between the Cup-holding Montreal Wanderers and Ottawa. In Ottawa's penultimate game against Montreal's Shamrocks, disaster struck when Cyclone Taylor's right foot was sliced to the bone between ankle and heel.

With only four days between matches, it looked like Taylor was finished. Ottawa's fans (and the Montreal Wanderers) worried over Taylor's fate. But on Wednesday, March 3, 1909, a crowd of 7,500 — some of whom had traveled to Ottawa from as far away as Halifax and Philadelphia — rocked the roof of the third incarnation of Dey's Arena when Fred Taylor skated onto the ice, his foot bandaged, his skate boot protected by extra leather.

During the warm up, it seemed as if Taylor was dragging his foot and would at best be a hobbled star. When the game began, however, the Cyclone started to whirl, executing his sinewy, high-speed rushes despite his grievous injury. True to form, the showman Taylor capped his performance with a dramatic end-to-end rush through the entire Wanderers team, then fired home the third of Ottawa's eight goals from a bad angle. He was a hero.

Hoisted aloft by the delirious crowd, the Cyclone was now Ottawa's new prize. He had brought the city its first Stanley Cup since the glory days of the Silver Seven and had won his first ever. The talk that summer was that the future belonged to Ottawa because of the Cyclone on skates, but talk was all it was. The following season, Taylor would again dazzle in Ottawa, but as the enemy, for now that he had shown his stuff in Canada's capital, Taylor was ready to spin the wheel of fortune in the free market.

And a belligerent market it was. The game that had attracted 40 curious onlookers to the Victoria Rink in Montreal 30 years earlier was now a big-and-getting-bigger business. In the boardrooms of the hockey clubs, a war was about to break out that would lead to the beginning of professional hockey on North America's Pacific coast, and to the creation of one of the world's most fabled teams, the Montreal Canadiens. It would also make Fred Taylor the richest player in the game.

—⁓—

In the summer of 1909, Senator Michael O'Brien was in an anxious mood, wondering just when his Renfrew Creamery Kings, owners of the Federal Hockey Championship, would have their crack at the big time. Stanley Cup trustee William Foran publicly promised "next year," but when next year came, the promise had vanished into thin air. So, in the winter of 1909, O'Brien dispatched his 24-year-old son, Ambrose, to Montreal to politely ask the Eastern Canada Hockey Association to let Renfrew into the party.

Ambrose, a University of Toronto graduate and used to the ways of the city, showed up at Montreal's Windsor Hotel on November 25, 1909, eager to present his case. The assembled committee from Montreal's Shamrocks and Wanderers, along with those from Ottawa and Quebec, had more important business to deal with than some upstart from the boonies. So they made young Ambrose wait in the lobby while they argued about money.

The Montreal Wanderers' new owner, Patrick J. Doran, wanted to move his team from their Westmount Arena on Wood Street to the smaller Jubilee Rink — which he just happened to own. The other owners wrinkled their noses. Doran's move to smaller premises would shrink the 40-percent share of profits they took from each other's gate receipts. So they came up with a simple fix. They would form a new league called the Canadian Hockey Association, with teams in Ottawa, Quebec, and three in Montreal: the Shamrocks, Nationals, and a team called All-Montreal. Doran and his Wanderers could have their tiny rink and its tiny revenues because now they were on their own.

As Ambrose O'Brien sat waiting in the lobby, Montreal Wanderers forward and team official Jimmy Gardner came out of the meeting in a thundering cuss. Clapping his eyes on the heir to the O'Brien fortune, Gardner had a brilliant idea, one that would eventually lead to the birth of the NHL. Since the O'Briens already had teams in Haileybury, Cobalt, and Renfrew, they could take in the Wanderers, and add a new team in Montreal, one made up of francophones. With these two powerful urban tenants, this new league could destroy the killjoys in the other new league, the CHA.

Even though the mainly francophone Montreal Montagnards had been together for over a decade, a new league actively promoting a French Canadian team was radical. On December 2, 1909, the meeting that changed everything was held in the old St. Lawrence Hall on Montreal's St. James Street. Ambrose O'Brien joined forces with P. J. Doran, Wanderers' officials James Strachan, Dickie Boon, and Jimmy Gardner, along with Tommy Hare from Cobalt, and the mining magnate Noah Timmins of Haileybury, to form the National Hockey Association.

Ambrose's millionaire father, Michael, shouldered financial responsibility for all franchises save the Wanderers, and Tommy Hare of Cobalt put up security for the French Canadian team. The club that would become one of professional sports most fabled was born the following day, and the francophone community was ecstatic. *La Presse* published a handsome photo of manager Jack Laviolette and proudly exclaimed that the new team would carry *"le nom de Canadien."*

Despite this exciting and progressive development, some gloomsters thought the quality of those wearing Canadien colours might be lacking. "French-Canadian players of class are not numerous," sniffed the Anglo *Gazette,* and "there will be some stiff bidding for men ... [since] neither league recognizes the other, and there is no National Commission to stop raids of the one league on players of the other."

The raids began with gusto. Jack Laviolette, who had once spirited Didier Pitre away from Montreal to play for the riches of the International Hockey League, now set about pursuing his talented friend for *Les Canadiens* and signed him to a contract. Laviolette's problem, however, was that the "Cannonball" had also signed a contract with the Montreal Nationals of the rival Canadian Hockey Association.

The matter wound up in court, which had never seen a breached hockey contract, so the lawyers had to dig into the world of Canadian theatre and American baseball contracts to seek out a precedent. In an irony that would be savoured by any NHLer who has endured ego-wounding salary arbitration, Pitre answered the Nationals' claim that he was unique by saying that "there are many others in the city who are able to occupy the position of cover-point." Mr. Justice Bruneau agreed, ruling that a citizen could not be forced to act against his will, and so Pitre could play for whomever he wished. He wished to be a Canadien.

Yet the Canadiens' first year of existence was hard, and they won only two of their 12 games. As the *Gazette* had rightly predicted, competition for players was stiff. With the O'Brien family's coffers stocking the enterprise, the upstart National Hockey Association went on a gleeful raiding party, returning with the Canadian Hockey Association's greatest stars.

The O'Briens' own Renfrew franchise signed defenseman Lester Patrick for $3,000 a season, which Patrick made conditional on the signing of his brother Frank, for another $2,000. Art Ross, who had starred for Kenora and who knew the value of a dollar as the twelfth of 13 children born to the wealthy factor of a Hudson's Bay fur-trading post, signed a contract with the Haileybury Comets for $2,700.

The richest dish on the menu would be Fred Taylor, who gleefully started his own bidding war. Having won the Stanley Cup with Ottawa the year earlier, and well aware that he could bring a crowd to its feet with one of his standard, dazzling, rink-long rushes, Taylor laughed at the $1,500 the O'Briens were offering him to bring Stanley Cup leadership to their team.

After the Cyclone's negotiating skills spun them in circles, the O'Briens considered themselves lucky to be paying the maestro $5,200 for the honour of his presence in 12 games — a salary that was $2,700 more than Prime Minister Wilfrid Laurier was earning. Then, as now, the PM was providing entertainment to editorial writers, while Taylor was providing entertainment to the masses. And that, in the democratic marketplace, had more recoupable value.

The O'Briens' expensive crew of puck-chasers no longer seemed to fit their team nickname of "Creamery Kings," paying homage to the region's wonderful butter. They were now big league, and their new name would innocently foreshadow the status of players more than half a century away. The team would now be called "The Millionaires."

The team that was bought to win the Stanley Cup began by losing its first match 11–9 to Cobalt. Still, the *Renfrew Mercury*'s hockey man had reason to hope, noting that Taylor's rushes, "while very spectacular, lacked result because of the failure of the forwards combination." The Millionaires fared better when *Les Canadiens* came to town, winning their second outing 9-4. Newsy Lalonde's rushes were "in the Taylor class," said the *Mercury,* and before the month was out, people could compare them as teammates, for Lalonde would be wearing the red and white of the Millionaires.

In February of 1910, Taylor went to Ottawa to play his old team for the first time. The town was abuzz with the prodigal's return, and Taylor wound them up by making a jest which would spiral his reputation into the realm of myth. Taylor was an expert backward skater, a skill he mastered as a youth after losing a skating race to a speed skater, who had skated backward while the fleet Taylor skated forward. While chatting in the *Ottawa Citizen* newsroom — hardly a den of confidentiality — Taylor teased cub reporter Tommy Gorman in the presence of Ottawa goalie Percy LeSueur, vowing to skate backward through Ottawa's defense, then score a goal.

Though Gorman (who would go on to manage the Senators himself) indicated Taylor was kidding, not everyone saw the joke. On February 12, 1910, 7,000 Senators fans — the largest crowd yet to witness a hockey game in Canada — came out to shower Fred Taylor with their affection for jumping to Renfrew and then mocking them. Curses, lemons, horse manure, and empty whisky bottles rained down on the former favourite son, one bottle smashing near Taylor's feet and propelling him to centre ice, out of throwing range.

Along with his partner Lester Patrick, Taylor played a superb game, but at the end of regulation time, the score was tied at five and he still hadn't scored a backward goal. In the 10-minute overtime, Ottawa scored three times, and while Taylor made many spectacular rushes, he never got a shot on Ottawa's Percy LeSueur. The hero was a chump and was duly hooted out of town.

One month later, on March 8, 1910, the Cyclone tried again, and this time Taylor's joking boast would come true. The *Renfrew Mercury* reported that he skated down ice "in his usual fine fashion," then "turned, going backwards, he skated a piece and then sent the shot home to the Ottawa nets with skill and swiftness." Taylor's goal was backhanded, not backward, but it was one of 17 that the Millionaires scored as they embarrassed Ottawa 17-2. And so the fable of Taylor's "backward goal" was born.

It is easy through the distance of the years and the promotional juggernaut that constantly overwhelms today's hockey fan with "The Next Great One" to lose sight of just how powerful Taylor's public image was. Two days after his bravura "backward" performance, the Cyclone was leading his Renfrew team into the ultimate test of anyone's star power: the Big Apple.

Taylor had been to New York City before. On his first visit in the spring of 1908, he led his Ottawa Senators to two exhibition victories over the Stanley Cup champion Montreal Wanderers at the posh St. Nicholas Arena. The sober *New York Times* was giddy with the delights of Taylor's hockey genius, and bestowed the highest honour an American publication could give: they favourably compared the Cyclone to an American baseball god, calling Taylor "the Ty Cobb of hockey."

The Cyclone was such a popular draw that New York promoters inserted the immutable clause that Taylor be part of any hockey package coming to St. Nick's. And so it came to pass that Taylor led the Renfrew Millionaires into Manhattan in March of 1910 to play three matches against an all-star team picked from the Montreal Wanderers and Ottawa. In case any New Yorkers hadn't been paying attention, the *New York Evening Telegram* called Taylor "the most exciting player in hockey" and put his talent in a context the American psyche would immediately grasp. "Considering that he is paid $5,000 for playing just a dozen games, he is unquestionably the highest paid player in team sport," gushed the *Telegram*. "His salary shames what is paid our star baseball players for a full 154-game season."

When the Millionaires weren't enjoying the bright lights of Broadway, they were sweeping the three-game series, collecting $1,500 in prize money and a heady sense that there was a great big life of possibility beyond the rich comforts of Renfrew. Still, the prize that mattered the most was Lord Stanley's Jug, and despite their expensive talent, the Millionaires still couldn't buy the damned thing.

They were also in financial trouble. Renfrew finished the 1910 season nearly $20,000 in debt, and at the annual meeting of the NHA other teams worried about the increasingly high cost of running a professional sports franchise. In an oddly familiar sequence of events, the owners tried to close the Pandora's box they had opened.

Among their items of business that day in late November 1910, NHA owners opted for corporate sponsorship, adopting the Spalding puck as the league's official puck; they refashioned league matches into three 20-minute periods in order to extend concession sales; and they tried to staunch the flow of red ink by imposing a $5,000 total salary cap on each club.

The players were angry, and speculation rose that a hockey strike was brewing. On November 25, the *Montreal Herald* published a letter from Art Ross which pointed out that, among the so-called suffering teams, the Wanderers had "paid on the average from $10,000 to $14,000 a year in salaries since they first started the pro game." Ottawa was even richer, paying "from $10,000 to $25,000." In a familiar lament, Ross implored "All the players want is a fair deal ... The players are not trying to bulldoze the NHA, but we want to know where we get off at."

The clubs were adamant, with Ottawa President D'Arcy McGee saying his club had recorded a deficit, even though they had taken in $25,000 in revenue and paid out $15,000 in salaries. The players were not fooled and issued an ultimatum to pay up or else they would start their own league. Ambrose O'Brien suggested the clubs could afford a salary limit of $8,000, but the frustrated players pursued their idea of a new league, only to discover that the rinks were all under contract to the NHA. They could start their own league if they wished, but they'd be back outdoors, playing on frozen ponds for free.

It turned out that the owners were not exaggerating their financial difficulties. At the end of the 1911 season, the once-glittering Renfrew Millionaires dropped out of hockey altogether. Cobalt and Haileybury dropped out, too, having discovered — as others would do after them — that buying a Stanley Cup is easier said than done. Their loss, however, meant Toronto's gain, as Hogtown hockey finally entered the big leagues when Toronto interests took over the two O'Brien franchises.

While the O'Briens failed to bring the Jug to Renfrew, their efforts would pay other dividends for the game and lead to many more Stanley Cups for other places. They had made possible the Montreal Canadiens, and they had showcased the hockey talents of Fred Taylor, and of Lester and Frank Patrick. It was those latter two visionaries who would now take up the torch to make professional hockey a sport spanning not just the country, but the U.S. border, too. Once again, Fred Taylor would be there.

In the spring of 1911, Lester and Frank Patrick's father, Joe, decided to take up an offer from a British syndicate and sold his British Columbia lumber business for $440,000 — a fortune in a time when for $25,000 you could buy a 10-room house not only in the fashionable West End of Vancouver but on Beach Avenue, with an unobstructed view of English Bay.

The Patrick brothers, fresh off the bounty of the National Hockey Association's experiment with high-salaried hockey, had differing ideas about what their father should do with his money. Practical Lester thought Joe should limit his hockey involvement to watching from a safe distance. Frank, the visionary, remembered his time in New York City with the Renfrew Millionaires and Fred Taylor, where the big St. Nick's rink with its artificial ice packed in all those people to see this wonderful sport. He thought about the boom that was the south coast of British Columbia, and about how all those prosperous Canadians might be lusting for the chance to plunk down their gold in the service of the national winter drama. So he told his father to wager his fortune on artificial ice arenas on Canada's Pacific coast. To the astonishment of all, Joe Patrick agreed with his younger son.

Joe and Grace Patrick raised the scions of hockey's "Royal Family" in Quebec, along with four other children. The Patrick brothers, along with future Hall of Famer Art Ross, would play shinny on the frozen rinks of Montreal's Westmount. It remained Lester's creed that trying to finesse a block of wood or tin can through the hacks of players wielding tree branches would teach a player more about hockey than any chalkboard or lecture ever could.

The Patrick brothers rose through the ranks of Montreal hockey and learned business off the ice. Teenage Lester served as stick-boy for visiting teams at the Montreal Arena and, with Art Ross, scalped 35-cent reserved tickets for as much as a dollar. Lester and Frank eventually made it into McGill University, but Lester's gifts were for hockey and basketball, not book learning. While Frank was captaining the varsity squad, Lester was winning the Stanley Cup in 1906 and again in 1907 with the Montreal Wanderers.

While the brothers were earning big money with Fred Taylor in the NHA, their father was doing likewise in booming British Columbia.

With the construction of new railway lines, virgin timber was accessible as it never before had been. With much of eastern and middle North America now logged out, would-be timber barons like Joe Patrick came west, staking out one-square-mile forest claims for the rent of $114 a year.

On December 7, 1911, the Patrick brothers used their father's timber fortune to proclaim the birth of the Pacific Coast Hockey Association, with teams in Vancouver, Victoria, and New Westminster. With just over half its population living in cities, British Columbia was the most urbanized province in Canada, and in 1911, the region surrounding Vancouver was in the middle of a growth spurt. In 10 years, Vancouver's population had grown from 27,000 to 100,000, with 13,000 more people living in New Westminster and another 35,000 in the Greater Vancouver area.

It was in this prosperity that the Patricks would build their castle, the Vancouver Arena. For $27,000, Joe Patrick bought a parcel of land on Coal Harbour, looking onto Stanley Park, Burrard Inlet, and the spectacular North Shore mountains. When a public subscription to finance the rink failed to scare up investors, Joe Patrick took out a $100,000 mortgage for the Vancouver Arena, which would eventually cost him $275,000.

With a capacity of 10,500, Vancouver's was the largest indoor arena in the world, bigger by 500 seats than Madison Square Garden in New York, the reigning champ. The ice in Vancouver would be big, too, 90 feet by 220 feet, making it the largest of the five artificial ice surfaces then in existence, one fueled by the world's largest refrigeration plant and ice-making machine.

Frank Patrick, 26, became the Pacific Coast league's president, and managed and coached Vancouver, while Lester, 28, ran the show in Victoria. As the O'Briens had done before them, the Patricks went on a feeding frenzy of other teams. Of the 23 players in the PCHA, 16 of them came from the NHA, for as Lester admitted, the Patricks offered players "more money than they could dare refuse."

At 8:45 P.M. on January 2, 1912, the Patrick brothers' dream became real in the spanking new 4,200-seat Victoria Arena, built for a comparatively modest $125,000. The brothers' parents, Grace and Joe, along with 2,500 fans, stood as the national anthem, "God Save the King," was played when B.C.'s lieutenant governor entered the arena to perform the ceremonial face-off of the puck. With the Victoria squad in red and white, and New Westminster in black and orange, the first professional hockey game ever played west of Ontario and Michigan began. And it was a hit.

"Ice hockey [delivered] all the thrills the west had heard of," cheered the *Victoria Times-Colonist*. Vancouver's Province took a swipe at the provincial capital's hubris, saying "it did not take the Islanders long to appreciate the beauties of the game though they did not like it too much when Jimmy's Gardner's Royal City crowd shoved over an 8–3 beating on Lester Patrick and his hired talent."

Three nights later across Georgia Strait, the Vancouver Millionaires made their debut with a veteran, stellar squad boasting the great Newsy Lalonde, as well as Si Griffis and Tom Phillips, who had been crucial to the Kenora Thistles' Cup victory in 1907. Frank Patrick himself suited up on defense, where he would set a record for the new league by scoring six goals in a game against New Westminster in March of 1912.

Despite the gleaming talent and local enthusiasm for the Patricks' bold project, the Millionaires' home opener in the world's largest indoor hockey palace on Friday, January 5, 1912 was only half-full, with 5,000 Lower Mainlanders turning out to watch the Millionaires defeat New Westminster 8–3. Frank Patrick knew (as owners know now) that in order to pack his new pleasure dome, he would need the biggest name in the game: Fred "Cyclone" Taylor.

Taylor would play in Vancouver in March 1912, but not for the Millionaires. True to form, the Cyclone decided to test the balmy coastal waters first by making a third-period appearance on behalf of the East All-Stars, playing against those from the Patricks' league. To the roars of the 8,000 fans, and with the score tied at three, Taylor set up the winning goal, then set up the insurance marker, in case anyone had missed the point. For a brand-new hockey town, it was like catching Wayne Gretzky in his prime for 20 minutes, then watching him wave good-bye.

As Taylor skated off the ice with visions of bags of gold dancing in his head, Frank Patrick began the wooing game by waiting until Taylor was back in Ottawa. Indeed, Patrick's initial overture was a model of pith and irony. "Dear Fred," he telegrammed to the wily showman. "Having a wonderful time. Wish you were here."

Taylor was having his own particular brand of fun, waging contractual war with Sam Lichtenhein, the hot-headed manager of the Montreal Wanderers. After the Renfrew Millionaires folded, the team was redrafted by lottery. The surviving clubs drew the rights to players who would otherwise be hustling shinny games against gormless kids at the local pond. The Montreal Wanderers thought that they had won Taylor, but little did they know what they were up against.

Taylor refused to report to Montreal and went back to Ottawa, taking up his job in the Civil Service, and more importantly, taking up residence in proximity to Thirza Cook, his intended bride. He told the furious Lichtenhein that he was a "free agent" and not a piece of chattel. Amid his righteous rhetoric was a scheme, for Taylor planned to cut a sweet deal with the Ottawa Senators. Sam Lichtenhein thought otherwise, and in March of 1911, one of early hockey's more remarkable encounters took place, at once high drama and low farce. In of all places, Boston.

Since the Cyclone's reputation among American hockey fans was huge, Boston hockey promoters were delighted that the recently ex-Renfrew Millionaire would be wearing the Ottawa Senators' colours against the team he refused to play for, the Montreal Wanderers. On the night before the Boston game, with 6,000 tickets sold to eager Beantowners, Sam Lichtenhein unleashed his demons of revenge: Cyclone Taylor belonged to him, and if he dared to show his face in this match, there would be no match.

With the promoters soiling their shorts, and the packed Boston Arena waiting to cast eyes upon the greatest hockey player on earth (or so they'd been told for years by the New York press) the Stanley Cup champion Senators' line-up was announced by a man with a megaphone standing at centre ice. Cyclone Taylor would be playing.

While a livid Sam Lichtenhein scuttled from the stands to stop this outrage, his captain, Art Ross, made a fast decision to defy his manager, and led his players onto the ice. Improbably, the recently wed Lester Patrick was in town, having taken his bride, Grace, on his idea of a honeymoon tour to the great hockey cities of Eastern Canada and the United States. When the promoters discovered that Lester was in Boston, they figured $50 might divert him from sweet romance to referee the game. It did.

The ref's allegiances were to Art Ross, his boyhood pal, and to Cyclone Taylor, the man whom Lester and Frank knew they had to get for their fledgling league. As Sam Lichtenhein ran along the boards, Lester Patrick hustled both centres together and dropped the puck to start the game. Lichtenhein could only watch in fury as his nemesis Taylor scored three goals to lead Ottawa to a 7–5 victory.

Sam Lichtenhein vowed to put the cur Taylor in his place. When the man who had defied him not once, but twice, tried to sign up with the Ottawa Senators for the 1912 season, Lichtenhein struck a note familiar to Fred Taylor. He so put the fear of free agency into his fellow NHA owners that they sent a message to any other rebels by suspending Cyclone for an entire year. If the greatest player in hockey wouldn't play for Sam Lichtenhein, then he wouldn't play for anyone.

Thinking he'd crushed Taylor, Lichtenhein's blood pressure could have powered the lights in the Montreal Arena when he discovered that Taylor had turned the tables. He had convinced the Senators that unless they paid him the exorbitant sum of $1,200 to serve his one-year suspension in Ottawa, he might not be around when his suspension was lifted.

While Taylor was the pioneer for all those players who today sit out until they get a contract that they feel reflects their worth, he in the end didn't play for the Ottawa Senators, though he did take their money. By the beginning of the 1912–13 season, Frank Patrick's overtures to Cyclone had marinated in Taylor's fertile brain. And the fact that, in these days of more modest salaries, Patrick would make Taylor the highest-paid player in the game at $1,800 a season convinced the Cyclone to head west. At last.

On December 5, 1912, Fred Taylor rolled into Vancouver on the train. While there was no snow or howling winds as there had been when Taylor made his first pro journey to Houghton, Michigan, Taylor's greeting party had a similar message to the one that met him eight years earlier: practice would be in three hours.

At age 27 and the most celebrated player in hockey, Taylor had just one Stanley Cup to his name, but the Patricks hoped that his superlative talent and powerful mystique — as Vancouverites 85 years later would hope with the coming of Mark Messier — would be enough to win another.

In an inspired move and hoping to exploit Taylor's creativity, Frank Patrick moved the Cyclone off defense and up to the forward line, making him a rover as he been in Houghton. Patrick was ecstatic at having the Cyclone, telling reporters "we have all the material necessary for three strong teams, and I want to state that we are not going to raid the Eastern clubs further."

Such was Taylor's fame that BC Electric laid on special trolley cars to transport 500 New Westminster fans into Vancouver to join the 7,000 others who had come out to see the wonder's debut. Taylor emerged as "Hero of Game," using his quicksilver speed and magical stickhandling ability to dominate the ice. Despite suffering severe stomach pains before the match, Taylor, who was rusty, scored one goal and assisted on several others as Vancouver spanked New Westminster 7–2.

Though the city loved him from the start, it didn't seem that way. While Taylor was sleeping off his first win as a Millionaire, his downtown hotel caught fire, and he had to flee through his window down a fire ladder. When he realized that he'd left his wallet back in his room, the thrifty Taylor tried to climb back up the ladder, but he was restrained by firemen. He would later claim that he never knew how much of his hard-earned cash went up in smoke, but in all likelihood, he knew the serial numbers on the bills.

The Millionaires' next home game, against Victoria, was a complete sell-out, the first time that 10,500 people had filled the Vancouver Arena, and the largest audience yet to watch a hockey game anywhere, ever. Things, however, got worse for Taylor. After his second game for Vancouver, his crippling stomach pains were diagnosed as appendicitis, and his doctor confined him to bed. Taylor escaped and suited up for his third match, where he put his appendicitis on hold long enough to score two goals and add three assists.

Indeed, things were going so well for the Patricks that both Lester and Frank were thinking of stepping back from their creation and letting their newly acquired talent shine. They also had a bigger world to conquer, looking south to launch their own gold rush in the fertile ground of Northern California. In December 1912, Frank Patrick announced that, in exchange for a quarter of a million dollars, the brothers had won the right to build a huge ice arena at the 1915 San Francisco World's Fair "so that visitors from all parts of the universe will be able to see Canada's great winter pastimes."

Such was the salesmanship of the Patrick brothers that, less than a year after beginning their expensive venture on the West Coast, they had managed to convince the Americans to stage an exhibit of winter events in a place where winter often means putting on a sweater. In the end, the outbreak of war canceled the grand plan, but the idea of hockey in the land of sun and surf would be resurrected over the next 80 years, with varying degrees of success.

Though they had lost $9,000 on their first year of Pacific hockey operations, the Patricks were thinking big in the right place: the far west was — and remains — all about inventing or re-inventing the self, and the statute of limitations never seems to expire. With the imaginative genius of Frank Patrick, and the organizational gifts of Lester, the West was theirs to be won, and what they needed to complement Lord Stanley's Park in Vancouver was Lord Stanley's Cup.

The Patricks' raiding of the NHA was over — for now — but they needed to convince the Stanley Cup trustees that their new league was as worthy to compete for the Cup as any other. So they arranged for an exhibition match between the Pacific Coast league champion Victoria Aristocrats and the Cup-winning Quebec Bulldogs, who consented to leave the frozen east to play a little indoor hockey on fake ice on the shore of the Pacific Ocean.

The National Hockey Association teams were now playing a six-man-aside game, having dispensed with the position of rover. The Patricks dismissed this innovation as a money-saving move, and two of the three exhibition matches in Victoria would be played under Pacific Coast rules.

The Quebec Bulldogs were led by centreman Joe Malone, a 23-year-old native of Quebec City, whose elegant stickhandling and scrupulous play earned him the nickname "Gentleman Joe"— considerable in an era when new rules made charging-from-behind and profanity offenses that could cost a player $5, and expulsion from the match. Malone's other nickname was "Phantom," for the finely featured, dark-eyed Bulldogs' captain had the ability to appear suddenly in the sights of a defenseman, seemingly on a leisurely skate, before bursting by the hapless rearguard, or faking him out with devastating finesse.

Yet the talents of "Phantom Joe" and his teammate "Bad" Joe Hall (whom Malone always maintained was unfairly named) were not enough to conquer the Aristocrats of Victoria. The Patricks had a point to prove, and their manager and founder, 29-year-old Lester, inspired his team with four goals over three games, to lead Victoria to a two-games-to-one victory. The fact the Patricks' team way out there on a B.C. island had outscored the reigning Cup champs 16–12 sent a message to the rest of the hockey world: the Pacific Coast Hockey Association was not some pampered experiment.

In 1914, the Patricks' league acquired more eastern stars. Didier Pitre arrived with his board-splintering wristshot and toasted fans between periods as he raised a pint of chilled champagne to restore his equilibrium. Frank Nighbor, "The Pembroke Peach," escaped from his Toronto team and also joined the Millionaires. Nighbor, who would become famous for his poke-check, was originally scorned as too small to play hockey — until he came off the bench to score six goals in his first game.

The Patricks were about to get closer to fulfilling the rest of their dream, but it wouldn't include Cyclone Taylor, or at least, not quite yet. As champs of the PCHA, Lester Patrick's Victoria Aristocrats would get the first crack at the Jug by playing the Cup-holding Toronto Blueshirts in hockey's first transcontinental, professional Stanley Cup match.

While most hockey fans imagine Toronto to have been a hockey temple filled with oracles since the first puck was dropped, the professional NHA game had only established itself in Hogtown the same year the Patricks began their league on the West Coast.

Though Toronto was the first Eastern Canadian city to install artificial ice, the Patricks had been busily re-inventing the game. In 1912, they introduced numbered hockey jerseys, and freed their goalies from their shackles. Under the Patricks' new rules, the net-minders no longer had to play the puck standing, but could now fall and flop in any manner they chose, so long as they didn't throw their sticks or pass the puck with their hands.

The Patricks' most brilliant innovation came after being frustrated by repeated, game-killing off-side calls in the 1913 exhibition "World Series" against Quebec. Frank and Lester conceived of dividing the ice into three zones, bisected by "blue" lines 67 feet apart. Players would be allowed to pass the puck forward in this zone, at once injecting the game with a powerful tactical dimension, and speeding up the action. Either from envy or from complacency, the eastern mandarins decided that their players were still forbidden to skate ahead of the puck carrier until further notice.

The three-game 1914 series alternated between the old eastern rules and the fresh new western ones, but the latter failed to impress the Torontonians, and crowds dwindled, some mocking the Patricks' innovations as nothing more than "lacrosse on ice." People were intrigued, however, by Victoria's substitute forward Jack Ulrich, a deaf mute, who the papers generously reported was not hampered by his affliction in his two substitute appearances. In a close series, the Toronto Blueshirts swept the three games, but now that the Patricks had been allowed to play for the Cup, they knew they would be back.

The bright promise of the twentieth century came to a bloody halt in August 1914, when Britain declared war on Germany and dragged Canada into a mass slaughter that resonates still. Despite newspaper headlines to the contrary, the war would not be over by Christmas.

Vancouver sent the highest number of young men off to war of any city on the continent, and of the 55,000 Vancouverites who went, half were killed or wounded. The Patrick brothers tried to march off to defend the honour of Belgium when the Kaiser's army invaded, but the Canadian government blocked them, deeming the Patricks' Pacific Coast league to be an entertainment "crucial to sustaining morale during the war." It was an astonishing reminder of the psychosis of war, for while one young Canadian could be deemed expendable for a yard of foreign soil, another was too priceless to let leave his patch of ice.

Fred Taylor was blocked, too, for his job as an immigration officer made him essential to the national interest. In the spring of 1914, Taylor had been in the middle of a quasi-military operation in Vancouver's harbour, when a Japanese ship, the *Komagata Maru*, was refused permission to dock with her cargo of immigrant Sikhs. For two months, the ship sat festering in the harbour. When Taylor saw the ship sail away at the point of the Irish Fusiliers' guns, he was relieved, but, as he said later, "nobody was proud" of one of Canada's shameful racial incidents.

That fall, Taylor went back to his night job and suited up for the powerhouse Millionaires. Though Vancouver had lost Didier Pitre to the Canadiens, they gained Duncan "Mickey" Mackay, honourably discharged from the army for being underage. Frank Patrick's inclination was to ignore the letter from the 18-year-old Mackay asking for a contract, but he gave the kid a chance. The quick-breaking, stylish centre known as the "Wee Scot" led the league with 34 goals over 17 games in his rookie year, while the Cyclone came second with 23 goals. The Vancouver Millionaires were the 1915 champions of their league, and now, at home, they would challenge the Ottawa Senators in the first Cup match played west of Winnipeg.

The Senators felt they had traveled too far, arriving on the Pacific coast in a state of disorientation. The *Vancouver Province* reported that the sea-level altitude conspired with the temperate climate to make the Senators sluggish, and in the first game, played under western rules, the Millionaires skated circles around Ottawa in front of 7,000 fans in the Vancouver Arena, winning 6–2.

Ottawa's "Punch" Broadbent scored three goals in the second game, but Hugh Lehman, Vancouver's 30-year-old goalie, grew stingy. Nicknamed "Old Eagle Eye," Lehman was famous for his sorties up the ice, and rumour had it that he once scored a goal. While Lehman shut out the Senators for the rest of the game, Cyclone Taylor matched Ottawa with three goals of his own, and Frank Nighbor added two in Vancouver's 8–3 win.

Despite Ottawa's efforts to stop Mackay, Nighbor, and Taylor, the third and final match was a blowout, as Barney Stanley rose to the top for the Millionaires, scoring four goals. Unimpeded by Ottawa's defense, Mackay and Nighbor each scored a hat trick, and Vancouver won 12–3. After sweeping the best of the east in three games, and outscoring them 26–8, the Millionaires were, as the *Vancouver Province* announced, "world champions." Each player collected $200 as his part of the prize money, and Lord Stanley's Jug had its first home on the West Coast. Years later, Lester Patrick would tell the scribes of Manhattan that the 1915 Vancouver Millionaires were "the best hockey team that ever stepped onto the ice."

And they were more than that: they were a symbol of entrepreneurial nerve rewarded. A mere four years after starting their Pacific Coast league, the Patricks had won professional hockey's highest prize. Not only that, but they had now established hockey both across the country and across the border, for the brothers had sold their New Westminster team to Portland, Oregon, and would soon put one in Seattle.

The Patricks had also changed the sport with their expansive vision, and their innovative rules, and they would go on to invent the playoff system, for which one *New York Times* columnist, Arthur Daley, said "they should have a monument raised in their memory for that one idea alone." While the Patricks were not the first to spend money on players, they had managed to do what the O'Briens of Renfrew never could: win the Stanley Cup, and christen their league with legitimacy.

Fred Taylor was now at the top of the hockey world. At 31 years old, the Cyclone was regarded as the best hockey player on earth, though he had reached his final hockey pinnacle. Taylor would never win another Cup, but fittingly, he scored a hat trick in his final professional appearance on March 11, 1921. Later in his long life of 94 years when he looked back on his magnificent career on ice, the Cyclone also saw that Cup-winning Millionaires team as his best, and one of the best ever. "Every regular on that team that took us to the Stanley Cup series — Si Griffis, Mickey Mackay, Frank Patrick, Barney Stanley, Hughie Lehman, Frank Nighbor, and myself—made the Hockey Hall of Fame. This has never happened to any other team." The boy who was once banished from the OHA for refusing to play in the big time had become a legend.

4

The Warriors

Of all the athletes who went off to fight the First World War, it is the story of two hockey players that captures the bloody triumph and disaster of a generation. One is a tale of luck; the other of fate. One, of the rising professional game; the other of a genteel and privileged amateurism. Yet when seen together, the stories of Conn Smythe and Hobey Baker form a picture of both doomed youth and the tough-minded spirit that would survive the war and prosper. One would become a symbol of the glorious ideal; the other, a symbol of the profane reality. The lives of both warriors would change the game they loved, and in between them came a war at home, which would give pro hockey the shape it knows today.

Conn Smythe was a swaggering bantamweight chancer, a poor runty boy who somehow always wound up as captain of whatever team he was on — simply because he wanted it so much. Despite being schooled at Canada's elite Upper Canada College, Smythe was no member of any old boys' club. He hated the school and what it stood for, saying later that he made his own sons go there because he knew that, if they survived, they would never again be in awe of any of the great family names, power, or social standing. No, Conn Smythe, the son of a Belfast Protestant journalist turned freethinking Theosophist, was a self-made man. And being so meant that the cost of losing is one's self. It was a cost Conn Smythe would not even entertain.

Hobey Baker, a classically handsome American pilot, came from an aristocratic Philadelphia family, the kind Conn Smythe would have loathed on sight. Being a privileged American at the turn of the twentieth century gave Baker a lofty height from which to view the world, and, from where he stood, the world was his. Sporting prowess, friends, women, fame, and victory came so easily that he didn't have to think about it — until it was gone. And the war came along to let him win again.

From the summer of 1914 until the autumn of 1918, the world was enslaved by the Great War. Young men and women, of all colours and creeds, marched from their homes to fight for — or more appropriately, survive — an ancient ideal of imperial integrity. The conflagration swept Western Europe, Russia, and the Middle East, and when it was over, the 20 principal belligerents had killed at least 8.5 million of the world's youth. On average, 5,600 soldiers were killed on each day of the war.

If any robust athletes had been ambivalent about the merits of dying young in some foreign field, a Canadian recruiting poster depicted square-jawed men driving a team of swift horses through a landscape more like the Canadian West than the muddy carnage of Flanders Fields. "Artillery Heroes at the Front Say 'Get Into A Man's Uniform,'" said the caption, the alternative not too subtly implicit: stay home and be a coward.

So hockey players traded in their hockey colours for the khaki of war and learned what wearing a "man's uniform" meant. The rising young star Allan "Scotty" Davidson, who had won the Stanley Cup in 1914 with Toronto, was killed at Ypres while trying to rescue a wounded officer. George Richardson, who had starred for Queen's University, was one of the 624,000 Allied troops obliterated during the Battle of the Somme in 1916. In December of 1915, Captain James Sutherland, who had coached Richardson when he wasn't advocating Kingston's claim as the birthplace of hockey, issued a message in his capacity as president of the Canadian Amateur Hockey Association. Showing the same kind of allegiance to a bloodless ideal of warfare that was all too prevalent in British rhetoric, Sutherland exhorted each young Canadian hockey player to take up arms and "play the greatest game of his life." Despite the ghastly casualties and obscene descriptions of the daily slaughter filtering back home, the old rhetoric equating war to a game would not die, though the athletes most certainly would.

"One-Eyed" Frank McGee, the most sterling of the Ottawa Silver Seven, answered the call to glory, managing to enlist in the army as a lieutenant despite his disability. As family legend has it, when asked to cover his right eye and read with his glass left eye during the army's eye-chart test, McGee merely switched hands and kept reading out of his good eye. Given that everyone in Ottawa knew that the famous hockey star McGee had only one eye, it was the McGee family's political clout that sent him into a carnage he had no business going to. As a silent protest of the sham, the doctor who "judged" McGee fit for active service refused to lie on McGee's medical chart. He just left blank the spot asking about the condition of McGee's blind left eye.

On September 16, 1916, McGee was killed, age 37, in action at Courcellete, another casualty of the savage Battle of the Somme. Predictably, his *Ottawa Citizen* obituary commended him for "jump[ing] into the greater and grimmer game of war."

Since Canada, as a member of the British Commonwealth, followed the mother country Britain into the carnage on August 4, 1914, it was Conn Smythe's war before it was Hobey Baker's. In the early winter of 1915, Lieutenant Conn Smythe, ex-captain of the University of Toronto Varsity Junior hockey team, had just route-marched his 40th Canadian Field Artillery "Sportsmen's" battalion from Niagara to Toronto with explicit orders from his commander, Major Gordon Southam. Ten of Smythe's troops happened to be among the finest hockey players in Ontario, and Southam, whose family was consolidating its hold on the Canadian newspaper business, wanted Smythe to get them into the mighty Ontario Hockey Association.

Smythe was one of those characters who makes things happen, though he often had the help of fabulous coincidence or luck of the kind that Charles Dickens would have loved. Despite proclaiming their hospitality to soldier teams, the OHA owners gave Smythe a hard time, for in the short, hot-eyed 20-year-old soldier, the owners saw a rube who was going to save them all a little money.

The four Toronto teams in the OHA Senior group all played at the city's Mutual Street Arena. Even so, one team had to be the home team, which got a higher percentage of the gate. In the early part of the season, league attendance was so small that it often seemed as if the players outnumbered the fans. The cunning OHA men gave Smythe's team the first four home dates, so they could take the later, richer ones for themselves.

The greedy OHA owners didn't figure on something that would define Smythe's life: patriotism. A soldier team playing hockey while an awful war raged in Europe was the kind of thing Torontonians wanted to support, and 2,500 of them watched the soldiers lose their first game, 6–1. The OHA men, though, watched in dismay as the soldiers won big at the box office.

The gunners soon found their skating legs and went on to win their next two games. After paying the team's start-up debts, Smythe discovered the soldiers had made a $2,800 profit from those very gate receipts that weren't supposed to exist. With a big game coming up against their archrival Toronto Argos, a team who'd beaten the soldiers twice in overtime, Major Southam confided in his young lieutenant that their next game would be their last. They were shipping out.

And then along came along an offer whose irony equaled its opportunity. A Toronto steel magnate, grown rich from supplying bomb and shell factories, proposed a wager against the soldiers. Smythe, a gambler to the kernel of his flinty soul, ventured $100 on his team, but the steel merchant scoffed. Smythe was always one to take a risk, but he couldn't blow the team's grubstake without authority from above. Fortunately, Major Southam was with him, so Conn Smythe forked over the entire $2,800. The death merchant was shocked. But he matched it.

There was now $5,600 — or more than three times what Cyclone Taylor, then the world's highest-paid hockey player, was earning for a season — riding on a single match.

Before the game, Smythe made a speech to his troops—one of many that he would make throughout his life. The emotion of it was not a Henry V "once more unto the breach" but came from the cold truth: Smythe told his gunners that every blessed cent they had in the world was riding on this game. If they lost, they lost everything.

The gunners came out blazing. Driver Quinn Butterfield, an Orillia native, scored two goals in the first four minutes. After nine minutes, the soldiers were up 4–0 on the Argos. By the time it was over, Butterfield had scored two more goals, and Smythe's team was on the right end of an 8–3 rout — as well as a lot of money. In addition to the

$5,600 Smythe had won on the bet, a record crowd of 6,378 people generated another $1,106 in gate receipts.

With the $6,706 in booty, worth roughly 15 times what it is today, Smythe was giddy with riches, and grand plans were made. When the troop arrived in England, every man going on leave would be given some of the winnings to spend. The rest was earmarked for a lavish Christmas dinner for the 200-strong battery — one to be held every Christmas for the rest of the war.

An omen of doom came early, for the magical match had been stained by a brawl in the stands between rival fans, and one of the 40th Battery's men was badly injured. In another small tragedy of war, the injured soldier asked Smythe and his mates to keep his wounds a secret, or else he might not be allowed to ship out to fight. They did, but there would be one less man at Christmas dinner, for the injured soldier died at sea of massive internal bleeding.

As the war blasted on, there were fewer and fewer of Smythe's troops at Christmas dinner. Every senior officer in Smythe's battery was killed or badly wounded, as was Quinn Butterfield, who Smythe said would have risen to stardom in any league in the world. And as for the enterprising young lieutenant, Conn Smythe, he was killed, too. Or so it seemed.

In November of 1917 the Toronto papers reported that Lieutenant Conn Smythe was "missing in action," a macabre euphemism that usually meant the missing soldier had been so effectively blown to bits that identification was impossible. Smythe had tried his best for self-preservation in the muddy, rat-infested trenches. When he heard that the Royal Flying Corps was looking for artillery officers to train as aerial spotters, he saw that his way out was up.

One of his flight instructors was the future Canadian air ace Billy Barker, who so hated teaching duty that he scared the student pilots senseless by taking them for sphincter-loosening rides. When that didn't get Barker posted to the Western Front, he buzzed some senior officers so closely they had to lie flat on the ground to avoid decapitation. Barker was then sent to Italy, where his adversaries were so poor that he didn't even bother counting his kills. Finally, he used the old buzzing trick again, this time giving the King of Italy a close shave, and so Barker got his wish. He was sent to the Western Front, where his talent at killing in the air filled his chest with medals, including the exalted Military and Victoria Crosses. Barker's zeal for combat and delight in flouting authority deeply impressed Conn Smythe, and he would later make Barker the president of the Toronto Maple Leafs.

Once Smythe got his wings, he discovered that being a pilot of an artillery observation plane had its own risk, the first one being the plane. Nicknamed "The Incinerator," the two-seater planes had the unnerving habit of catching fire all by themselves. Canadian infantrymen would make bets each time an "Incinerator" took off to see if it would explode on its own, or with the help of the Germans.

Smythe went down in flames courtesy of the enemy. On a day so cloudy it was difficult to perform any artillery observation, Smythe and his observer were hit by gunfire. Their plane went into a flat spin, so Smythe cut the engine and put the nose down, looking for a place to land. Throughout his life, Smythe was a fierce Protestant, and his religious beliefs influenced how he treated his hockey players. His Catholic observer was on the opposing side of the debate, and Smythe frequently argued religion with him. Now, as their plane dropped toward the ravaged earth, the ruined trees jutting up as lethal spikes, the observer asked Smythe what was going to happen. Smythe answered that finally, they were going to find out who had been right about the afterlife.

Not quite. Managing to pancake the plane into a shell hole behind German lines, Smythe and his observer made their way toward a man waving at them in a friendly manner. Only when they could see the whites of his eyes did they realize he was a German soldier, and the scrappy Smythe began screaming at him for this unsporting trick. The German answered back by shooting Smythe twice at point-blank range, but the bullets were deflected by Smythe's rage and pierced only his flying coat. Before the German could take better aim, one of his comrades tackled him. Canadians were of more value alive than dead.

So the two downed flyers were bundled off to an interrogation conducted by General Rupprecht, the Crown Prince of Bavaria. As Smythe recalled in his memoirs, *If You Can't Beat 'Em in the Alley*, things went well until the Crown Prince suggested he'd make a fine Canadian governor general after the war. This was too much for the patriotic Smythe, who shouted at the aristocrat, "For God's sake, you don't think you're going to win the war, do you?" That was the end of Smythe's Q&A, and he and his observer were bundled off to serve out the rest of the war in a series of German prison camps. It was the kind of backhanded luck that would follow Smythe throughout his life.

Ironically, though Smythe made one attempt at escape and was soon captured, his real brush with death came when he tried to learn the harmonica, something he'd always wanted to do. Figuring that prison camp was a good place to practise, Smythe played "Home Sweet Home" incessantly until finally a German guard shoved his rifle through the bars and conveyed to Smythe that one more note of that wretched song would ensure Smythe never saw home sweet home again. Smythe abandoned the harmonica on the spot, and the hockey world would be the better for it. Or at least, more interesting.

While the future builder of the Toronto Maple Leafs was stuck in prison camp, another soldier hockey team was making headlines back home. The summer of 1916 had seen the beginning of the Battle of the Somme, a grotesquely ill-conceived plan that led to a five-month slaughter which killed 24,713 Canadians. As a result of British military ingenuity, young Canadian men were signing themselves up to charge German cannons, and many hockey players were among them.

In one of the most remarkable hockey stories of the war, the 228th Battalion, also known as the "Northern Fusiliers," took up where Conn Smythe left off and delighted Toronto hockey fans with some of best players around. Sergeant Eddie Oatman, 27, had cut his professional teeth with the Quebec Bulldogs in 1911, before moving out west to join the Patrick brothers' New Westminster team, which then became the championship Portland Rosebuds. Sergeant "Goldie" Prodgers, an auburn-haired, amiable youth of 25, had recently scored the Stanley-Cup–winning goal for the Montreal Canadiens, a team which had also boasted big 21-year-old Sergeant Amos Arbour and popular 25-year-old Captain Howard McNamara. His older brother, Captain George McNamara, 28, had distinguished himself on defense for the 1912 champion Toronto Tecumsehs and more recently for the Blueshirts, while Lieutenant Art Duncan, 25, had starred for the 1916 Vancouver Millionaires.

Lieutenant Gordon Meeking, whom the *Toronto World* called "the greatest little goal-getter ever seen in the OHA," added firepower, while

Lieutenant Roxie Beaudro added the wisdom of the veteran, having been a member of the 1907 Stanley-Cup–winning Kenora Thistles. The squad's only neophyte was the goalie, Private Howard Lockhart, who received his first taste of the professional game when the 228th Battalion skated onto the ice in their special khaki uniforms on December 1, 1916, before the Duke of Devonshire, governor general of Canada, and 5,000 spectators. In case there was any doubt as to their worth, they crushed a team of All-Stars 10–0.

After the soldiers gave a 10–3 shellacking to another All-Star team featuring Newsy Lalonde and Didier Pitre, the other NHA teams had been given fair warning. A cartoon in the *Toronto World* depicted the 228th's muscular Captain Howard McNamara running roughshod over his opponents, while Germany's fretful Kaiser Wilhelm looks on, exclaiming to his chinless wonder of son: "They tell me this *man* is coming over to visit us with the Canadian devils." To which the son reassuringly replies: "As an officer, papa."

The 228th went on an astonishing run, outscoring their first five opponents 40–20. In early January 1917 they were leading the NHA — of which they were full members—before suffering their first defeat at the hands of the Montreal Canadiens. The team had captured the imagination of a public desperate to see their army boys as invincible, but in mid-February, they were gone, called off to war. "The soldier team is thru for all time," mourned the *World,* in a dispatch sounding more like an obituary. "They always played clean hockey, and always put their best foot forward. One can hardly say more than this. Doing one's best is all [that] can be asked of mortals in this world of sadness."

When the 228th received their marching orders, they led the league with 70 goals and sat in third place in the standings, with one win less and one loss more than both Ottawa and Montreal, with the Canadiens, who would go on to compete for the Stanley Cup, claiming first place on their better goals average. Even though this infantry battalion had been changed to a "construction" battalion due to the incompetence of their officers (an odd criterion, considering the competence of some masterminding the bloodbath), the departure of the Northern Fusiliers for France wasn't as poignantly glorious as it might have seemed.

Just 10 days after the Toronto papers were piping the boys off to war, star forwards Eddie Oatman and Gordon Meeking turned up in

Montreal. Both had been unceremoniously discharged in St. John, New Brunswick, because they "would not become efficient soldiers." Even worse, Oatman claimed that he was never a "real member of the battalion" and had only been recruited to play hockey for them.

As such, he was now demanding the $700 still owed to him as part of his $1,200 salary. Meeking's argument was one not of money, but of rank, having been promised a lieutenant's commission in exchange for playing hockey, and even being allowed to wear the officer's uniform.

When the battalion was ordered overseas, Meeking was ordered into a private's uniform, as his "commission" had never been approved. The soldier team, it seemed, was part propaganda stunt, part the same old battle between management and itself, with the lives of the players thrown in for good measure.

As 1917 lurched on, that battle heated up to a crisis point. At stake was the future of the professional game, or rather, the division of the spoils. When the smoke had cleared, the league that would eventually dominate professional hockey was born. As with most things concerning pro hockey at the time, the birth was a difficult one.

Toronto Blueshirt owner Eddie Livingstone, a gifted antagonist, had demanded that the other NHA owners accommodate him with a five-team, home-and-away schedule when the 228th shipped off. The NHA refused, preferring a four-team league with three clubs in Quebec and one in Ottawa.

The ornery Livingstone would not go quietly, saying that he would retaliate by selling his players to the highest bidder. Against this news were dark rumours that the other clubs wanted to form their own league. So, when Quebec's financial problems caused it to pull out of the NHA, the league's directors met at Montreal's Windsor Hotel on November 6, 1917, to unravel, as the *Gazette* hoped, the "professional hockey tangle."

Frank Calder, a fearless Montreal sportswriter who had exposed the appalling conditions at a Montreal horse-racing track and roundly condemned professional wrestling fixes, had become secretary to the now disbanded NHA and chaired the ominous meeting. A dramatic motion was raised to avert the extinction of professional hockey in the land, which could only be done if the "Canadiens, Wanderers, Ottawas, and Quebec Hockey Clubs unite to comprise the National Hockey League."

The motion carried. Just as the meeting was moving on to new business, William Northey came barging in. Eddie Livingstone had cut his losses and unloaded his beleaguered Toronto franchise to the directors of the Montreal Arena Corporation. Northey, representing those worthies, now wanted into the new league. As if by magic, Quebec's financially troubled representatives offered to withdraw to make room for Toronto — on one small condition. They needed to disperse their players to other teams, in exchange for a little ready cash.

The *Toronto Star* wasn't fooled. "The professional hockey situation is cleared up to-night and Toronto is to have a place 'in the sun,'" the paper jauntily announced on November 28, 1917. "All the secrecy and back-door stuff was camouflage to cover up the distribution of the Quebec players to the best advantage."

And with that, the Quebec Bulldogs — who had won the Stanley Cup in 1912 and 1913 — were parceled off. The Montreal Canadiens picked up "Gentleman" Joe Malone and "Bad" Joe Hall, while the other Bulldogs were sold throughout the "new" league as if they were chattel, for $700 a man. Frank Calder was elected president and secretary-treasurer of this phoenix National Hockey *League* at an annual salary of $800, on the understanding his decisions were final and binding — in order to give the league "stability." And shut down any hint of rebellion.

In the hotel corridor outside the meeting, young *Montreal Herald* sports reporter Elmer Ferguson rushed up to the first man to exit, begging to know what had happened to the fate of the game that was supposedly coughing blood onto the ice. "Not too much, Fergie," the laconic Frank Calder replied, before stepping onto an elevator and into pro hockey history. The National Hockey League was in business.

—⁓—

A few hours earlier in the same hotel, the martial chorus of *"La Marsellaise"* rang out to welcome the 73-year-old Sarah Bernhardt, once upon a time the world's most celebrated stage actress. The one-legged Divine Sarah, now in a wheeled sedan chair, had come to Canada on a Victory Loans fund-raiser. In thanking the nation for its war effort, the woman who had suggested line changes to George Bernard Shaw and Oscar Wilde, said contributing to the Victory Loan program would help the Allies bring about "the independence of nations and the crushing out of barbarism."

As the *Montreal Daily Star* reported, "there was something about the way Madame Bernhardt said that word 'barbarism' that showed the feline ferocity of the woman who has seen her countrymen slaughtered." For even though the word "victory" was flowing more loosely from Allied lips now that the Americans were in the fight, there was still a fight going on.

In the spring of 1918, a young American pilot wearing the colours of the redoubtable *Escadrille Lafayette* was looking to get into that fight, lusting after the chance to compete once again on a grand stage. Indeed, it seemed as if the grand stage had been invented for the likes of Hobey Baker.

Hobart Amory Hare Baker was America's first hockey superstar, a man whose talents were so grand that one game in which he played was advertised as "Hobey Baker and six players representing Princeton University." With his patrician Philadelphia lineage, his sporting excellence, his physical splendour and natural humility, Baker cut such a glamorous figure that his adoring fellow Princetonian F. Scott Fitzgerald would try to distill his essence into fiction, basing the character "Allenby" on Baker in his debut novel, *This Side of Paradise*. "He was an ideal worthy of everything in my enthusiastic admiration," wrote Fitzgerald, "yet consummated and expressed in a human being who stood within ten feet of me."

Hobey Baker learned to play hockey in the first decade of the twentieth century at the elite St. Paul's School in Concord, New Hampshire, where schoolboy variations on hockey had been played since the late 1870s. The United States had a thriving amateur hockey culture, and the upper-class prep schools in New England supplied the Ivy League universities with their future stars.

Young Baker's communion with the heavens was literal, as he would stay out on the ice alone until the only lights in the sky were the moon and stars, learning how to feel the puck when he couldn't see it. Baker was just a 15-year-old winger when his schoolboy squad beat the Princeton University team 4–0.

In the autumn of 1910, Hobey Baker entered Princeton himself, though it almost didn't happen. His parents' divorce had been costly, and had Baker's older brother Thornton not abdicated his place in favour of the gifted Hobey, the bigger hockey world might never have known Hobey Baker's name.

Baker's first athletic career at Princeton, however, was that of "football star." It was a time when football was still an unpadded relative to rugby, a fluid affair that encouraged the long run. Baker was able to move at will through opposing forces with elegance and speed, and as a member of the freshman football team once galloped the length of the field against archrival Yale to score the winning touchdown.

Baker would eventually become the All-American captain of Princeton's football team and carried with him two significant honours: he had never fumbled a punt, nor had he played on a team that lost to Yale. Such was Baker's fame that on the day Woodrow Wilson was elected president of the United States in 1912, he stopped by the Princeton field to watch Hobey Baker practise.

As John Davies reveals in his regal biography *The Legend of Hobey Baker*, Princetonians were so in awe of the self-effacing Baker that they regarded him as out of this world. "With his wavy blond hair, his flashing blue-gray eyes and straight features he was handsome as a Greek God," said one contemporary. "In height he was about five-feet-nine and I don't believe he ever exceeded in weight 160 pounds. He was one of those athletes who are never hurt."

Despite his prodigious athletic gifts, Hobey Baker's first love was hockey. Playing at the position of rover, he would begin in his own end, circling his net two or three times to gain momentum for a goal-to-goal rush. The crowd would rise to their feet, and friend and foe alike would fill the arena with shouts of "Here he comes! Here he comes!" Baker's speed was such that he could blast past an opponent without having to try to fake him out, his shot so heavy that he could score from the centre of the ice, and his sense of fair play like a second skin. *The Boston Journal* said the 21-year-old virtuoso "is without doubt the greatest amateur hockey player ever developed in this country or in Canada."

Since Princeton didn't have its own rink, the Tigers played their "home" games at New York City's St. Nicholas Rink, whose marquee would boast "Hobey Baker Plays Here Tonight" just in case anyone hadn't heard. The St. Nick's rink had been built in the late 1890s, its $300,000 tab sponsored by such paladins as the Vanderbilts, the Astors, the Choates, and the Morgans. The result was a 75-foot-high model of luxury, built of ornamental brick, and boasting a spectators' gallery, clubrooms, a grill-room, and a restaurant.

St. Nick's special feature was its 16,000 square feet of artificial ice. The need for fake ice was a hardship to which the New Yorkers were enviously resigned. After all, said the *New York Times*, "Canadians ... simply have to build a house, put a watertight floor in it, turn on the water, and let Jack Frost do the rest."

The St. Nick's method for making artificial ice — though secret — was simple: the 200-by-80-foot rink floor was laid over water pipes, which flooded the rink to five inches deep. A series of pumps then forced a "freezing fluid" through the pipes, making the ice smooth, and much harder than that formed in "natural ice" rinks because it was uniformly frozen, and maintained that way throughout the match.

As a state-of-the-art facility, St. Nick's attracted a swank Manhattan crowd, and when Hobey Baker played, the limousines stretched from Columbus Avenue to Central Park West on 66th Street. The ladies wore their best jewelry and the men their finest evening clothes, because going to see Hobey Baker was a high-society event. Even so, all that rich, cool New York sophistication would explode into squeals and hurrahs when Baker took off down the ice on one of his magical rushes.

Yet for all his talents and fame, Baker was uncommonly modest. The garish rink signs in New York and Boston that advertised his presence upset him, and he sometimes refused to play until they were removed or were changed to emphasize that he played for a team. A reporter who asked Baker what he should say about the young god's athletic gifts was met with the reply "You would oblige me by saying nothing at all."

Fittingly, Hobey Baker played his last collegiate hockey game in Canada, on the last day of February 1914. The University of Ottawa team had already beaten the Tigers once that year in New York, but this game at Ottawa's Dey's Arena was a big one: at stake, the Intercollegiate Hockey Championship of America.

The Princetonians were met at the train station like the visiting dignitaries they were and put up in the comfort of the elegant Château Laurier. The game itself was an occasion: the governor general's Foot Guards band played the national anthems of the two countries, while Canada's Martin Burrell, minister of agriculture, dropped the ceremonial puck. The American consul, one Colonel Foster, was content to look on with Yankee pride at Baker, "the swiftest amateur in the game today ... the cynosure of all eyes."

There weren't as many eyes clapped on the young American star as had been predicted, for just half of the anticipated 5,000 fans showed up to watch the two squads struggle on poor ice. Indeed, the ice was so bad (a frequent reality on natural ice, given Mother Nature's whims) that skating through the slush was difficult and stickhandling almost impossible.

Baker, however, wasn't bothered by any of this, and his superb and tireless skating made fans hungry for a future pro career, even though he and his Tigers went down to a 3–2 defeat to Ottawa, a collection of rugged Irish Catholics coached by a priest.

Baker's Princeton hockey career was over, but his legacy was grand: 27 wins and just seven losses. When he graduated in the spring of 1914 with a B- average Bachelor of Letters, Baker was voted the man who had done the most for Princeton, the best all-round athlete, the best football player, and the best hockey player.

Upon graduation, Baker did what many American aristocrats had done before and after and went to work on Wall Street. His desk job with J. P. Morgan bored him senseless, and the golden athlete took up smoking to alleviate the tedium, masking his cigarette-breath with penny candy. To add to his woe, executives would bring important clients in to peek at Baker, as if he were a trophy. "That's Hobey Baker," they would whisper, and Baker's ears and neck would burn in embarrassment.

Baker sought release by playing for the St. Nicholas Rink's amateur team, five of whom were so wealthy that they had their own valets, though Baker's rich friend Percy Pyne loaned him a manservant to speed Baker's exit from the locker room into the nocturnal delights of Manhattan.

The St. Nick's team played against rough-housing Canadians on the city's "Irish American" squad, tough players who thought Baker an overrated society toff asking to be knocked down a peg, something which they happily did. After one such battering, Baker limped into the opposing team's dressing room to shake hands and thank them for the game. "Thereafter we decided never to do anything like that to Baker again," recalled a Canadian player. "He was the cleanest and best hockey player, as well as the finest gentleman I ever met."

Montreal thought so, too. On December 11, 1915, Baker and the St. Nick's team played the Montreal Stars for the Art Ross Cup for international amateur play (donated by the same man who would give the NHL the Art Ross Trophy). Baker scored twice and set up three goals to lead St. Nick's to a 6–2 victory. The next day, the Montreal papers were in a forgiving mood, saying, "Uncle Sam has had the cheek to develop a first-class hockey player ... We didn't want the St. Nick's to win, but Baker cooked our goose so artistically that we enjoyed it."

Lester Patrick, no stranger to hockey talent, enthused that Hobey Baker was the only amateur he had seen who could have been a star in his first game of professional hockey. Baker was even offered $3,500 to come to Canada and turn pro, but he only played for love, and refused. While a poor boy like Conn Smythe would chase a buck wherever he could, Baker didn't have to. He could afford to be an amateur.

Still, Baker's New York life was unfulfilling, and, craving the pure speed and glory that defined his college years, he embraced the chance to go to war. As Conn Smythe's flying instructor Billy Barker buzzed generals to get what he wanted, Hobey Baker buzzed the crowd at Princeton football games, reminding everyone that he was still there, up in the air, keen to chase glory once again.

Baker joined the *Escadrille Lafayette*, a squadron formed by volunteer American pilots in April 1916. Based in France as part of the French Air Service until 1918, when it became part of the U.S. forces, the Lafayette Squadron was renowned as much for the glamour of its officers' clubhouse as for the talents of its pilots. By the time Baker arrived in April 1918, the worst air battles of the war were over, but this did not diminish his competitive instinct. In May he shot down an enemy plane over Ypres and received France's *Croix de Guerre* for "exceptional valour under fire."

Lieutenant Hobey Baker, who had also set the record for the steepness of an ascent in an airplane, was promoted to captain and commander of the new 141st Pursuit Group. He cut a swashbuckling figure, even winning the heart of a beautiful American nurse, only to have her affections cool, perhaps because of his devotion to his mistress, air combat.

Baker's squadron's planes arrived in October 1918, decorated in the orange-and-black colours of Princeton, with a Princeton tiger standing over a spiked German helmet that had been painted on each fuselage. Baker "officially" shot down two more German planes to put his tally at three, and though he was two shoot-downs short of being proclaimed an "ace," Hobey's unofficial total of enemy kills ominously numbered 13.

Baker dug into the metaphors of sport to describe war, calling the clouds his "ice fields," and saying that he flew instinctively, as he would "dodge instinctively when running with the ball in open field." But there would no more aerial goals or touchdowns for Hobey Baker when the war to end all wars finally shuddered to a conclusion on November 11, 1918. Once again, time had run out on his kingdom.

Baker met his orders to return to the reality of growing old in the United States with frustration, pleading to remain in France. He was refused. On a cold, rainy December 21, 1918, Baker was due to catch the train to Paris to ship home. He told a Princeton colleague serving with him that he wanted to take "one last flight," a serious breach of aviation superstition lest the "last flight" prove fatally prophetic. Baker's friend tried to dissuade him, but Hobey was adamant.

When he got to the hangar and discovered a recently repaired plane, he decided to take it up, despite vigorous protest from his ground crew. So Baker pulled rank: as commanding officer he couldn't ask any other man to test fly a repaired plane.

Baker took off into the drizzle, then, scarcely 20 feet off the ground, gunned the motor and pulled up into a *chandelle*, a nearly vertical climb that tested the limits of any plane of the day. He leveled off and was approaching a little clump of trees just a quarter of a mile away when his roaring engine spluttered into silence. The plane's notoriously fickle carburetor had failed again, and Baker's formidable instinct had a split second to respond: crash land the plane or try to turn back to base.

Not wanting to "wash out" the ship on his last day in France as the senior pilot and commanding officer, Hobey tried to impose his will on the machine to make it fly. He could not. Baker crashed, and his horrified comrades came running to wreckage, getting there in time for him to die in their arms. He was no longer an athlete who never got hurt. He was 26 years old.

It was long rumoured that the magnificent Hobey Baker — the only man to be elected to both the College Football Hall of Fame and the Hockey Hall of Fame — had committed suicide rather than return to a life of relentless anti-climax. He did not, but rather tried to win "one more game," while he had the chance. Like so many young athletes in that terrible war, he lost.

An anonymous poet would express it in more mythic terms, on Baker's gravestone in suburban Philadelphia. Even though the poetry of irony was now fully entrenched in the literary canon, where the idea of it being sweet and fitting to die for your country had been buried deep in the mud of war, the verse summing up Baker's brief, shining life pays tribute to its glory, and not the lies by which a generation died.

> You seemed winged, even as a lad,
> With that swift look of those who know the sky,
> It was no blundering fate that stooped and bade
> You break your wings, and fall to earth and die
> I think some day you may have flown too high,
> So that immortals saw you and were glad,
> Watching the beauty of your spirit's flame,
> Until they loved and called you, and you came.

Shortly before the armistice on November 11, 1918, on the edge of the Western Front just east of the famous battlesite of Mons, a young Canadian private named George Price sat in the village of Ville-sur-Haine, watching as officers counted down the seconds until the nightmare was over. Two minutes before peace broke out, a German sniper fixed Price in his sights and shot him dead. Of the 68,300 Canadians killed in the war, Price was the last killed in action on the Front, the victim of a singularly cold-blooded murder that punctuates the futility of all the killing that preceded it.

The war's end, however, meant life to another Canuck, 23-year-old Lieutenant Conn Smythe, who had survived his stint in prisoner-of-war camps and now headed home. Smythe's troop train finally pulled into the North Toronto station in Rosedale in February 1919, and his fiancée, Irene, was there to meet him — along with her chaperoning father, who worried their reunion might fall into lusty debauch.

In an irony at once moving and surprising, there was no such danger. The man who had killed, who had been wounded and shot down, and who survived nearly 14 months as a German prisoner, was still a virgin. Despite opportunities to escape from the war in brief couplings with willing foreign girls (including one at a French train station when an attractive middle-class Frenchwoman invited carnal embrace in the half-hour before Smythe's train pulled out) Smythe demurred. He had "saved" himself for Irene.

Much at home had changed in his absence. Smythe's father had moved into a new home with a new wife, and Smythe now had a new baby half-sister. As if that wasn't challenge enough, young men and women returning from the war did not come back to parades of glory and arms outstretched in gratitude, but to an uneasy, weary society.

While the warriors were away, Canada had seen the invention of the passport and income tax, and British Columbia had restricted liquor to "medicinal purposes" in 1916, a reality that galled more than one soldier returning from Hell in search of a drink. B.C. also spearheaded women's suffrage in 1916, permitting women to vote in provincial elections, and to be elected to the legislature. A year later, the country extended the franchise to war nurses and the immediate female relatives of soldiers and extended it to all Canadian women in 1918, if they, like their male counterparts, were white and over 21.

Hockey, too, had changed since Smythe had been at war. The NHA was dead, the NHL was born, and an American team, the Seattle Metropolitans, who played in the Patrick brothers' Pacific Coast league, had become the first American team to win the Stanley Cup when they knocked off the Montreal Canadiens in March 1917.

Conn Smythe, like the good Protestant boy he was, looked inside himself to take stock. "Four years of my life were gone, and I hadn't done a thing yet," he recalled. "But I was going to make up for it, of that I was damn sure."

Indeed, he had been uncommonly sure since childhood. When Smythe was 11, his mother died of complications brought on by alcoholism. At her funeral it was discovered that her son, Constantine Falkland Cary Smythe, had never been baptized. Seizing the opportunity, he discarded the loathed "Constantine" and renamed himself Conn, spending the rest of his life creating the world in his own image.

Now he had the chance again. Though never among the top players on any of his teams, Smythe was a hockey man from his clipped military mustache right down to the spats he would soon wear. He was a leader because he could see where he wanted to go.

The Jazz Age was about to pop its champagne cork, and the world would enter a time of garish prosperity and limitless ambition — or so it seemed. The feeling in the air was one of optimism, of breaking free of a dark age into one of light. The young NHL was hungry for money, and hockey would catapult itself into much brighter lights with new teams in Toronto and Boston and New York. Hobey Baker had set up New York for the big time, and though he was now a marble head in the pantheon of dead young heroes, Conn Smythe was very much sweating and cussing and scheming down on Earth. And the poor boy wanted everything Mammon had to offer.

5

THE GOLDEN ONES

The time between the First and Second World Wars is often called hockey's "golden age," an era of grand hockey players whose exploits would be played out in the biggest rink yet, courtesy of the NHL's ambitious expansion to the United States. While nostalgia's amber haze can soften the harsh and exalt the ordinary, this "golden age" indeed saw a cast of characters whose lives seem more classically proportioned when compared to the gold-plated stars of today.

Perhaps this is just nostalgia fooling us; perhaps it's because the stars back then had to travel farther and harder to reach their zenith. Those of today are often anointed in childhood and led toward ineffable riches, the price being that their every move is scrutinized by an all-seeing media. This relationship is suitably Faustian, for the hockey titans need the media to sell their products, and "product endorsement" deals form a significant portion of their incomes and their images.

Hockey's golden ones of the 1920s and '30s were not seen through the eye of the insatiable media machine, but they were heard: in the crackly, excited cadences of Foster Hewitt, sitting high in his gondola at Maple Leaf Gardens, giving people huddled around their radios from St. John's to Victoria to Detroit a picture of hockey's glorious era. Or they were hymned in print by a generation of sportswriting Homers, who didn't have television or the internet to contradict them, and could let their tales of the heroic icemen soar on the oxygen of legend. Howie Morenz and "Tex" Rickard and Conn Smythe and Frank

Boucher and Eddie Shore and "King" Clancy and the Conacher brothers shone for a generation, not because they were seen on TV highlights each night, but because their triumph came from more than the ice. It came because they were so human.

—⁓—

Of all the epic characters who passed through hockey in the two decades of peace after the Great War, there is one man who embodies both the exuberance and despair of the time, and so he is both beginning, and end. But he nearly didn't begin at all.

In 1906, Howie Morenz was an inquisitive four year old poking into the mysteries of a kettle of potatoes on the stove when he slipped. The kettle tipped, splashing boiling water onto his legs and scalding him so badly that his older sister Gertrude said, "We never thought he'd walk again, let alone play hockey."

Howie Morenz not only walked again, he learned to skate, although glory didn't come instantly. When Morenz made his debut as an eight-year-old goalie in Mitchell, Ontario, 21 pucks found their way past him in one game. It would be his only appearance in goal.

When Howie was nine, his family moved to Stratford, Ontario, where, as a fast and flashy forward, he would win the nickname "The Stratford Streak." He also showed prodigious gifts at baseball, and his mother, wanting to give the boy some culture, signed her genius up for piano lessons. By all accounts, Morenz preferred to keep his musical talents hidden, refusing to practise anything other than "One-Fingered Joe" to prevent injuring digits better suited to hockey and ball.

In the summer of 1917, the 14-year-old Morenz felt he could break open trench warfare in favour of the Allied forces, who had been stuck in the bloody mud of the Western Front for nearly three years. When Howie failed to turn up for both lunch and dinner, his frantic mother called the police. On a bit of inspired detective work, the constabulary caught up with Morenz in Toronto, where the slight lad had convinced a credulous recruiting officer for the Governor General's Horse Guards that he was in fact 18. Mrs. Morenz descended in maternal fury upon Hogtown and Howie's cavalry career was over.

When Morenz really was 18 years old, he took a job as an apprentice machinist in the Stratford railway shop. The federal government had now consolidated five smaller, financially troubled regional railways to make one big unit called the Canadian National Railway. In the spring of 1922, Morenz scored nine goals for Stratford's CNR team in the Montreal Canadiens' stomping ground, the Mount Royal Arena.

The referee of that match had once played amateur hockey for the Canadiens' coach Cecil Hart, and he called his old mentor with the news that an astonishing talent had been revealed. The Canadiens' co-owner, Leo Dandurand, was skeptical. If Morenz was so good, why hadn't a Toronto team already signed him? Nevertheless, he dispatched Hart to watch Morenz play, and when Hart reported back that "The Stratford Streak" was even better than they said, Dandurand took the next train to Stratford.

But there was a problem. Like Cyclone Taylor before him, Howie Morenz didn't want to leave the comforts of small-town Canada for the big city. Stratford was his duchy, where he starred at baseball in the summer and hockey in the winter. Besides, he already had a good job. It's a logic hard to comprehend today, when not many jobs compare to the pro hockey star's dilemma of pulling down millions for working 15 minutes a night, 82 nights a year.

Young Morenz also had debts. As freewheeling with his money as he was on the ice, he owed $800, which was more than enough to buy a swank car. Leo Dandurand came up with a brilliant solution. How would young Howie feel about a $2,500 annual contract and an $850 cash signing bonus — to get rid of those debts, with change left over? Howie Morenz signed the contract.

Not long afterward, Dandurand received a telegram from Morenz announcing that he had changed his mind about playing for the Montreal Canadiens. He wanted out of his contract. Now that Dandurand had seen the future of the franchise, he was having none of it. So he told Morenz politely, but with nuance, that Montreal was counting on him.

Morenz didn't quite get the drift and responded by returning Dandurand's cheque, along with a note, claiming he couldn't accept the pro offer due to reasons of family and work. The truth was that Morenz's father didn't want him playing hockey for a living.

So Leo Dandurand invited Morenz to Montreal for a blunt face-to-face. If the kid broke his contract, he told Morenz, then the mighty Dandurand would make sure Morenz never played hockey for anyone, anywhere. Morenz broke into tears, and his own truth spilled out with them. He wasn't good enough for the Canadiens, and the team would be sorry they ever set eyes on him. Dandurand remained unmoved. Howie Morenz would be a Montreal Canadien, or he would be nothing.

Morenz played his first shift with the Canadiens on Boxing Day 1923, in Ottawa's new rink. Before a record crowd of 8,300 fans, Howie Morenz scattered any self-doubt by scoring a goal, the first of the 270 he would notch in the NHL. "Morenz skated right at me, going like hell, shot the puck, and knocked me on my ass," recalled young Frank "King" Clancy, who was on defense for Ottawa. "I told him if he tried it again, I would cut his head off. He laughed and said he planned to do it again. Know what? He did."

After beating Vancouver, champs of the Pacific Coast league, Morenz and the Canadiens took on the Calgary Tigers for the 1924 Stanley Cup championship. With the "Little Giant" Aurele Joliat and Billy Boucher on his wings, Morenz centred a blazingly fast line. In two games against the Tigers, the Joliat-Morenz-Boucher line accounted for eight of the Canadiens' nine goals. Georges Vezina allowed only six goals in six playoff games, and earned two shutouts. Aurele Joliat came in third in playoff scoring, Billy Boucher came second, and Howie Morenz came first, with seven goals.

The man who didn't want to play professional hockey — and certainly not in Montreal — wound up drinking champagne from the Jug in his first season as a pro. In that one image lay Morenz's glory, and his doom. The stage on which the reluctant hero would play out his drama was about to get much bigger.

—◦◦◦—

In the autumn of 1924, the NHL, just seven years old, sold its first American franchise. Nearly 20 years had passed since Doc Gibson and his enterprising friend James Dee had organized the world's first professional league in the United States, and now pro hockey once again needed the big rich country that spawned it. They set their sights on Boston.

When the NHL was formed in 1917, the Boston Amateur Athletic Association's hockey team was the defending champ of the American Amateur Hockey League. College hockey had been played in and around Boston for decades, and the city was a natural for the pro game, boasting a critical mass of fans that not only knew the game but loved it. One of those fans was Boston grocery tycoon Charles Weston Adams, who had sponsored an amateur hockey club until he discovered — as his Canadian counterparts had done years earlier — that the other so-called amateur clubs were slipping gold into the gloves of their players.

The wealthy Adams was the perfect target for the NHL, and so he was wooed with what would become a pattern: an invitation north to see a real pro hockey game. Adams accepted and wound up seeing the 1924 Stanley Cup Finals between Calgary and the Canadiens. Dazzled by the light show put on by Howie Morenz and company, Adams went back to Boston reeling, like a tourist who has glimpsed Shangri-La and will never be the same again. "When he returned home," said his son Weston, "he told us this was the greatest hockey he had ever seen. He wouldn't be happy until he had a franchise."

The NHL was happy to oblige the millionaire, and the Bruins were in business later that autumn, making their debut against another new club, the Montreal Maroons. The Maroons, ironically, had been created for Montreal's Anglo community, which, after dominating Montreal hockey for a half century, had been without its own pro team since 1918 and had grown restless at seeing its rightful glory stolen by the upstart francophones wearing the *bleu, blanc, et rouge*. Under the creaking rafters of the Boston Arena, where Cyclone Taylor had performed his magic show years earlier, the Bruins beat the Maroons 2–1, on December 1, 1924, their home opener. Like many a new franchise running on adrenaline, the wins were few and far between, and the Bruins finished in last place their inaugural season, with only six of them. The Maroons beat them by three wins and wound up second last.

Pro hockey's return to the land of the free was no sentimental journey. In the autumn of 1924, the NHL had one shaky franchise in Hamilton and three dependable clubs in Howie Morenz's Montreal Canadiens, the Toronto St. Pats, and the Ottawa Senators. As pro hockey players knew 20 years earlier, and as the NHL knows a little too well today, there's gold south of the 49th Parallel. In order to survive, the NHL knew that it needed more than Boston. It needed to tap into the 120 million potential customers who lived under the Stars and Stripes. Or at least a good chunk of them.

It would not be an easy mission, for the United States had invented the Golden Ones, those sporting titans who lured the masses from their dens to spend their hard-earned coin watching games. "Babe" Ruth was "The Sultan of Swat"; the tragic Lou Gehrig was on his way to becoming the "Pride of the Yankees." Galloping Ghost "Red" Grange was haunting the gridiron; Jack Dempsey was pummeling lessons into all comers in the "sweet science" of boxing.

Still, hockey had reason to hope. The United States in the 1920s was paradise for those who wished to find a marketable, profitable commodity and monopolize it. In the absence of anti-trust legislation, and with reduced business taxes and government tariffs protecting U.S. manufacturers, the prospects for tycoons of any stripe were rosy.

The man or the woman getting off shift at the factory wasn't thinking about monopolies and cartels. They dreamed of spending their income on the moving pictures, or sitting by the fire with their favourite radio show, the one kindly sponsored by Company X, a development which in turn made the advertising industry an even more lucrative enterprise. Hockey needed to advertise, as it needed to take some of those entertainment dollars from American hands and feed them into the league. Baseball had done it for years, and the National Football League had joined the party in 1921. If hockey didn't set up shop in the world's greatest marketplace, there might not be any money left.

In order to show they were serious, the NHL knew that they were going to have to conquer the biggest, most glamorous market in the world. Fortunately, they had union-busting Howie Morenz and a little old-fashioned gangsterism to help them.

In the autumn of 1925, three months before hockey's glitzy professional debut in New York, a banquet luncheon at the swank Biltmore Hotel welcomed the NHL to the Big Apple. Or rather, it welcomed the Hamilton Tigers to New York. When the Tigers had the effrontery to go on strike over playoff money five months earlier, the NHL responded with enlightened concern. They sold off the entire team to one William V. Dwyer of New York City for $80,000 — crushing the Tigers' Bolshevism by clothing them in the red, white, and blue jerseys of the New York Americans.

Bill Dwyer was a man well placed to handle pro hockey's affairs in New York. As one of the city's most powerful bootleggers, Dwyer had made a bundle slaking the thirst of a country parched by Prohibition, and many society swells were grateful to his mission. Yet on that night in December 1925, when pro hockey made its glittering Manhattan debut, Bill Dwyer was not applauding in the stands. Bill Dwyer was in jail.

Just days earlier, Dwyer was arrested as the head of a booze ring, whose multimillion-dollar smuggling operation had greased the palms of more than a few government officials. He would get two years in prison for his sins, still maintaining his innocence.

Dwyer was being economical with the truth. Ships, trucks, warehouses, nightclubs in New York, a casino in Miami, and racetracks in Montreal and Florida were all part of Dwyer's flourishing portfolio. He also kept company with a collection of New York gangsters who would make any contemporary screenwriter happy. Mob figures "Dutch" Schultz, "Legs" Diamond, and Owney Madden all called Dwyer friend. Since Dwyer also owned the Forrest Hotel on 49th Street, New York Americans' players had to dodge the molls and hitmen talking shop in the lobby when they went to collect their paycheques.

Bill Dwyer actually loved hockey, having been taught the game by William MacBeth, a Canadian friend who worked for the *Herald-Tribune*, but by the time hockey's opening night rolled around, Dwyer had been airbrushed from the party pictures. The "role" of the Americans' proprietor aptly fell to one George Rickard, a former soldier of fortune, saloonkeeper, gold prospector, and now ace boxing promoter known to polite society as "Tex."

Rickard had been the prime mover behind the new (or third) Madison Square Garden, for upon discovering that its predecessor was to be razed for one of the hundred skyscrapers that muscled up the city's fabled skyline of the 1920s, he assembled a team of business luminaries he called his "six hundred millionaires" and broke ground for a new arena at West 50th Street and 8th Avenue in January of 1925.

Rickard had no interest in putting fake ice in the new Garden, mainly because he had no interest in hockey. So Tom Duggan, director of the Montreal Maroons (and reputedly Bill Dwyer's bootlegging partner), reprised the strategy that had worked so well on Boston's Charles Adams. He invited Tex up to Montreal to see the game as it should be played. Rickard's vision would be helped with a few pre-game cocktails in civilized post-prohibition Canada. And if the hooch wasn't enough, Duggan had a secret weapon called Howie Morenz.

By the time the game started, Rickard was afloat on a sea of high-proof goodwill and suitably primed to watch the exalted Morenz and his Canadiens take on the Ottawa Senators. At first glance, Morenz didn't seem like all that much. Only five-foot-nine and 165 pounds, with thinning hair and perennial five-o'clock whiskers shadowing his amiable, earnest, sometimes puzzled face, Morenz liked to wander out of position as if playing a game in his imagination and not on the ice. He looked like somebody's uncle who had stumbled into the rink by mistake.

Like all great players, Morenz *was* inside his head, seeing the ice the way no on else could. As Rickard looked on, Morenz would pounce on the puck and speed along with it on his stick as if he had invented his own laws of physics. The showman Rickard, awestruck, wanted to put ice in Madison Square Garden then and there, on one condition: the wizard Morenz would have to play in the opening game in New York.

Which is how Stratford's unwilling son came to perform his magic in Manhattan that December 1925, watched over by disgraced Bill Dwyer's proxy Tex Rickard and some of New York's highest society names in the 17,000-seat Madison Square Garden. They had descended from their Park Avenue penthouses to witness what the *New York Evening Post* called the "favourite child of Canada": hockey.

Despite the muscle of its protectors in Manhattan, hockey came to New York City with a familiar mix of trepidation and swagger, for New York was the big time, a place that had seen the best that spectacle had to offer. The Garden opening was as splashy as it gets, making the front pages of the papers and giving the seen-it-all Manhattanites a good dose of pomp and splendour, with Canada's Governor General's Foot Guards band, in their red coats and bearskin hats, playing "God Save the King" and a West Point cadet band answering with "The Star Spangled Banner."

The crowd was spangled too, for, as the *New York Times* marveled, "in the tiers of flag-draped boxes was a social register representation which was something entirely new in New York's long history of the events of sport." Indeed, an extraordinary collection of power and wealth and glamour had shown up to watch a bunch of Canadians play hockey: moneybags Quincy S. Cabot, Jr., could hit up Mr. and Mrs.

E. F. Hutton for investment tips; Mr. and Mrs. Adolph Ochs could pick up gossip from Mrs. Franklin D. Roosevelt for their newspaper, the *New York Times;* Mrs. Charles Tiffany could compare her lustre with that of circus magnates John Ringling and William Barnum.

The reason professional hockey fit so nicely into this world of pearls and playboys was because the St. Nicholas Rink had raised the curtain a quarter of a century earlier to showcase the upper-crust talents of the Ivy Leaguers, the most dazzling of them being Hobey Baker. Where most Canadian lads had taken their lumps on frozen ponds, American boys more often than not learned the game at the posh private schools of Groton, Exeter, and St. Paul's, then pursued it at Harvard, Princeton, and Yale. It was only natural that their supporters should come to the games in limousines.

Both amateur and pro Canadian teams had made regular pilgrimages to New York City to top up their bank accounts, and New Yorkers had fallen in love with the Canadian panache. Now, with the debut of the "Amercks," they had their very own Canadians wearing the red, white, and blue.

Though they had been sold across the border for being rabble-rousing chattel, the former Hamilton Tigers didn't seem to mind. Billy "Captain Yonkers" Burch and Jake Forbes, who had led the Hamilton strike, had done very well for themselves as commie labour organizers, each pulling down $20,000 on three-year deals with the Americans at a time when the players' bank manager would be lucky to make $2,000 a year.

Despite scoring first, the Amercks were as much in awe of Morenz and the Canadiens as the crowd was. In their fiery red jerseys and aflame with foreign mystique, the Flying Frenchmen were the seductive marauders from the exotic French Catholic domain to the north — the great joke being that the most fabulous of the Frenchmen were not French at all.

Billy Boucher — three-quarters Irish — scored two Montreal goals. The "Little Giant" Aurele Joliat — the son of a Swiss Protestant — delighted crowds with the curious black-peaked cap that he wore as he streaked along the wings, waiting for a pass from Morenz. And it was Morenz — of German Swiss stock — who was the star of the show, the man that had made this night possible. Morenz obliged his celebrity by scoring a goal and showing off his speed and making casually brilliant plays that flushed the cheeks of many a debutante. When it was over, the Canadiens had a 3–1 win and the Prince of Wales Trophy, presented to them by New York's mayor-elect James J. "Beau" Walker for safekeeping until the end of the year.

The night had been a blazing success. Even the young and sophisticated *New Yorker* magazine was seduced—in a New York kind of way. "The Garden takes well on ice; bands and fancy skaters in the intermission soften hard hearts," ventured the journal, before adding its know-it-all caveat. "With an equipment like the Garden, badminton could be made to drive crowds into a frenzy. As my taxi driver said, Rickard is no fool."

With an irony that would shiver the bones of any hockey player, the Garden's opening had been sponsored by the city's Neurological Institute. Prices had been hugely inflated for the occasion, with box seats going for $11.50 and a place in the gods for $10 less (tickets for regular Amercks matches would run from $1.10 to $3.85). The high-rolling crowd didn't care, spilling out of the Garden and on to the Biltmore Hotel, where they could brush up to the players in person, and even snatch a dance with the light-footed Howie Morenz to Paul Whitelaw's renowned orchestra. Morenz loved to dance, and he even played a musical instrument of his own, the ukulele, on road trips. He would be the life of any party that would have him.

Morenz, the big fish reluctant to leave the small pond of Stratford, had fallen hard into the ecstasy of being the high priest of the hockey temple of Montreal. He took winning and losing so personally that either would keep him up all night, drunk to celebrate scoring or setting up the winner, or drunk to self-recriminate for losing a face-off or some such other failing, real or imagined. To win in the Big Apple on such a night would have seen Morenz at the height of joy, having fussed before the mirror in his room at the Waldorf-Astoria; changing his tie once or maybe even three times for the party; making the angle of his spats just so; and being the first to call for more champagne, and the first to drink it.

Howie Morenz had put hockey in New York by showing Tex Rickard the game's poetry. The fact that Rickard was himself drunk at the time makes the conquest all the more potent, for come the cold light of dawn, he had no regrets. He wanted to see Morenz again. The American papers were so captivated by Morenz they cast him in the only terms they could understand, calling him "The Babe Ruth of Hockey." Morenz had put the NHL under the limelight in the biggest show on Earth, and now they wanted more. It would take another singular Canadian to give it to them.

———

By the end of 1925, the National Hockey League had launched a full-frontal assault on American hearts, with teams now in Boston, New York, and Pittsburgh. In 1926, the Cougars won a franchise in Detroit, with former Pacific Coast star Jack Adams hanging up his skates to take the position of coach and manager. In November of that year, Major Frederick McLaughlin, a 49-year-old patrician who had been to Harvard and played polo, used part of his inheritance from his father's substantial coffee fortune to bring a hockey team to Chicago.

And there was a team that could be had. The Patrick brothers' Portland Rosebuds, who had played for the Stanley Cup in 1916, were on the block. Despite his wealth, McLaughlin formed a consortium to offset the cost, then paid $200,000 for the privilege of moving the Buds to Chicago — a staggering sum considering the Americans had cost $80,000 the year before, and the Montreal Canadiens had been picked up in the fire sale of wrestler George Kennedy's estate for $11,000 just seven years earlier.

The hot-eyed, gung-ho McLaughlin also used $150,000 in operating capital to stock his team, for the Patricks' experiment with the Pacific Coast had died, and the brothers were selling off their players from their now-defunct franchises for a grand total of $300,000.

McLaughlin had been the commander of the U.S. Army's 33rd Machine Gun Battalion during the First World War, which was itself part of the 85th Blackhawk Division. The major had also followed the exploits of the aboriginal Chief Blackhawk, whose tribe had been active in what was now Illinois. With his wife Irene Castle, a celebrated ballroom dancer, designing the team's red, black, and white uniforms with its Chief Blackhawk's head logo, McLaughlin moved the Rosebuds to Chicago, and called them the "Black Hawks," installing them in the 6,000-seat Chicago Coliseum. The Hawks' first home was well primed to receive an expansion franchise, having been the scene of many livestock fairs and thus used to manure, but the seasoned players of the Hawks' pulled off a respectable first season, finishing in third place and making it to the quarterfinal of the Stanley Cup playoffs.

Back in New York, Tex Rickard, though, was restless. He had seen the New York Americans flourish beyond expectation in their first year — finishing with one win more than Howie Morenz's slumping Montreal Canadiens, who weren't all that fabulous in 1925–26 and wound up in the basement. Better still, the Amercks were turning great box office. So Rickard reckoned that both the Garden and the city were big enough for another team, one he would own.

The NHL, so pleased with the gate success of the Americans, saw even greater revenues in granting Rickard's wish. A sportswriter joked that the new team should be called "Tex's Rangers," and with that one of pro hockey's great franchises was born. The only man not cheering was Bootleg Bill Dwyer, who had not signed a lease to be a double act, yet couldn't do much about it from his Georgia prison cell.

Dwyer wasn't the only one with a problem, for while Terrific Tex had a franchise, he did not exactly have a team. Fortunately, there was an ambitious young war veteran from Toronto looking to make his mark on the big time, a man who had already established his reputation for gambling. And who, having risen from the dead on the battlefield, had a certain messianic zeal.

In 1926, Conn Smythe was a 31-year-old amateur hockey manager who had caught the attention of Boston Bruins' owner Charles Weston Adams in a typically brash way. Two years earlier, Smythe rolled into Boston with his University of Toronto Varsity squad and promptly began a lifelong feud with Bruins' coach Art Ross. Smythe humbly suggested that his crew of college boys could wallop Ross's rookie Boston Bruins, who had only won two of their games in the first half of a 30-game schedule.

Ross did not take up the challenge, but Smythe's team then went on to sweep its games against Boston colleges, drawing crowds so large that those who couldn't get into the Boston Arena had to be restrained by mounted police. When Tex Rickard had a franchise but no team, Charles Adams pointed him in the direction of the guy who had put on such a show in Boston — Conn Smythe.

Even though Smythe had been going to Toronto St. Patrick's games for years and would tell anyone who cared to listen that he knew the book on all the players in the NHL, his real advantage was his amateur hockey experience. He had been able to see players on their way up to the pros, and when he took his amateur teams on barnstorming tours to places the NHL thought too out-of-the-way, he saw players who would otherwise have been missed altogether.

Smythe's first quarry for the Rangers was the goalie Lorne Chabot, who, at six-foot-one and 185 pounds was, in that era, unusually large for a netminder. In the spring of 1926, Smythe's Varsity team lost the Allan Cup to Port Arthur — or rather, to Port Arthur's big goaltender Lorne Chabot. This convinced the diminutive Smythe that bigger, in this instance, was indeed better, and Chabot would prove him right by posting 10 shutouts in his first season with the Rangers.

After snagging Chabot, Smythe set off to Minneapolis, where he bagged defensemen Ivan Johnson and Clarence Abel from a semi-pro league. Johnson had been a cook in a railway camp and was thus nicknamed "Ching" (a sanitized version of a derogatory term for a Chinese person), while Abel's Welsh ancestry was honoured with the all-purpose "Taffy."

Neither Johnson nor Abel went quietly. Each time Smythe was close to a deal with Johnson, the player would break off to phone his wife, who was apparently a contract expert. After a dozen such interruptions, Smythe made Johnson sign first, then phone home to see if he was still married. Abel proved even more difficult, so Smythe held the player hostage on his rail car as his train pulled out of the station with the next stop 250 miles away. Abel saw his imminent future with great clarity, so he signed, then jumped off the moving train.

Conn Smythe then went after two prospects of the Montreal Maroons, the brothers Bill and "Bun" Cook. Indeed, the two wingers were on their way to Montreal when Smythe cut them off at the pass in Winnipeg, and won them over to his Rangers with signing bonuses totaling $5,000. Bill Cook told Smythe that there was good centre named Frank Boucher who had been sold to Boston, and so Smythe bought the former Mountie for the Rangers, then nearly burst a vein when he clapped eyes on Boucher at the Ottawa train station — all 135 pounds of him, fully fed.

Among the greatest playmaking centres the game has known, the dark, handsome Frank Boucher hailed from a famous Ottawa sporting family, who, despite their French surname, were hardy and spirited

Irish. In a family of eight children, four of the six Boucher brothers became hockey stars: Bobby with the Montreal Canadiens, Vancouver, and Edmonton; Billy with the Canadiens; George with Ottawa; and Frank with Ottawa, Vancouver, and New York.

Oddly enough, Frank Boucher's decision to play pro hockey came from a stint in the Royal North-West Mounted Police — after first being rejected. Though an inch under the regulation height of five-foot-eight and a year younger than the force's minimum age of 18, Boucher and a friend who had already been accepted wrote to the RNWMP Commissioner to explain that Boucher's father was a big man and a famous rugby player, so chances were good that young Frank would grow a bit. He didn't.

Though he loved his police work as a member of the Lethbridge, Alberta, detachment, tracking down commies during the "Red Scare" and busting opium dens in Chinese laundries, Boucher loved hockey more. For $50 he bought his release from the Mounties to sign with Ottawa, then wound up with Vancouver's Millionaires, whom he led to back-to-back championships. His adoring fans christened the former cop "Raffles" (after the gentleman thief of fiction) because of Boucher's elegant and clean play at centre.

When Conn Smythe was finished, he had built the Rangers for only $32,000, and he had done it from Toronto, striking at forgotten players on different parts of the continent. Even so, the insular, jealous pro hockey world sneered that Smythe's Rangers were just a bunch of jumped-up amateurs. If he had been serious about winning, he would have gone after Toronto St. Patrick scoring ace "Babe" Dye, a man not shy about telling the world how good he was. The insulting gossip, which may well have originated with Dye, made Smythe burn, for he felt he had created a *team* — not a back-up chorus for an ego-centric player.

The Rangers' president Colonel John Hammond, stung by the embarrassing suggestion that Manhattan was icing a small-town product, used it as a reason to clash openly with Smythe at the team's training camp in October 1926 in Toronto. Shortly afterward, Smythe was summoned to Toronto's Union Station, there to be greeted by Hammond and the wily Lester Patrick.

Just as his creation was about to show what it was worth, Smythe had been fired, and Patrick hired. To add insult, Hammond announced he was withholding $2,500 of Smythe's $10,000 fee. Since Smythe hadn't moved to New York, he wouldn't need to claim moving expenses. The man who became not all that affectionately known as "The Little Pistol" had been hoodwinked. He would be avenged.

In one of those fateful turns that always seem to colour the great — or are perhaps caught by those with an eye to self-mythologizing — Smythe tossed Tex Rickard's invitation to the Rangers' home opener into the garbage bin. His wife, Irene, quickly retrieved it, for an expense-paid trip to New York would be the perfect payback for all those nights she had spent alone with the children while her husband was off in Podunk inventing the Rangers.

Smythe, still fuming about being cheated, ushered his wife into Rickard's box at the Garden while the Rangers and the Stanley-Cup–holding Montreal Maroons were in their pre-game warm-up. Rickard had always been impressed by the self-confident young Canadian and teased Smythe about the team he had built, wondering if the Rangers could stop the Maroons from breaking double digits on the scoresheet. Smythe was having none of it and spared no modesty in telling Rickard that the Rangers would win the game.

New York went up 1–0 when Bun Cook flipped a goalmouth pass over to his brother Bill, who popped it over the Maroon's "Praying" Clint Benedict, a goalie who liked to play on his knees. But Montreal's rangy forward Nels Stewart, a deadly shot, answered back. Sports-writers joked that Stewart couldn't skate and he couldn't check, but once the puck was on his stick and he could see the whites of the goalie's eyes, then he was as fatal to goalies as "Old Poison," his nickname. Not tonight, though, for the Rangers' big netminder Lorne Chabot proved to be an antidote and preserved New York's slender lead.

As a delighted Smythe watched his Rangers hold off the Maroons, the Montreal club grew ornery, with Harry "Punch" Broadbent and Earl "Babe" Seibert throwing their weight around. The "team" that Smythe had created responded as a team, and even 135-pound Frank Boucher, who would win the Lady Byng Trophy *seven* times for his gentlemanly play, jumped into a couple of brawls. It was this sense of collective purpose that led the Rangers to their first victory in their first home game.

An ecstatic Tex Rickard offered Smythe a job as the team's vice-president, but with characteristic diplomacy Smythe blustered that he wouldn't take another breath for those "cheapskates." Rickard did not know that Hammond had chiseled Smythe out of $2,500, and when Smythe told him the sorry tale, he ordered Hammond to pay up.

Now armed with his $2,500 grubstake — or half a year's salary for an elite player — Smythe prudently invested the lot on a college football game between Toronto and McGill. As he had done when betting on his own soldier team during the war, Smythe won big, doubling his money.

When the Rangers came to town to play the St. Pats, the bookies said that New Yorkers' defeat of the Maroons was a little practical joke courtesy of the hockey gods. Smythe, drooling, got 5 to 1 odds on the winning Rangers, and in three days had parlayed $2,500 into $10,000 — worth 10 times that in today's economy. It was time to pay another visit to John Paris Bickell.

Bickell had listened to Smythe's pitch to transform his ailing Toronto St. Pats a few months earlier, and while Bickell supported the young man's nerve, his partners balked at giving money to this come-by-chance amateur. Philadelphia had made an offer to buy the St. Pats for $200,000, and Smythe argued that if Toronto lost its franchise, it would be a long time before it got another one. Bickell listened and made Smythe a deal on two conditions: he would stake his $40,000 interest in the team if the young hotshot could round up investors to make up the other $160,000. The second condition was the kicker — Smythe would have to take over the team.

Smythe put down his $10,000 gambling win and found enough investors to front the rest of the cash. Once again his Belfast Protestant genes rose up, and Smythe found the "St. Patrick's" name and their green-and-white uniforms a little too redolent of the audience they were supposed to attract. Taking the colour scheme from his University of Toronto varsity squad, he dressed his crew in blue and white. Since there was already a minor hockey team called the Maple Leaves, Smythe renamed his crew "The Maple *Leafs*" in patriotic homage to the emblem worn by Canadian soldiers on their uniforms in the First World War. As a brazen "by the way," Smythe promised to win the Stanley Cup within five years. The Jug, however, would come sooner than he thought.

The Rangers that Smythe built thrived under the canny Lester Patrick, who kept perspective with a glass of cocoa and an early bed, stopping his ears against the city's 10,000 speakeasies tempting a Jazz-Ager with sin. The 1927 Rangers finished first in the NHL's American Division, and Bill Cook beat out Howie Morenz for the NHL scoring title, with 33 goals in 44 games. The next year, Smythe's Rangers had made it all the way to the grand prize competition, playing the 1928 Stanley Cup Final against the Montreal Maroons in one of the strangest Stanley Cup Finals in history — one that not even Conn Smythe could have reckoned.

With "Hail, Hail the Gang's All Here" lustily ringing out from the Montreal fans, the Maroons were keen to go up two games to zip on the Rangers. Early in the second period, Montreal's victory looked sealed when Nels Stewart fired a bullet into Rangers' goalie Lorne Chabot's left eye, spurting a stream of blood onto the ice, and speeding Chabot to the Royal Victoria Hospital.

Since most teams didn't carry an extra goalie, Lester Patrick asked the Maroons' for permission to use one of the spectators, Alex Connell, the standout goalie for the Ottawa Senators, or another netminder for a minor league team. The Maroons said no.

Patrick, whose cunning and thick mane of silver hair earned him the nickname "The Silver Fox," then did something that seemed unusually impulsive: he pulled on Chabot's gear — which fit perfectly except for the skates — and went into the net himself.

Patrick's grand gesture was not as harebrained as it seemed. Twenty-five years earlier, when his Brandon goalie was sent off for fighting (in those days, goalies served their own penalties) Patrick took his place in net, stopping the only shot the Ottawa Silver Seven managed. He pulled on the pads twice more in 1922, when Victoria's goalie Norm Fowler was sent off for fighting, and newspapers called Patrick "the Praying Colonel," after his martial demeanor when he knelt to block a shot. On that April night in Montreal in 1928, though, the 44-year-old Patrick was indeed praying that Nels Stewart wouldn't slam a puck into *his* face.

Though Stewart did put one past him, Patrick stood his ground, and Bill Cook evened the score for the Rangers. The game went into "unlimited" overtime. After twice repelling the Maroons from flat on the ice, Patrick watched as "Ching" Johnson took off with the puck. There was a scramble in front of the Maroon net, and Johnson passed to Frank Boucher, who fired the puck home.

The 13,000 Montreal fans, who had begun cheering for the Rangers partly because Patrick had once been a Montreal Wanderer, but mainly because of his nerve now, rose in laudation. The Rangers carried their coach off the ice and onward to a Stanley Cup victory — the first American NHL team to take the Jug. The old warrior had strapped on his armour and made Conn Smythe's promise come true: his team *had* won the Stanley Cup. In just its second season of play.

—✠—

After Lester Patrick's overtime heroics, the NHL governors met in New York to change the rules. President Frank Calder could make a substitute goalie available to any team in case of emergency at a cost of $200 per game, plus the sub's traveling expenses. A 10-minute overtime period was introduced, and if the game was still tied, it would go into the books as a draw. Foreshadowing contemporary league policy, the president was authorized to fine "not less than $200 and not more than $1,000" any player who gave a negative "statement" to the press about the conduct or ability of any league or club official, or any other player.

The biggest hockey success story in the United States came from Boston, where under the guidance of the old Montreal rich kid, Art Ross, the Bruins' 26 wins were the best in the NHL in 1928–29. It was a fine way to celebrate the beginning of their tenancy in the new Boston Garden, built above the city's North Station, allowing fans to take the elevated train right into the scene of the action.

Hockey had become so lucrative that the man behind this shiny new hockey palace was none other than Tex Rickard. Originally called the "Boston Madison Square Garden," the $10-million building was to be the second of seven "Gardens" that Rickard planned to build across the United States, but in the end, the Boston rink was his last.

With 14,448 seats, the Garden was a tightly packed venue that soon earned its nickname, "The Zoo," with its second-balcony seats seeming to hang over the ice, making it easier for fans to aim their approval — or displeasure — at the play down below. Indeed, at the Bruins home opener at the Garden on November 20, 1928 against the Montreal Canadiens, 3,000 more fans than the building had seats for squeezed in to create a mob atmosphere the *Boston Herald* called "the re-enaction [sic] of the assault on the Bastille."

Though the Bruins lost that game to the Canadiens, they finished first in the American Division, before exiting in the Stanley Cup semi-final. And they were loaded with talent. Ralph "Cooney" Weiland, just five-foot-seven, centred six-foot-one "Dutch" Gainor and six-foot-two Aubrey "Dit" Clapper, whose odd nickname resulted from his childhood difficulty at pronouncing his middle name, Victor. The trio was so explosive that by the following year they had been dubbed "The Dynamite Line."

Trios of players were now winning nicknames because the sport had evolved into one of substitution. As usual, the idea had been pioneered by the Patrick brothers and had met with resistance back East, but its eventual acceptance resulted in the shifting of nicknames. Where once the whole team had earned a flattering sobriquet — the "Little Men of Iron," the "Silver Seven"— forward lines now took on identities of their own: the "Kid Line" in Toronto, the "A Line" in New York, and the "Kraut Line" in Boston being a few.

Goalies were usually nicknamed by size, and Boston's Art Ross always claimed that he'd picked up Cecil "Tiny" Thompson "sight unseen" from Minneapolis. If true, it was one of the greatest blind plays of his hockey career, as Thompson would win the Vezina Trophy four times in his 10-year campaign with the Bruins.

Helping Thompson frustrate the opposition were Lionel Hitchman and Eddie Shore, one of the finest defensive pairings ever iced. Hitchman had won his first Stanley Cup with Ottawa in 1923, one month after he had turned pro. The six-foot defenseman was a favourite target of hockey's version of an axe murderer, Sprague Cleghorn, who once narrowly escaped life-banishment from hockey for his on ice-violence, and whose own wife swore a warrant out against him for domestic abuse. Cleghorn had cost Hitchman several of his teeth and countless concussions, yet "Hitch" was a clean, tough defenseman who took care of business in his own end and left the pyrotechnics to the original "Mr. Hockey," Eddie Shore.

Ornery, swashbuckling Eddie Shore was an eccentric hybrid of entertainer and philosopher, who made it to the big time from the disbanded Edmonton Eskimos of the Western Hockey League and quickly became a favourite of the raucous Boston Garden. As intimate as a bearpit, the Garden's fans screeched and pounded within spitshot of the players, who often responded in kind. If the Garden was "The

Zoo," then Eddie Shore was the zookeeper, bringing the hoarse groundlings to their feet with his ramrod-straight rushes, then setting up a Boston marksman for the kill with a sweet pass of the puck. Nearly half a century later, Shore suggested that his generosity to his teammates was not an act of noble selflessness. He claimed that if he shot the puck — and even if he scored — manager Art Ross would fine him $500. Given that Shore scored 12 goals in 1926–27, his first NHL season, either he had an endless supply of cash or his legendary mocking wit was very much alive.

Shore was also one of the toughest pieces of meat in the butcher shop. He used to tell sniffing reporters that he was born neither in Fort Qu'Appelle, Saskatchewan, nor in Regina, but in an oxcart on the road between the two towns. He suffered his first of 14 broken noses at age nine, while trying to tame a wild Shetland pony for a timid friend. When the colt reared, Shore's nose became a geyser, but dizzy, retching, blood flowing down his chin and onto his coat, he refused to yield to the bucking pony, and won. The bloody triumph serves as metaphor for the hard way that was Eddie Shore's, but there's one to match each of the 978 stitches he took during his long hockey career.

Despite his wounds, Shore was remarkably free of scars, a combination of vanity and his own medical philosophy which demanded clean stitching, then intensive massage of the wound to prevent scar tissue. At his first NHL training camp in 1926, the rookie Shore responded to the taunts of the veteran Billy Coutu by knocking him out. Shore was hurt, too, his ear split down the middle and flapping in the breeze. A team doctor wanted to amputate, but Shore would have none of it. He found a cooperative doctor who would sew the ear back together, and took a mirror as his only anesthetic — so he could watch and direct the doctor's stitching. "I was just a farm boy," he later told a reporter. "I didn't want my looks messed up. I made him change the last stitch: he'd have left a scar."

The man Lester Patrick called "The Human Gyroscope" had an overstock of self-confidence, even when it wasn't warranted. With the darkness of Quebec or Ontario whizzing by the team's train on road trips, Shore would take his tenor saxophone and play duets with his teammate Frank Frederickson. While Frederickson was an accomplished violinist, Shore was a rank amateur who only knew how to blow hot air. When modesty didn't stop him, Art Ross did, threatening to throw Shore and his sax under the train if he didn't shut up.

Bald, flinty-eyed Shore was also a consummate actor, rousing the home side and goading the enemy. He was so famous that he, too, earned the handle "The Babe Ruth of Hockey," and though he preferred to call Ruth "The Eddie Shore of Baseball," Shore could fill a rink with his name alone. *Collier's* magazine wittily observed that Shore's popularity came from "the hope, entertained by spectators in all cities but Boston, that he will some night be severely killed."

Shore's celebrity and vanity conspired with manager Art Ross to create one of hockey's more bizarre stunts. With his team already on the ice, Shore would skate out to "Hail, the Chief" wearing a toreador's cape, accompanied by a valet. The servant would unveil Shore, and friend and foe alike would howl in pleasure or derision. The New York Americans put a stop to this travesty with a sophisticated tool: satire. After Shore had done his routine, the Americans skated out carrying a rolled-up rug, which they dropped at centre ice. When they unrolled it, out popped their pointy-eared forward Charley "Rabbit" McVeigh, primping and preening and blowing dainty kisses to the crowd. It was enough to end Eddie Shore's toreador strut.

It didn't, however, end his fondness for capes. Shore was decked out in tails and a long black cape on the night of January 2, 1929, as he took leave of a dinner party in Brookline, Massachusetts. He was heading for the train station to meet up with his team as they set off for Montreal, but his taxi became stuck in the gridlock of a car accident. Shore knew that Art Ross would find this a thin excuse for missing the team train. Since there were no more trains to Montreal that night, and a winter storm brewing that had grounded airplanes, Shore borrowed a big Pierce Arrow touring car and its chauffeur from his wealthy host.

The duo drove straight into a blizzard. The city-boy chauffeur wanted to retreat, but Shore, who had practised hockey on days so foul that hoarfrost formed on his shoulders, laughed the chauffeur into the backseat, and took the wheel himself.

Nearly 24 hours after he set out, Eddie Shore arrived in Montreal. Practically delirious from sleep deprivation and the rigours of blizzard-driving, Shore accosted his teammates Clapper and Weiland in the lobby of the Windsor Hotel and made them promise to wake

Lieutenant Hobey Baker found in WWI aerial combat the same thrills he had once found on the ice, as the United States' first "hockey superstar." Despite repeated overtures to play professional hockey, Baker steadfastly refused, and with his athletic gifts, his matinee idol looks, and his untimely death, he became cast as the ideal hero.

below, top: Undaunted by The Great Depression, Conn Smythe took a mixture of luck, vision, and some muscular persuasion to build Maple Leaf Gardens in less than six months. Located at Carlton and Church Streets, the Gardens became the temple at which people worshipped English Canada's Team. HOCKEY HALL OF FAME

below, bottom: Invented by Conn Smythe, and led by GM and coach Lester Patrick (standing, center), the 1928 New York Rangers won their first Stanley Cup in only their second season. Patrick poses in uniform, a right he earned in Game 2 when he pulled on the pads to substitute for injured goalie Lorne Chabot. HOCKEY HALL OF FAME

facing page, top: Conn Smythe (seated, far right) had transferred from Toronto's aristocratic Upper Canada College, which he hated, to Jarvis Collegiate in 1910, when he was 15. Though usually the smallest member of any squad he was on, Smythe's intensely competitive spirit and entrepreneurial nerve made him one of hockey's giants. HOCKEY HALL OF FAME

facing page, bottom: The Montreal Maroons were the world's premier hockey city's "other" NHL team, and often its best. Led by future Hall of Famers Nels "Old Poison" Stewart and goalie Clint Benedict, the Maroons competed from 1924–25 until 1937–38, winning two Stanley Cups in their relatively brief existence. HOCKEY HALL OF FAME

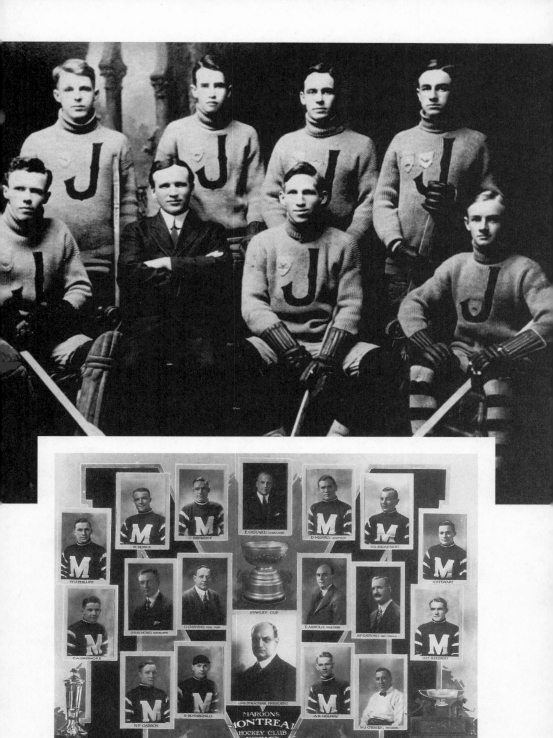

facing page, top: The 1932 Toronto Maple Leafs, making a rare appearance in their civvies, take to their pipes to ruminate on their first Stanley Cup championship. Significantly, brash owner Conn Smythe (middle row, 3rd from left) boasts the longest pipe, while Francis "King" Clancy, the Leafs' heart and soul (kneeling, center), holds one of the shortest. HOCKEY HALL OF FAME

facing page, bottom: When Conn Smythe teamed rookies Charlie Conacher (left) and Harvey "Busher" Jackson (right) with seasoned Maple Leaf warrior Joe Primeau (center) in 1929–30, one of hockey's greatest threesomes was born in the "Kid Line". In the Leafs' first Stanley

Cup–winning season of 1931–32, the Kid Line accounted for 75 of the team's 155 goals. HOCKEY HALL OF FAME

above: A teenage Howie Morenz, "The Stratford Streak," (seated, second from left) looks solemn with his championship Stratford junior team. Morenz initially feared leaving the safety and small-pond stardom of Stratford when the Montreal Canadiens forced him into their colors in 1923, but once in Montreal, Morenz's brilliant play made both the team and the city his own. HOCKEY HALL OF FAME

far left: Howie Morenz's body lies in state in March 1937, in the Montreal Forum, where his brilliance had transported fans to hockey heaven over fourteen seasons, twelve of them as a Canadien. More than 50,000 people walked past his casket before his funeral, and a quarter of a million more lined the route to the cemetery, to watch their fallen hero pass by one last time.
HOCKEY HALL OF FAME

left: The Detroit Red Wings' superstar Gordie Howe jokingly shovels pucks into a net in a team publicity shot. In his astonishing 25 seasons with the Wings, Howe shoveled 786 pucks into opposing nets, winning six Art Ross Trophies as the NHL's leading point scorer, and six Hart Trophies as the NHL's MVP.
HOCKEY HALL OF FAME

bottom: General manager and coach Jack Adams (center ice) speaks to the Red Wings at a 1950s training camp. In his 35 years with the Red Wings, Adams masterminded twelve regular season titles and seven Stanley Cup championships. Despite his nickname of "Jolly Jack," Adams could be tyrannical and mean. In the end, his efforts to control his dynasty ended up dismantling it.
HOCKEY HALL OF FAME

following page: Fearless, combative "Terrible" Ted Lindsay fights off a checker with the same grit that he fought all of his battles. When Lindsay showed too much fortitude in his efforts to establish a strong NHL players' association, the nine-time All-Star left winger and team captain was exiled to the lowly Chicago Black Hawks as a warning to other "troublemakers."
HOCKEY HALL OF FAME

him in half an hour. Dutifully, at the appointed time, the two Bruins poured ice water on the slumbering Shore, and he struggled out of bed and to the Montreal Forum, where he scored the only goal in a 1–0 Boston victory. Bruin manager Art Ross celebrated Eddie Shore's Herculean triumph by fining him $200 — for missing the train.

Three months later, Eddie Shore and the Bruins beat the Rangers for the Stanley Cup — their first. It was the first time in its 36 years that Lord Stanley's Dominion Challenge Trophy had not seen a team from that Dominion even play for it. Thanks to the talents of Howie Morenz and Conn Smythe and Eddie Shore, hockey was now as much an American success as it was in Canada. Hockey's Golden Ones had found a place in the land where the streets were paved with gold.

As the good times roared in Uncle Sam's house, so they did for Sam's northern cousin. In 1928, a billion dollars of exportables were coming out of the bountiful Canadian Shield, and Canadians were buying more and more goods and stocks with the alchemy of credit. But then Canadian wheat prices fell on the international market, and the fastest growing region of the country stumbled. In New York, the stock market crashed, and all those paper millionaires and credit-worshippers were either wiped out, or in a deep, dark hole.

Nature, as if to remind the world of real power, brought a drought in the west, and crops failed. Men and women hopped boxcars looking for work, and many people left their weekly grocery line-up for the relief line-up. Hockey would have to put in overtime, acting as an arena for the hopes and dreams of those who had little to hope for and dream on.

True to imperious form, Conn Smythe was going to take care of hopes and dreams in Toronto. By October of 1927, Smythe had listened to the acumen of his Leaf defenseman and friend Clarence "Happy" Day, a 26-year-old University of Toronto pharmacy graduate, and added nine new players. Smythe also appointed his old flying instructor, Lieutenant-Colonel W. G. "Billy" Barker, Canada's "most decorated soldier" of the First World War, as the Leafs' first president, seeing in Barker a potent public relations symbol.

Barker's mission from Smythe was to instill a sense of heroic purpose to the new Leafs by giving them rousing locker-room speeches.

The fearless, irreverent Barker, however, was plagued by a demon Hobey Baker had anticipated: postwar life was dreadful. Many veterans, who could never express the horror to a world that didn't really care to know, escaped in drugs and drink, and Billy Barker carried a case of ginger ale with him at all times to ward off his own temptation to alcohol. It didn't always work.

One night before an important game, Barker had to go Hamilton, and found himself out of ginger ale. By the time he got back to Toronto, he was so drunk that his car skidded out of control and flipped on Jarvis Street. Nevertheless, the man who had 50 enemy kills to his credit, who had won the *Croix de Guerre*, the DSO and bar, the Military Cross, two Italian Silver Medals, and who had been mentioned three times in dispatches, showed up in the Leafs dressing room, his torn clothes covered with blood. "He didn't give a bad speech at all," Smythe recalled, "on the importance of morale."

Smythe's loyalties only went so far, and he didn't see the humanity in Barker's problem, only the weakness. So he let him go. In 1930, Barker — with echoes of Hobey Baker — was killed in a freak air crash, when a new plane he was testing stalled in mid-air. Fifty thousand people lined Toronto's streets that March to watch his coffin pass in the largest public funeral the country had ever seen.

Conn Smythe was seeing nothing but signs of life in his second pro hockey creation of the decade. He found aggression in left winger Irvine "Ace" Bailey, who would lead the league with 22 goals and 32 points in 1929. He found comportment in "Gentleman" Joe Primeau, a young centre whose clean play would win him the Lady Byng Trophy. He found loyalty and gratitude in goalie Lorne Chabot, saving him from New York, where Lester Patrick felt he was going gun-shy after again being hit in the face by a puck.

Smythe paid $8,000 to Pittsburgh for the toughness of back-checking left winger Harold "Baldy" Cotton, and found a defensive marvel in the Toronto Marlboros' Reginald "Red" Horner, a big aggressive blueliner with a devastating shot and a bodycheck so beautiful it could only have come from nature. Indeed, Smythe called Horner "the greatest bodychecker I ever saw."

In 1930 Smythe brought up a feisty, carefree youth from the juniors. Harvey "Busher" Jackson had scarcely reached his teens in the mid-1920s when Frank Selke, coach of the Toronto Marlboro

Juniors, brought his team to practise at Toronto's Ravina Rink. Jackson had won the right to practise in the rink in exchange for clearing the ice, and when Selke tried to shoo the boy away, the silver-footed Jackson embarrassed the Marlies, who couldn't take the puck away from him.

Selke loved Jackson, and nearly half a century later called him "the classiest player I have ever seen ... Good-looking as a movie idol, six feet tall, weighing some 202 pounds, Jackson was as light on his feet as a ballet dancer. He could pivot on a dime, stickhandle through an entire team ... and shoot like a bullet, either forehand or backhand."

Jackson's linemate, Charlie Conacher, was one of 11 children born to Irish Protestant immigrants who lived on Davenport Road, a place he described as "one of Toronto's high-class slums of the 1920s." Even though his father had a job as a teamster, Charlie Conacher's family had to rely on *Toronto Star* food hampers at Christmas. His eldest brother, Lionel, had to leave school in the eighth grade to take a job to help support them all — an experience faced by many families at the time.

It was Charlie's beloved brother Lionel who inspired him to take up hockey. Lionel, at six-foot-one and 200 pounds, was nicknamed "The Big Train." He would go on to become Canada's athlete of the first half of the twentieth century with sporting feats that seemed impossible then, and are not possible now.

Lionel's middle name, "Pretoria," came from a British victory over the Boers in 1900, the year he was born. With a battle as a namesake, Lionel took up other sports with ferocity. At age 16, in his first season as a junior, Lionel won junior hockey's cherished Memorial Cup, and hockey wasn't even his best sport. After hitting the winning home run to give his baseball team the 1920 Toronto championship, "The Big Train" raced across the street to save his lacrosse team from a 3–0 drubbing by scoring all four goals in a 4–3 victory.

That same year he also won the Canadian light-heavyweight boxing championship, and in his first game with the Toronto Argonaut football team, he scored 23 of the team's 27 points. The following year he spent an afternoon helping the Argos win the Grey Cup, then that evening played defense in a senior hockey game.

With 500 stitches in his face and head, and a nose that had been broken eight different ways, Lionel once wittily understated that "my appearance cannot be said to be aristocratic." His sporting genes were as regal as they come, and Charlie Conacher had them, too. He idol-ized his older brother, and so when Lionel made the NHL, Charlie worked on his skating so hard that he thought his "legs would drop off."

To a family so poor they didn't have "enough money to buy tooth-paste," hockey meant money, and Charlie Conacher was going to get it. He scored on his first NHL shift, but at the end of his rookie year, doc-tors discovered he had a ruptured kidney, removed it, and told him his hockey days were gone. Conacher responded by leading the league in scoring with 31 goals — three more than the wizard Morenz, and in two fewer games.

At six-foot-two and 195 pounds, Conacher was a giant at a time when the average NHL size was six inches and 40 pounds less. He was also enormously well endowed, and teammates swore that his penis hung 14 inches — in repose. Conacher's teammates never tired of joking about his size, and would bring visitors to the dressing room for a pre-game view. When a teammate brought in a priest to witness Conacher's miracle, he finally had heard enough, and chased them out by breaking the second commandment.

With Joe Primeau at centre and Conacher and "Busher" Jackson on the wings, the trio would became famous as "Kid Line." Between 1931 and 1935, Conacher would lead the league in scoring twice, and Jackson once.

Even with "The Big Bomber" Conacher, team-builder Smythe felt his team was missing one secret ingredient — the irrepressible Francis Michael Clancy. Such a notion was rank heresy in Toronto. Clancy wore the colours of the Ottawa Senators and carried the loathing of everyone who called themselves Leafs' fans. He was even despised by the Leafs' genial captain, "Hap" Day, and to make the issue moot, Clancy said he would rather suit up for Hell than for the Leafs.

Clancy had scored 17 goals and 23 assists, an extraordinary feat for a defenseman of that era, and he planned on continuing to do so in his hometown. After all, his father had been one of the greatest rugby footballers Ottawa had known in the 1890s, so good at rolling the ball out of the scrum with his heel that he was nicknamed "The King of the Heelers." Clancy junior used to joke that he was just "King of the Heels," but his hockey was so good that he too was nicknamed "King."

Though Clancy and Ottawa loved each other, the Senators were suf-fering because people couldn't afford to come to games. Word leaked that the "King" could be had — for $35,000 and few choice players. It was a prohibitive sum in the Depression, and the best the Leaf directors could do was offer $25,000. Conn Smythe needed another $10,000 and so he turned to an old, faithful source: gambling.

Smythe didn't expect all that much from his filly Rare Jewel, which was not surprising since the horse had never won anything. On race day Rare Jewel's odds were about the same as those for pennies falling from heaven. Even so, Smythe bet a wad on his filly, and her trainer and one of Smythe's gambling cronies each slipped the horse a flask of brandy. And so, running on hooch, Rare Jewel won her first and only race, and Smythe found himself nearly $11,000 richer. He had more than enough to buy a "King." And now he had a Stanley Cup contender.

Still, Smythe wasn't content. The Leafs had been playing, as had the St. Pat's before them, at the 8,000-seat Arena Gardens on Mutual Street. Built in 1911–12 for $200,000 by a consortium of businessmen led by Sir Henry Pellat (whose house Casa Loma is still a Toronto landmark), the "Mutual Street Arena" was now too small and too dowdy for what Conn Smythe had in mind. He wanted a place that was more than a drafty hockey arena, but rather a "venue" where people could dress up and go as if they were attending the opera, or, in later years under Harold Ballard, the circus.

Despite the crushing Depression, Smythe sent his assistant Frank Selke and star forward "Ace" Bailey out on the hustings to solicit corporate largesse. Eaton's came through with a parcel of land at the corner of Church and Carlton in exchange for $350,000 and a stock option. Given that this building would become one of the two most cherished hockey temples in the world, the fact that it was on Church Street only added to its allure.

To give his Leafs a voice, Smythe would build Foster Hewitt a broadcast booth wherever he wanted. Hewitt had reluctantly invented hockey broadcasting by taking an amateur-hockey radio assignment that no one else wanted as a 23-year-old cub reporter in 1922. Hewitt's first game had been broadcast from a glass box at ice level, made foggy with his own breath. He even had to use a telephone as a microphone and was constantly interrupted by telephone operators demanding to know what number he was calling.

Despite this, Hewitt had become North America's "Voice of Hockey" and knew that no glass box was going to give the Leafs their due. So he climbed the stairs of the new Eaton's building and gazed down at pedestrians until he found his perfect view of the action from the fifth floor. It was from this height that he would call the deeds of the icemen, hanging from Maple Leaf Gardens' rafters in a silver tube romantically dubbed "the gondola."

When money ran short, Selke and Smythe convinced the trade unions to take payment in shares, and on June 1, 1931 the ground was broken. The Gardens had been designed by the prestigious firm of Ross and Macdonald, who were behind Union Station and the Royal York Hotel, two of Toronto's most muscular and imperial buildings. An average of 700 workers used 77,500 bags of cement, 600 tons of reinforcing steel, 760 tons of structural steel, and 750,000 yellow bricks, with the bricks coming from Conn Smythe's sand pits. The Gardens' distinctive domed roof stood out as a beacon, at its apex 150-feet high, and beneath it sat 12,500 people, none of whom were farther than 65 feet from the ice.

The Gardens cost $1.5 million, and it was finished in an astonishing five months, largely due to the fact that its utilitarian interior — despite its bowling alley, billiards room, full gym, and the two full-time painters who daily touched up any blemishes — was not going to make the cover of any architectural digest. Even so, it had a human scale and perfect site lines, and on November 12, 1931, the bands from the Royal Grenadiers and the 48th Highlanders played "Happy Days Are Here Again" to an audience of more than 13,000, many of them in evening dress. As the Gardens' president J. P. Bickell tried to make a speech at centre ice, exuberantly impatient shouts of "Play hockey!" came roaring back from up near the rafters, where many of the men who had built the place were sitting, eager to see if the one-dollar common shares they had in the building were going to be worth anything.

The Leafs lost that first game to the Chicago Black Hawks, but they would make those concerned blue-collar shareholders breathe easier by making it to the Stanley Cup Finals in their first year in their new home. Fittingly, their opponents were Smythe's other team, the New York Rangers, and the Leafs beat them in Madison Square Garden. The second game went off in Boston, for Tex Rickard had made a deal giving the Ringling Brother's Circus tenancy of Madison Square Garden every April. Thus the Rangers got bounced to Beantown, and the Leafs went with them.

With former Pacific Coast star Dick Irvin behind the bench, Jackson, Conacher, Clancy, Bailey, Frank Finnigan, "Baldy" Cotton, and "Hap" Day all weighed in with goals as the Leafs outscored the Rangers 18–10 to win three straight games, the last one in front of their frenzied hometown fans. Almost five years earlier, Smythe had promised to take revenge on the Rangers who cheated and belittled him by winning the Stanley Cup at home. It was the kind of bright, shining deed that made the darkness outside seem unreal. But the darkness was real enough, and no hockey rink wall could keep it out.

By the time the Depression was entrenched, pro hockey had seen some rough years, and entire leagues had disappeared, leaving the Golden Ones a smaller frozen pond to play on. The Patricks' Pacific experiment was dead, and from 1927 the NHL had been the only game in town.

In 1934, NHL President Frank Calder promised the hockey world that the illustrious Ottawa Senators would never leave Canada because the American teams would never allow it. Hungry Canadians were blaming the Americans for starting this damned Depression with their mania for speculation and credit, and then with their loan recalls and crushing tariffs. Promises about hockey teams were worth as much as stock certificates.

The truth was that Ottawa, a team that had won four Stanley Cups in the Roaring Twenties and finished in first place seven times, was indeed going south, to splash the American eagle across their jerseys in St. Louis. In the spring of 1935, the truth was even worse: the franchise that had known some of the greatest players the sport had ever seen — the Franks McGee, Nighbor, and Clancy — was now finished. The team's players could join the one-in-three Canadians looking for work.

Or rather, looking to survive. People were making coffee out of roasted rye wheat, soap from bear oil and moose fat. They were making clothes from flour and sugar sacks. With no health insurance, and an unemployment insurance scheme just passed in Parliament, people were on their own.

The Ottawa Senators / St. Louis Eagles weren't the only team to go down the chute. The Pittsburgh Pirates had moved to Philadelphia in

1930 and were dead after a season. Indeed, more misery and death were on the way.

Women's hockey, however, soared on the glory of the Preston Rivulettes, one of the finest teams that Canada has ever produced. Women's college hockey had disbanded in Ontario in 1933 due to the Depression, but amateur groups played on, seeking small victories wherever they could. From 1930 to the 1939, the Preston Rivulettes won big, amassing 10 championship titles in both Ontario and Quebec, as well as six national champion titles. The Rivulettes took on teams from across the country, tying three times and losing only twice in the 350 games they racked up over 10 years.

Led by forwards Hilda Ranscombe and Marm Schmuck, and backstopped by Nellie Ranscombe, the Rivulettes were originally a softball team who decided in 1930 they needed another sporting challenge and took up hockey. Throughout their career, the Rivulettes and other women's hockey teams were hard-pressed to meet traveling and equipment expenses, and the Depression only added to the misery. When the Rivulettes beat the mighty Montreal (women's) Maroons in 1936, only 168 fans turned out, leaving the Rivulettes with $150 less in anticipated gate receipts, and the indignity of paying $5 a woman to their "host" Maroons for provisions at their post-game victory "party."

In the NHL, the mood was not the least bit festive, with the darkness falling first on December 12, 1933.

The Leafs were two men short against the Bruins in the Boston Garden when Toronto coach Dick Irvin sent blue-chip defensemen "King" Clancy and "Red" Horner out with the stickhandling "Ace" Bailey to kill off the penalties. Bailey put on a virtuoso display, ragging the puck for an entire minute. Tiring, he shot the puck into the Boston end to get a breather, and Bruin avenger Eddie Shore embarked on one of his famous rink-long rushes.

Shore got as far as King Clancy, who used the old trick of tapping the front of Shore's skates to send the Bruin skidding along the ice on his knees. Clancy calmly picked up the puck and took it back the other way, while Shore, kneeling on the ice, waited for another penalty call against Toronto. When none came, he steamed his way toward the nearest Leaf.

Ace Bailey was leaning on his stick, trying to catch his breath, when Shore ploughed into him from behind, knocking Bailey's feet from under him. Bailey's head hit the ice with the sound of what Leafs' assistant Frank Selke described as a "pumpkin cracked with a baseball bat." The Boston Zoo went wild.

As defenseman Horner rushed to Bailey's aid, the blood from Bailey's head flooded the ice. Horner caught the smirk on Eddie Shore's face and crumpled Shore with a punch, while Conn Smythe did the same to a Boston fan who screamed that Bailey was faking it. Smythe's old enemy, Art Ross, gleefully had him arrested for assault.

After 16 stitches were threaded in the back of his head, Shore went to the Leafs' dressing room to apologize. Bailey, fading into unconsciousness, forgave "Mr. Hockey" by saying, "That's all right, Eddie. It's all part of the game." But the game was now deadly serious.

The Boston team medic, Dr. Kelley, took one look at Bailey and said, "If this boy is a Roman Catholic we should call a priest right away." Frank Selke, who was in the room, recalled that Bailey opened his eyes and demanded to be put back in the game. "They need me," he said.

By the time Conn Smythe was released from jail at 2:30 A.M., journalists were already composing Bailey's obit at his Boston hospital. Still, there was hope, for Dr. Kelley had found the two American brain surgeons who might be able to save Ace's life. As luck would have it, they were in Boston, attending a conference.

Over the next two weeks, the surgeons performed two intricate, risky operations on Bailey after discovering he had not one concussion, but two. The surgeons were not optimistic, and reporters thought Bailey as good as dead.

So did Bailey's father, who had gone down to Boston to kill the man who had killed his son. Frank Selke, who was in Toronto but still ordered to stop Ace's father by Conn Smythe, ran through a list of everyone he knew in Boston, finally hitting upon Bob Huddy, a man who shared Selke's hobby — raising exotic birds. Even better, Huddy was a Boston policeman, and soon found Bailey's father drunk in his hotel bar, loudly promising to fill the devil, Eddie Shore, full of lead.

Mustering all of his Irish wiles, Huddy asked the old man if he wasn't the father of "Ace Bailey ... as good a player as ever shot a puck!" The man proudly allowed that he was and accepted Huddy's invitation to have a drink with him. Huddy soon had Mr. Bailey's gun and gently escorted him to the train station, ordering the train conductor to keep Bailey on board until Toronto as a matter of national security.

As the deathwatch continued outside Bailey's hospital room, reporters heard the nurses trying to revive the fading Ace by slapping him and begging him to fight on, because his team needed him badly. At 2:30 in the morning, a haggard nurse emerged from the room and told the scribes they could all go home — Ace Bailey would live.

Two months later, the NHL held a benefit game for the Ace at Maple Leaf Gardens, featuring a squad of All-Stars against Toronto. Each player skated out to receive his All-Star jersey from Ace himself, who seemed as if he had come no closer to death than any other healthy 31 year old. The Gardens fell silent when Eddie Shore skated up to accept his sweater, and in the spirit of forgiveness and sportsmanship, Ace Bailey shook Eddie Shore's hand.

The emotion of it all released a cheer from the fans that seemed to rattle bits off the Gardens's roof and down onto Carlton Street. Though Ace Bailey would never play professional hockey again, his All-Star benefit planted an idea which would become a reality in the next decade. And Bailey's head injury also introduced the protective helmet to the game — an idea embraced only at first by Eddie Shore.

—⁓—

As if to remind everyone that mortality was a fragile thing with Hitler and Mussolini rampaging in Europe, and the Depression ravaging the world, the original golden person in Montreal was now just sadly mortal. From 1926 to 1933, Howie Morenz had led the Canadiens in goals. He had led them to back-to-back Stanley Cups in 1930 and '31; he had won three Hart Trophies as the NHL's most valuable player; and he was twice the league's leading scorer. But the speed and panache that had put hearts in mouths and ice in Madison Square Garden had faded with injury and age and excess.

With only eight goals in 30 contests in 1935, the 32-year-old "Hurtling Hab" was taking up room on the team that he once wanted no part of, and then came to define. Now the Canadiens wanted no part of their once-mighty prince, and sent him into cruel exile in Chicago.

Morenz and Montreal fans were devastated. His linemate and attendant lord, Aurele Joliat, had won the 1935 Hart Trophy, and felt the loss as badly as Morenz. "I couldn't tell you how many goals I scored merely by having to tip in a puck that he passed to me from the corner behind two opponents," he said. "Morenz just ran out of gas completely when he was 32 or 33, and that was it."

Morenz had some satisfaction in the last game of the season, when he scored for the first time against his beloved *Canadiens,* and the Montreal Forum stood as one in ovation — in part for Morenz, in part for the beginning of their own nostalgia.

Yet Morenz's fortunes turned with his exile. Part-way through the 1936 season, "The Stratford Streak" had been traded from Chicago to the Rangers, back to the place he had lit up just a decade earlier as the proudest of the Flying Frenchmen. The neon of Broadway seemed to light up Morenz's faded glitter, bringing back some of his old magic.

Watching from Montreal, Cecil Hart was delighted. Hart had coached Morenz and the Canadiens to their Stanley Cup triumphs in 1930 and '31 (and in 1923 his father, Dr. David Hart, a veteran of the 1886 Fenian Raids as well as first president of Montreal's Zionist society, had given the NHL its trophy for the most valuable player). Now the Habs wanted Hart back behind the bench, and he saw a bargaining chip that would restore the cosmic order. Like Tex Rickard's offer when he first saw Morenz play and agreed to put ice in Madison Square Garden if Morenz would play in the first game, Hart said that he would return to coach the 1937 campaign on one condition: he wanted the glorious Howie Morenz back just one more time.

The Montreal fans and Morenz were on a second honeymoon, for the man who had taken the Canadiens' fortunes personally was home to look after them. Once again Montrealers would see Morenz keeping brasseries afloat after a Canadiens' win, or forbid the thought, a loss. Losing was a bad word indeed now that Morenz was back on a line with his pal Joliat, with one last a chance for glory in the only place that really mattered.

Those who saw Morenz play against the Black Hawks on the night of January 28, 1937 must have felt they'd climbed into a time machine and gone back to the beginning. There was Morenz, a half-smile playing at the corners of his mouth as he dashed here and twisted there, making improbable things happen between ice and steel and rubber and wood.

Just like he used to do, Morenz broke through the Chicago defense and sped after a loose puck that had slid into the end boards. Chicago defenseman "Big Earl" Seibert chased him, and would never forget it.

"When he came down the ice, he was like the wind," Seibert remembered. "There was no way I could catch up with him, but I was able to force him behind the net. Then he tripped and the tip of his skate got caught in the boards, and I hit him. There was no other way of stopping him."

The sound of Morenz's snapping bones echoed through the Forum. The leg that had once been so badly scalded that his family thought he would never walk again was now broken in four places.

Both the French and the English papers in Montreal reassured their readers that Morenz was only through for the season, but Aurele Joliat knew differently. "I cried that night. I knew he wouldn't be back," Joliat recalled 34 years later. "We were very close, and I knew that Howie was worried about the fact that he might burn himself out early ... but ... he could only play full-out. When his leg shattered that night, I knew there was no way he could come back. He was through and we all knew it."

From his bed in St. Luke's Hospital, Morenz the *bon vivant* put on a hearty public front, joking with visiting players and drinking heavily from a supply of whisky and beer they brought him, and which the hospital allowed. Morenz was drunk most of the time, and a letter to his family suggests the optimism of someone who is struggling with reality. "The x-rays show a vast improvement and I've only been here a week," he wrote. "I sure would have liked to finish the season, but fate gave me quite a blow. You can bet it's not going to get me down."

Yet the increasingly dismal prognosis *was* getting Morenz down. He had to be restrained in a strait-jacket after suffering a nervous breakdown. He worried to his cherished teammate Joliat that his lavish way of living had left little money for his wife and children. Morenz wept, and, pointing to heaven, confided that he'd watch the Canadiens win the Stanley Cup "from up there."

On March 8, 1937, Howie Morenz tripped while walking to the bathroom, hitting his head on the floor. The resulting coronary embolism stopped his heart, age 34, but Aurele Joliat saw beyond the cold science. "Howie loved to play hockey more than anyone ever loved anything, and when he realized that he would never play again, he couldn't live with it," said Joliat. "I think Howie died of a broken heart."

The day after his death, New York's Rangers and Americans lined up on their respective blue lines at Madison Square Garden, and

10,000 people stood in bowed silence as a lone bugler played the "Last Post." In Montreal, 2,000 people filed by Morenz's casket at the funeral home on the night after his death — Westmounters in expensive cars and furs; little boys with their hockey sticks; sombre, tough working men, caps in hand as they held back the tears.

Morenz's body was placed at centre ice of the Montreal Forum, with four Canadiens' teammates forming an honour guard. More than 50,000 people walked past his casket in the four hours before his funeral, and a quarter of a million more — many of them sobbing — lined the route to the cemetery. "The Stratford Streak's" funeral had eclipsed Billy Barker's as the largest public event yet seen in the history of Canada.

The Canadiens held a benefit game for the Morenz family the following year, raising over $11,000. Howie's Montreal uniform was auctioned off for $500, though the sweater was returned to his son, who had turned 10 the week before, and had once served as the Canadiens' mascot. Collections for the family totaled $20,000, but the money had to be put in trust, and because of the low interest rates, the family only received $600 a year. A year after Howie died, one of his daughters died of pneumonia. His widow, Mary, only 29, couldn't take any more, and Howie Jr. and his surviving sister, Marlene, were placed in an orphanage.

In 1950, a Canadian Press sportswriters' poll voted on "hockey's greatest star during the first half of the twentieth century." Cyclone Taylor received three votes, Rocket Richard, four, and Howie Morenz, 27. The man called the greatest player ever by those who saw him play had won his last trophy from the grave. He had not wanted to play for Montreal at all, yet he had come to define an era. The original Golden One was dead. And the era was dead with him. The next three decades of pro hockey would see glory, but it would be dynastic, when three teams would rule the ice. Howie Morenz's beloved Canadiens would be at the pinnacle of the era, and maybe he was watching, from "up there."

6

THE WINGED WHEELMEN

From 1942 to 1967, the NHL was dominated by the Trinity: the Montreal Canadiens, the Toronto Maple Leafs, and the Detroit Red Wings. When the two Canadian teams weren't winning the Stanley Cup, the Red Wings were, becoming en route the most successful American NHL hockey franchise in history.

The story of the Montreal Canadiens is draped in the flag of Canadian francophone symbolism, and the story of the Toronto Maple Leafs is wrapped in a particular kind of Canadian anglophone patriotism, but the Detroit Red Wings' tale is a more nakedly American one of money and power. The flag that flew in the Motor City was the dollar sign, and while money built the Wings, it was also money, or the struggle for the power it brought, that ultimately took them down.

From 1949 to 1955, the Detroit Red Wings finished in first place every year, setting a record for professional sports teams. Under the managerial genius of Jolly Jack Adams, and the deep pockets of the Norris Family, they won Stanley Cups in 1950, '52, '54, and '55, a kind of interregnum between the dynastic triumphs of Toronto and Montreal. The Wings, in their regal red jerseys with white-winged-wheel logo, debuted players who would become legends long before they had hung up their skates: Ted Lindsay, Gordie Howe, and Terry Sawchuk.

Yet the Detroit Red Wings were also at the centre of a revolution, one that changed the way the business of hockey was conducted as much as Cyclone Taylor and the Patricks and the first pro leagues had done a half-century earlier. As if in some medieval fable gone wrong, the Wings soared because of their gilded patrons, but when it came time to share the wealth, the Wings' shining knights of the ice were vilified and exiled, shattering the illusion that hockey was about anything other than money.

━━━━

Jack Adams, the architect of the Detroit Red Wings, had learned about money and hockey the hard way, growing up poor way out on the western edge of Lake Superior in Fort William, Ontario. As a teenager, Adams had two newspaper jobs, and his afternoon route took him through the town's bars, where the lubricated miners and loggers were good tippers.

When one bar customer wanted to buy Adams a drink, the kid thought fast and asked the man for a cigar. Adams remembered that the man who looked after the local rink liked cigars, and he could trade one for a free skate. The rink guardian churlishly made Adams clean the ice with a shovel first, but he let him in for nothing, and cigars became Adams' favourite kind of tip.

He turned pro with the Toronto Arenas in 1917, winning a Stanley Cup. By 1919, he was so highly regarded that he was receiving urgent, if seemingly backhanded, telegraphic summons from Frank Patrick in Vancouver: "Situation desperate or would not wire you." Adams answered the S.O.S., and the fine, play-making centre was 24 years old when he impressed hockey men out on the rich west coast as a Millionaire. "Jack Adams carried the puck through the opposition defense," wrote the *Vancouver Sun* sports editor, Al Hardy, "with the ease and grace of Cleopatra's head waiter bringing in the morning java."

Adams played for Vancouver for two years before returning to Toronto. As a star centre with the Toronto Arenas in the 1920s, he was often the target of vicious attacks, and those who decry today's level of hockey violence can take small comfort in the fact that things have much improved. In one donnybrook against the Canadiens, Adams head was cut so badly by stick-swinging opponents that when his teammates took him to a Montreal hospital where Adams's sister was a nurse, she didn't recognize him.

After retiring as player in Ottawa, Adams headed south to Michigan. He would later say that the "smartest thing I've ever done in my life is to take out American papers. This country has been good to me and ... I am proud of my citizenship."

Adams loved the American entrepreneurial spirit and parlayed the fact that he'd just won the Stanley Cup into a job as coach of the Detroit Cougars for the 1926–27 season. When the Patrick brothers' daring Pacific Coast league folded, the Victoria Cougars moved into the Western league, winning the Stanley Cup in 1925. When the WHL folded in 1926, the Cougars' players were sold for $100,000 to the Motor City, which had been lobbying hard for an NHL franchise.

When Adams signed up with them, the Cougars were a disaster, finishing last of the NHL's 10 teams and losing $84,000 for their trouble. They even had to play their home games in Canada, at the Border Cities Arena in Windsor, Ontario, because their new building, the Olympia, suffered from construction delays. Cougar fans had to take a ferry across the river to the team's "home" games, with the added insult of paying a "war tax" to the Canadian government when they disembarked.

After emerging from receivership, the Cougars began the 1928 season in a new home with a new name: they would ply their trade in Detroit's brand-new $1.25 million Olympia Arena as the Falcons. Designed by the theatre architect Charles Howard Crane, who had created Detroit's "Orchestra Hall" which housed the city's symphony, the Olympia rose up on Grand River Avenue, boasting a Romanesque facade and a sophisticated refrigeration system which used 74,800 feet of pipe to carry the ice-making coolant beneath its floors. In a gesture to the mercantile spirit of the time (and the team), Crane had provided for 13 retail outlets along the Olympia's entrance way, thus attracting more money from the wallets of the 11,200 fans who would fill the rink.

Despite their name change, the Falcons were less than predatory, muddling through the league at the bottom, something their impatient fans exploited mercilessly. Not only were they booed by their own supporters at home, the Falcons were booed on the road by fans who, recalling the humiliation of "home game" trips to Windsor, would follow the team to Toronto or Montreal just for the pleasure of jeering them.

One Detroit player even endured humiliation in absentia. Samuel "Porky" Levine, a Toronto native, had strapped on the pads as the Cougars / Falcons' back-up goalie in 1928–29, until he was loaned to the Seattle Eskimos in the renovated Pacific Coast league. Jack Adams decided that the Falcons were slumping because Detroit had let Levine go, leaving them with just one goalie on whom to practise their skills.

Team management was unmoved and wouldn't let Adams bring back Levine, nor sign another back-up netminder. So Adams commissioned a plywood cut-out of the stocky five-foot-eight, 175-pound Levine, then dressed this wooden "Porky" in a full uniform with pads and skates, hauling him out to guard one of the nets during Falcons' practices.

Things were so bad both for the team and the economy that the Falcons sometimes let people into the rink in exchange for food. Jack Adams forked over his own money to help meet the payroll, putting it into perspective by mordantly joking that if the Montreal Canadiens had offered them their superstar Howie Morenz for $1.98, Adams wouldn't have been able to afford him. In November 1932, the Olympia Arena filed for bankruptcy, after defaulting on their mortgage to the Union Guardian Trust Company, who had ordered them to pay $776,770. It seemed as if hockey might be dead in Detroit. And then along came Jim Norris.

Norris, a big, loud, rich Montrealer, badly wanted his own team. He had sunk cash into Madison Square Garden, he had loaned money to the Boston Bruins, and he would come to be a co-owner of the 18,000-seat Chicago Stadium, the biggest in the NHL, all on his way to becoming the most powerful governor in the league. But Norris wanted more.

While Norris was a true lover of hockey, having played the game in Montreal, he also loved making money. Though the Depression destroyed the lives of many people, it opened the door to people like Norris, who had made a fortune selling grain futures short just before the stock market crash of 1929. When the market collapsed, the cash-rich Norris scooped up properties at bargain prices. Seizing his opportunity with the financially grounded Falcons, Norris bought both the team and their multimillion-dollar rink for a measly $100,000.

Norris's purchase of the Detroit Falcons was news to Jack Adams, who had resigned himself to their inevitable demise. Adams met the new owner, an imposing six-foot-two and 250 pounds (in a good month), to receive his marching orders. But Norris had other plans.

First, the big moneybags was going to keep the team alive, and second, Jack Adams could keep his job to see how things worked out. For a year.

Detroit's pro hockey club would now be called the Red Wings, and their jerseys would bear a winged wheel, reminiscent of Norris's sporting alma mater, the Montreal Amateur Athletic Association, the first winners of the Stanley Cup. All this was a pleasant surprise to Adams. With the new name and borrowed symbol there would at least be a semblance of a winning hockey tradition.

Better still, there would be money to spend on players. Even with NHL salaries capped at $62,500 per team, Norris gave Jack Adams $100,000 to buy players and develop a "farm" system to nurture talented juniors into the pros. Though Toronto and Montreal had feeder systems, the American teams were still of the opinion that you could always buy what you needed — a function of the fact the surviving American teams were owned by millionaires.

When Detroit beat the New York Rangers for the first time in 78 games in 1933, Norris did the unheard of and gave each player a $50 bonus — worth US$633 today, though its value was much higher then, when a dollar bill would buy a man a feast. The Red Wings also gave up their long train trips, which were frequently just tedious, cramped character tests fueled by mouldy sandwiches and drain-cleaner coffee. Now the Wings traveled by air, one of the first teams to do so, though the innovation scared all kinds of virtues into those Wings who were afraid of flying.

By the spring of 1936, if anyone asked what type of bird had red wings, a legitimate answer would have been the Phoenix. Just five years out of their seeming doom as the Falcons, the pumped and primed Wings had finished at the top of both their division and the NHL. Money had bought success, but the Wings wouldn't be satisfied until they had that last piece of silver.

First, however, they would have to go through the Montreal Maroons, with whom they were so evenly matched that their first game would change Stanley Cup history. When the two sides faced off in the Montreal Forum at 8:34 P.M. on March 24, 1936, a betting fan would have received long odds that the teams would still be playing five hours and 51 minutes later.

After three periods the game was scoreless. Near the end of the fifth 20-minute overtime, Detroit's big stickhandling centre Marty Barry fed left winger Herbie Lewis a lovely, game-winning type of pass. Lewis fired the puck past Lorne Chabot, now the man between the pipes for the Maroons. And the pipes sent the puck ricocheting back out.

After four minutes and 46 seconds of the *sixth* overtime period, the teams waved good-bye to the old record set by Boston and Toronto in 1933. Twelve minutes later — just short of the equivalent of three regulation games — Detroit's Normie Smith made his nintieth save. Hec Kilrea, whom Jack Adams had bought from Toronto for $17,000, was out on the ice with Syd Howe, whom Adams had snagged for $35,000 from St. Louis, and Modere "Mud" Bruneteau. Down the ice swept Kilrea on a two-on-one with Bruneteau. Then the "one" — Lionel Conacher — fell down.

Now the Wings had only the goalie in front of them. Even though "Mud" Bruneteau had notched just two goals for the Wings that season, he was looking to be a hero. So he took Kilrea's pass, faked out Chabot, and ended hockey's longest hockey playoff game at 2:25 A.M.

Thus blessed by destiny, the Wings beat Montreal in three straight games, then did the same to the Leafs to win their first Jug. The following year, with Jim Norris's cash and Jack Adams's shrewd, "win or die" style of management, the Wings became bar-betting favourites for generations to come as the first American team to win Lord Stanley's bowl in back-to back seasons.

But it wasn't enough. Serving as both coach and general manager, Adams also handled the team's PR and was still greatly vexed by the number of fans the Wings attracted from Southern Ontario. To Adams, this seemed like the bad old days with the Falcons, as these unruly Canadians would pollute the Olympia by cheering on Montreal or Toronto, while hurling abuse at Detroit.

So Adams, considering himself just another Canadian missionary to Mammon, decided that he had to educate the Motor City if its citizens were ever to be proper hockey consumers. He started writing a hockey column in the local press called "Following the Puck," which indeed might have been a problem for spectators in 1930s Detroit (and elsewhere). The ice was not yet painted white, and from the distance of the stands took on the colour of the grey floor beneath it. Ironically, the title of Adams's column hits on a contemporary American gripe about the trouble they have watching televised hockey today.

Even so, what educated Adams's American audience the most was winning. In 1943, the Red Wings would take the Jug again, which now gave them three championships in the 10 seasons since James Norris and Adams had rescued them from a place on pro hockey's list of dead teams. Detroit had rightly earned its self-imposed sobriquet, for as far as the United States went, it was now "Hockeytown."

―――

By the time the NHL had shrunk to a six-team league in 1942 due to war and economic famine, the league had granted each franchise the right to own all players who lived within a 50-mile radius of the team's home rink. This was good news for Detroit, for if the crow were to fly 50 miles northeast of Motown it would be soaring above the hockey factories of southeastern Ontario. Better still, it wasn't a hard and fast rule. If Toronto didn't want a fine young prospect who lived on Spadina Avenue, anyone could take him. And if the player was beyond anyone's 50-mile limit, then it was open season.

Jack Adams — whose outward hearty portliness earned him the nickname "Jolly Jack" but masked his inner darkness — had reached into Norris's deep pockets to set up a vast Red Wing farm system, one which allowed the club to compete with those talent feeder systems of Montreal and Toronto. While Adams was always happy to take credit for success, the real genius of the Red Wings dynasty in the 1950s lay in Carson Cooper and Fred Pinckney, Detroit's eastern and western scouts who trawled the nation's rinks, taking people their major scouting competition, the Leafs, either missed or had scoffed at.

One of those unwanted players was "Terrible" Ted Lindsay, who broke into the NHL with Detroit in the 1944–45 season, the pundits unanimous in their belief the five-foot-eight, 160-pound left winger would be pummeled into oblivion.

Afraid of no one, Lindsay's fierce play got him into many fights, occasionally even with loudmouthed fans, but he could trounce the best of them. Lindsay, though, was much more than a brawl-in-waiting — he was a goalscorer of the first order, a natural sniper who would make the NHL's First All-Star team eight times as the league's best left winger. Lindsay would win the 1950 Art Ross Trophy as the champion scorer, tallying 78 points in 69 games — despite having spent the equivalent of two-and-a-half games in the penalty box.

No one hated Lindsay more than Conn Smythe, who would run from rinkside to rinkside in Maple Leaf Gardens to scream abuse at Lindsay. The "Little Pistol" saw in the smart, bold Red Wing exactly the type of man Conn Smythe's army had a problem with. The other thing that drove Smythe crazy was that Lindsay, as a product of Toronto's St. Michael's College, should have been a Maple Leaf.

Lindsay was playing for St. Mike's in a 1943 game against the Toronto Marlboros when he was so badly cut in the calf by another player's skate that he would be out for two months. Nevertheless, a spectator whose son, Tom O'Neill, played for the Leafs told coach "Hap" Day about this marvelous kid on left wing. With Conn Smythe off at war, Day and Leafs general assistant Frank Selke showed up at a St. Mike's practice, unaware that Lindsay was sidelined. Mistakenly, they put another left winger on their "protected list."

Lindsay fought his way back to form like he was fighting for his life, and he made it back into the St. Mike's lineup. After a game against Detroit's junior team in January 1944, a grey-haired man came up to Lindsay, looking like the God of the Old Testament. He asked the 18 year old if he'd ever thought about playing pro hockey. Lindsay had been awaiting such an interrogation, and said yes, he most certainly had. Lindsay's questioner was none other than Detroit scout Carson Cooper. By the time the Leafs found out about their mistake, it was too late.

The Leafs also missed another St. Mike's boy, Leonard "Red" Kelly, who they thought couldn't skate, couldn't shoot, and was generally so bad that they demoted him to the junior team of their *farm team*. Once again, Carson Cooper saw what the Leafs couldn't, and Red Kelly made it to the NHL as a superb "offensive defenseman," whose rushes showcased his smooth, powerful skating, and his intelligent puck handling. Between 1950 and 1957, Kelly would make the First All-Star team six times and the second team twice.

Kelly's ability to defend without beating up the opposition won him the Lady Byng Trophy for sportsmanlike play an unprecedented four times, and in 1954 he became the first winner of the James Norris Memorial Trophy as the league's best defenseman, the trophy commemorating the Wings' founder, who had died in 1952.

The one Red Wing whom Carson Cooper didn't pluck from the wilderness was harvested by his western counterpart, Fred Pinckney, who invited a strapping young man from Saskatchewan to attend the Detroit training camp after the kid had been lost in the shuffle by the New York Rangers. When Jack Adams saw the 16 year old's training camp performance, he knew that "Gordie Howe was the best hockey prospect of that age I ever saw."

Still, the man who would earn the moniker "Mr. Hockey," who would etch his name into the ice across six decades of pro hockey, and who would come to define what hockey meant in "Hockeytown," nearly wasn't a Red Wing at all. Young Gordie liked the snazzy Detroit team windbreakers he saw at training camp, and Jolly Jack Adams promised to get him one, then forgot about his promise. But Gordie didn't forget.

When Adams offered Howe a contract the next fall, Howe wouldn't sign, saying Adams had broken his word. "Naturally, I was flabbergasted, and I asked him what he meant," Adams recalled. "'Well,' he said, 'you promised me a windbreaker and you never gave it to me.' You can't imagine how quickly I got that windbreaker. But that's how close I came to losing him."

While a windbreaker might have been a small thing to Adams, it was huge to Gordie Howe. Nine days after he was born in Floral, Saskatchewan, in March of 1928 — the sixth of nine children to Albert and Kathleen Howe — the family moved 10 miles down the road to Saskatoon, where Ab took a variety of jobs in construction. By the time the Depression had set in, Ab was making 40 cents an hour working as superintendent of maintenance for Saskatoon's city works.

There wasn't a lot of money for luxuries, and so Gordie Howe, like many another hockey star from days of yore, began his career on ice with the utmost humility. "It was during the '30s and we didn't have much," Howe's mother recalled. "A woman came to the door asking a dollar and a half for some things, which included a pair of skates. Gordie, who was four, would put on one skate and [sister] Edna the other and they'd go to Hudson Bay slough ... He was hockey, hockey, hockey all the time, even in July when he used to break shingles off the house practising shooting both right and left handed."

Gordie could not only shoot with either hand, he could also palm 90-pound sacks of cement while working on Ab's road crew, summoning murmurs of awe from the other brawny workers, who weren't all that easily impressed. That strength famously came to bear in a game against Montreal, when Howe scored a goal one-handed. But it wasn't just any one-handed goal.

First, Howe faked out Montreal's peerless defenseman Doug Harvey, who desperately spun and draped his stick over Howe as he charged the net. The six-foot, 200-pound Howe took one hand off his stick and used it to lever Harvey onto the toes of his skate blades. Then, with only one hand half-way down his stick, Howe swept in front of Jacques Plante, who followed the puck. Howe saw daylight and roofed the puck hard into the net, the bulging twine straining as if it had caught a cannonball.

Jaws dropped on the Red Wings' and Canadiens' benches. The next day, Howe's teammates tried the feat in practice, lining up pucks on the goal line, attempting to one-hand them into the top of the net. With no one harassing them and all the time in the world, they couldn't even raise the pucks off the ice.

And Gordie could use those Herculean hands to throw a devastating punch. His father later recalled in an interview with *Sports Illustrated* that when his son joined the Wings, "I told the wife 'I hope that boy never fights. He's got a blow that can kill a man.' That first night he played for Detroit, I put my feet up by the radio and listened to the game, and pretty soon Gordon was in a fight, all right. And he got in another. She was terrible [sic] upset, worrying he might kill someone. He got in fights about the first 10 games, and after a bit Mr. Adams calls him in and asks, 'Howe, you think you've got to beat up the entire league, player by player?'"

Jim Norris, also president of the International Boxing Club, then the controlling organization for North America's boxing, saw the strapping Gordie Howe naked in the dressing room and dollar signs spun in his head. "I could make you heavyweight champion of the world in 10 months," he enthused, before Jack Adams quickly intervened to remind the Wings owner that Howe was a hockey player, the kind they call the franchise.

Besides, Jack Adams had no great love for boxing. Influenced by the violence he experienced during his own playing career, Jack Adams exhorted his players to keep their gloves on. Fighting broke hands that could score goals, and besides, there were other ways to get revenge.

So Gordie Howe changed his style, and, as any player who ever went into a corner with him can attest, was as adept at communicating with his elbows as he was at making his point with the puck on his stick.

Jack Adams looked like a genius when he teamed "The Big Guy" with Ted Lindsay and Sid Abel to form another kind of "Production Line" in the Motor City, a line which would become one of hockey's most prolific scoring trios. "Old Bootnose" Abel served as the line's foreman, cooling down Lindsay and heating up Howe. In the winter of 1949, Abel, in his tenth NHL season, claimed that he was only continuing to play out of charity to keep the 24-year-old Lindsay and the 21-year-old Howe in the league. "If it weren't for me," he quipped, "they'd be in [the minors in] Indianapolis."

Lindsay's retort was suitably respectful: "Why he could sit in a rocking chair on the ice and score 20 goals a season the way we feed him." Even with Lindsay and Howe hobbled by injuries for the 1948–49 season, Abel would win the Hart Trophy as the league's most valuable player.

In the 1949–50 season, Gordie Howe began the kind of streak that makes a player a legend. For the next 22 years, Howe would score 23 or more goals a season, an astonishing statistic given that NHL players these days are thinking about renegotiating their contracts after a couple of 20-goal seasons. Ted Lindsay had a legend going of his own, scoring 22 or more goals each season from 1946–47 until 1958–59, only falling short in '54–55 when he was injured and '57–58 when he was traded.

In 1949–50, Howe potted 35 goals and added 33 assists to put him in third place on the scoring charts, one point behind Sid Abel, and 10 behind Art Ross winner Lindsay. The Wings were invincible. Until the night of March 28, 1950.

On that infamous night, the Maple Leafs — who had finished third — were taking it to the league champions in the first game of the playoffs. Midway through the second period, Leafs captain "Teeder" Kennedy was streaking along with the puck on his stick, when Gordie Howe came rushing at him from behind. From the corner of his eye, Kennedy saw that he was about to be steamrollered into the boards by Howe going at full tilt.

Kennedy put on the brakes to avoid the check. What happened next is still debated: Kennedy, corroborated by Wings goalie Harry Lumley, says that Howe simply tripped. Howe says that Kennedy's stick flew up just as another Leaf player ploughed into Howe, the butt-end of his stick clipping Howe on the edge of his right eye.

Howe crumpled, slamming his head into the oak hardwood boards, the side of his face smashing against the moulding running along the top. Blood gushed onto the ice, gruesomely now, for an innovation of the 1949–50 season had been to paint the ice white.

Howe, unconscious, was carried off on a stretcher. He had broken his nose, his cheekbone was smashed, an eyeball was scratched, and he had a concussion, with possible brain damage. Rumours swirled around Detroit that night that Gordie Howe was dead.

Doctors at Detroit's Harper hospital knew that Howe *would* be dead if they didn't take action. Suspecting a brain hemorrhage, they called in a famous neurosurgeon named Schreiber, and Jack Adams gave him permission to cut into the head of the Wings' great white hope.

Dr. Schreiber drilled a hole into Howe's skull, just above his right eye, and the fluid that had been building up on Howe's brain spurted out like a little geyser. Ninety minutes later Howe was out of surgery and under an oxygen tent: his situation serious, but no longer critical. The Red Wings players, hearing this news at 2:30 A.M., felt secure enough to go to bed. But Howe was not out of danger.

Back home in Saskatoon, Howe's mother, Katherine, listened as Jack Adams told her that Gordie might not live to see his twenty-second birthday, just three days away on March 31. Radio stations in both Canada and the United States made updates on Howe's condition a priority, while Saskatoon radio stations covered the event all night long, as if sitting vigil for a dying king.

The next day, dawn broke with good news. Gordie Howe would live. Better still, he would even be able to play hockey again next season. Howe's mother had rushed down from Saskatoon to be with her son, but the nurses blocked her from entering his room, fearing she'd make some weepy maternal fuss. In the end, it was Howe who cried when he saw his mother. It was a sure sign of life.

After losing both the "Big Guy" and the first game, the Red Wings literally took to arms, fighting two savage brawls that blooded them, then taking the Leafs into the overtime of a scoreless draw in the seventh game. When Leo Reise scored on Toronto's "Turk" Broda, the

Wings felt a surge of destiny. They had won the series for Gordie Howe; just four more wins would give them the silverware.

The Wings had lost the last two Stanley Cup Finals to Toronto, but their opponents, the New York Rangers, had not played in a Stanley Cup Final since their president had defiled the sacred Cup by burning Madison Square Garden's paid-up mortgage in it in 1940, bringing "The Curse" down on the Rangers.

Despite their years in the wilderness, the Rangers were not without talent. Buddy O'Connor, a five-foot-eight, 140-pound centre was fast and a gifted playmaker, much in the sparkplug mould of Aurele Joliat. O'Connor's talents had been eclipsed by "The Punch Line" when he played in Montreal, but in New York he flourished, winning the Hart and Lady Byng Trophies in 1948—the first NHLer to win both in the same year. O'Connor nearly won the scoring title, too, but lost that honour to Montreal's Elmer Lach by just one point.

Edgar Laprade, the Rangers' second-line centre, had won the Calder Trophy in 1946 as the league's Rookie of the Year. The same height as O'Connor and just 12 pounds heavier, Laprade was a relentless two-way player whose game was so gentlemanly that he played three full seasons without receiving a single penalty. In 1950, he was the Rangers' scoring leader, with 22 goals and 44 points, and won the Lady Byng Trophy for his sportsmanship.

New York's goalie Claude "Chuck" Rayner had posted six shutouts that season, despite playing behind an aerated defense. Rayner had always wanted to score a goal and he nearly did it against Toronto earlier that season, banking a shot off the boards and toward the Leafs' empty net. The puck just missed, but Rayner was nevertheless rewarded with a bigger prize: the 1950 Hart Trophy.

In addition to being cursed, the Rangers were known as the orphans of the NHL, evicted as they were each April by the circus, and forced to play all of their playoff games on the road. If that weren't enough, one of their principal owners was Detroit's boss, Jim Norris, and the Wings were his baby, often at the expense of the Rangers.

After losing the first game in Detroit, the Rangers decamped to their "home" rink of Maple Leaf Gardens, where they exchanged wins with the Wings before their third-line centre Don "Bones" Raleigh won them two games in overtime in Detroit. The Wings won the next game, but with three wins apiece, the Rangers were drooling at the thought of slaking their decade-long thirst with Stanley Cup champagne.

Then "The Curse" roared again. With game tied at three at eight minutes, 31 seconds of the second overtime period, Detroit's George Gee won a face-off in the New York zone and passed the puck to Pete Babando. His backhand shot from 15 feet out sailed into the top-left corner of the Rangers' net, and the Red Wings had won the Stanley Cup — their first since 1943, their first for Gordie Howe.

The Detroit Olympia shimmered with something like ecstasy when Howe walked onto the ice to celebrate with his teammates, a soft fedora on his scarred head. Ted Lindsay gently knocked the hat off so the crowd could see how close to death Howe had come. "I'll never forget the night he came back, more so than the night he got hurt," Sid Abel remembered. "The night we won it he got a standing ovation. We were all thrilled."

Gordie Howe recovered from his head injuries well enough to play in all 70 of Detroit's regular season games the following year, scoring 43 goals and adding 43 assists to win the Art Ross Trophy — the first of his six NHL scoring titles. And while Howe scored, Detroit saw the rise of another superlative talent whose job was to keep pucks out of the net, a skinny, moody Ukrainian kid from Winnipeg named Terry Sawchuk.

When Sawchuk brought his goaltending genius to the professional ranks in 1947, Jack Adams, the arch manipulator, gave the young man of modest means a $2,000 signing bonus. Scarcely able to keep his hands steady on the steering wheel of his car, Sawchuk sped to a Windsor bank to exchange this fabulous sum into something he could understand: 2,100 Canadian dollar bills. Once safely back at his motel, he threw the money into the air and danced as it fell around him. Life was finally looking sweet, and this was not Terry Sawchuk's usual perspective.

Sawchuk began his hockey career as a forward and was good enough to be the scoring champion of his "Bantam A" hockey team in Winnipeg, Manitoba. When his team's goalie quit, the coach decided to convert Terry Sawchuk to netminder since fate and practicality ordained it: Sawchuk had a spare set on pads at home, ever since his older brother had died at age 17 of a heart murmur.

Sawchuk was devastated by his brother's death. He couldn't believe that the card-playing rogue who'd taken him out in their father's car and let him have underage turns behind the wheel was gone. Now Sawchuk saw a way he could bring his brother back. By strapping on his dead brother's pads he could let his brother keep playing, too.

Sawchuk showed such talent that at 15 he was starting goalie for the Winnipeg Rangers, a team within the shopping compass of the Chicago Black Hawks. Sawchuk's father, a Ukrainian tinsmith, shrewdly told his son that when he signed the registration card that gave the major league clubs *de facto* ownership of junior prospects, he must always insist they give Sawchuk free agent status at the end of the year.

When "Baldy" Northcott, the former Montreal Maroon, came scouting for the Hawks, he offered Sawchuk a signing bonus, but the goalie's father said no. Chicago had no future, and his boy certainly did. The next day, a Detroit scout showed up and asked the same question. This time, Sawchuk's dad said yes.

A grim sort of destiny guided Sawchuk, who hoped to go to college after his junior career but took up pro hockey as a family necessity. When Sawchuk's father was laid up with a broken back for 18 months, Terry signed his first pro contract with Detroit's minor league affiliate, the Omaha Knights. During a game in Houston, a stick caught him in the right eyeball.

Instead of going out to celebrate his eighteenth birthday, Sawchuk wound up in the operating room of a hospital. The doctor decided to cut out his eye, then changed his mind. He would wait a day to see if there was any improvement. The delay saved Sawchuk's career.

With three stitches in his eyeball, the nervy Sawchuk went back into goal and shut out St. Paul. From then on, Omaha won 23 out of its 27 games and the league championship. Sawchuk won the Rookie of the Year award, then did it again the following season with Indianapolis of the American League.

Before the 1950–51 season began, Jack Adams sent Harry Lumley, the Wings' 24-year-old starting netminder, to Chicago, and this meant a promotion for the 20-year-old Sawchuk, though foreshadows of doom came early. On the day Sawchuk started his second game in goal for Detroit, Hall of Fame goalie George Hainsworth was killed in a car crash. Sawchuk would surpass Hainsworth's record of 94 NHL shutouts — becoming the first and so far only goalie to post 100, as well as playing more games and winning more than anyone else. But like Hainsworth, Sawchuk would also meet with a violent end.

For his first full season in net for the Red Wings, though, all Terry Sawchuk could do was stop pucks. A Detroit haberdasher offered the goalie a hat every time he shut out the opposition, and it cost him 11 of them. Sawchuk wasn't a hat man, so he wound up supplying the whole team on his way to winning the Calder Trophy—the first man to be named the finest rookie in three separate leagues.

Between 1948 and 1957, the Wings would finish first in the NHL eight out of nine times. They would win three Stanley Cups and most of the trophy hardware in the league. In 1952, they would roll through the playoffs without a single loss, the first team to do so, and in their eight-game rampage, Terry Sawchuk posted four shutouts.

When the Wings won the 1955 Jug in seven games over Montreal, the usually unflappable *Hockey News* spun the conspiracy theory that Detroit was going "to imprison the Stanley Cup forever." With Jack Adams's tyrannical but effective management, and Jim Norris's endless money, it looked as if Hockeytown just might be seeing a good deal more of Lord Stanley's prize. But there was another conspiracy theory afoot, with the usual suspects of money and power at its centre. The resulting battle would cause discord and destruction in the Wings locker room. And end their dynasty on ice.

—⁓—

The first shot was fired in 1952, by the Wings' old adversary Conn Smythe. The so-called Golden Age of the Original Six was really a gentlemen's club of three owners: Senators Raymond, then Molson in Montreal; Major Conn Smythe in Toronto; and the almighty Norris family everywhere else. In 1933, Norris bought the Chicago Stadium, along with Chicago real-estate tycoon Arthur Wirtz. Later, Norris became the majority shareholder of the Madison Square Garden corporation, which owned the New York Rangers. He also loaned money to Boston's perennial cadger Charles Adams. And the Norris family had more than a stadium landlord's hand in Chicago.

For some time, Conn Smythe had been badgering NHL President Clarence Campbell to reveal who *really* owned the Chicago Black Hawks, as the major couldn't stand the thought that someone had a bigger cash cow than he did. League insiders knew all too well that the lowly club was primarily owned by Detroit's Norris family, and that

Bill Tobin was just their front man to dodge league rules against owning more than one team.

Smythe suspected the Hawks were being allowed to languish so that their market value would fall to nothing, and the Norrises could pick up even more shares for a song. The splendid Toronto sportswriter Jim Coleman, whose father had been a director of the Montreal Canadiens, joked that the NHL really stood for "Norris House League."

Indeed, in September 1952, James Norris Jr. and Wirtz quietly bought the Chicago Black Hawks from the estate of Major Frederic McLaughlin. When the Red Wings' patriarch, James Norris Sr. died in December 1952, his playboy sons Jimmy and Bruce (who were half-brothers) were in a bit of a bind: they couldn't increase their stake in the Black Hawks without losing their stronghold in Detroit, and young Jimmy especially didn't want trouble.

A public fight with Smythe would reveal Jimmy Norris's interests in other NHL rinks, venues he needed to stage his money-spinning boxing matches. Even worse, Norris Jr. was already under investigation by the U.S. Congress for fight fixing, as well as for enjoying the company of people like Al Capone's hit-man Sam "Golfbag" Hunt and convicted Mob murderer Frankie Carbo.

So, bowing to a long tradition among the rich and mighty, the Norrises hid behind the distaff side and made their 25-year-old half-sister, Marguerite, president of the Red Wings. This was a particularly bold move at a time when newsreel shorts like "Detroit Hockey Wives" were entertaining the masses, one in which Red Wings' spouses sip tea and chat while occasionally glancing at a TV set showing their men playing hockey.

Indeed, pro hockey thought female participation best expressed through rinkside cheering and keeping the hearth warm. As Roy MacSkimming relates in his superb biography *Gordie Howe,* when Colleen Howe first met the Wings' Bruce Norris at a year-end team party, he showed his respect for his star player by drunkenly accusing Gordie's wife of "having affairs" on her "ski trips" instead of taking her rightful place at Wings home games. The truth was that Colleen Howe found skiing trips with her children and friends to be a more appealing prospect than being a slave to the Wings' harem of dutiful spouses, but Norris's caddish attack still made her cry.

This callous seigneurial attitude was hardly confined to Detroit. An American woman, impressed by a televised game in the mid '50s, phoned NHL President Clarence Campbell to propose a professional women's league. Her initiative was "tut-tutted" back to its nuclear family by Campbell's paternalistic insight that "hockey was too rough for gals."

It wasn't too rough, however, for Marguerite Norris, though the press did its novelty-act bit with puff pieces when she became Wings president. "No. 1 Ice Lady, Wings' New Boss Learned Hockey Hard Way as Goalie in Family Games," reads one, its accompanying photo showing Marguerite studying a book on hockey, befitting her blue-stocking station as a graduate of posh Smith College. The book had nothing on what Marguerite already knew about the way boys played — something she learned the hard way in family games. "I was the youngest so I was left no choice — I had to be the goalie," she told a reporter. "It was a couple of years before I found out that goalies wear shin pads. [My brothers] never told me."

Marguerite's tough schooling in the ways of hockey was good training for life as an NHL boss, especially when it came to Conn Smythe. The major tried to block Marguerite from sitting on the NHL Board, inventing a law that essentially said all NHL Governors had to have a Y chromosome. Marguerite outsmarted him by appointing his loathed rival Jack Adams as her proxy, giving "Jolly Jack" hand signals during board meetings to ensure that her wishes were carried out.

Smythe continued his campaign to discredit her, publicly questioning her management abilities and even decrying the befouled state of the women's washrooms at Olympia. As David Cruise and Alison Griffiths reveal in *Net Worth*, Marguerite got him back by asking Smythe what he was doing in the women's washrooms in the first place, then fired the coup de grace by mentioning to a Toronto reporter that Mr. Smythe seemed to be fascinated by the ladies' room in her stadium. Smythe dropped the matter.

Even though Marguerite had never seen the Wings play in the Olympia when she began as president in 1952, they took off under her smart, shrewd regime, and under her tenure, which lasted until 1955, had their best years of the '50s. There was, however, a problem. Marguerite Norris didn't like or trust Jack Adams and what had now become his egomaniacal destructiveness.

She wanted to promote coach Tommy Ivan, who had been the Wings' benchman since 1947, but she couldn't find a way to "talk" Adams into retirement. As both she and Ivan knew would happen, Ivan was poached by Marguerite's half-brother Jim, in Chicago, and Marguerite was without an ally. She walked the plank shortly after, courtesy of her yachting brother, Bruce. Now that the Wings were the biggest and best ship on the ocean, Bruce decided that he wanted to be captain. So Marguerite was cast overboard into "executive vice-president"— hockey's equivalent of a desert island.

Without Marguerite Norris to keep him in check, Jack Adams began to fiddle with the Wings, acting out his bizarre theory that a championship team only has a shelf-life of five years. Though Terry Sawchuk had won the Vezina Trophy in 1955 and backstopped the Wings to the Stanley Cup, Adams had seen enough of Sawchuk's dark moods and traded him to Boston, who hadn't won a Stanley Cup since 1941, and wouldn't do so anytime soon.

Adams's thinking was that he would move the talented young Glenn Hall to take Sawchuk's spot. Hall responded with aplomb, posting 12 shutouts in 70 games and winning the Calder Trophy. But Hall would soon be gone, too. As would the heart and soul of the Wings, Ted Lindsay.

On July 24, 1957, while hockey writers were sipping the joys of summer, and hockey fans were distracted with days at the beach, the Detroit Red Wings traded their 33-year-old former captain to the dreadful Chicago Black Hawks, who from 1949 to 1957 had finished dead last every season but one. Though Lindsay was hobbled neither by injury nor by time, he was punished for daring to stand up to the NHL's tyranny, and the implications of his trade would reverberate throughout the world of professional hockey for the next four decades.

Ted Lindsay had led the NHL in assists the year he was traded, with 35 goals and 55 assists, the best by a left winger ever. He had won the Art Ross Trophy in 1948 as the league's leading scorer. And he was universally feared for his warlike presence on ice.

As he prospered in Detroit, Lindsay started his own business and became more savvy about the ways of the world. Appointed in 1952 to the board of the NHL's Pension Society, Lindsay grew frustrated by the stonewalling of the NHL owners, who refused to let the players see the books to their own pension fund.

Though the NHL had been up and running for 35 years, its player pension fund had been in existence for only five. In October of 1947, the Stanley Cup champion Leafs played an "All-Star" squad, and the $25,865 from the game's gate receipts went to the newly established NHL Players Pension Fund. By the time Lindsay was demanding to see what he and his fellow players had in their old-age kitty, the players were contributing 20 percent of their average $5,000 annual salaries to the fund, while the NHL kicked in $600 a man, and did so from revenues from the All-Star Game, which the players played for free.

When Lindsay learned about the advances made by a pro baseball players association in the United States, he flew to New York to consult with the association's legal brains trust. He left the meeting with his head spinning, for the two labour lawyers had revealed how television revenue was going to be the future for pro athletes across the continent.

Televised hockey had been experimented with as early as February 11, 1939, in, of all places, London, England, when the third period of a match between Oxford and Cambridge at Earl's Court was broadcast by BBC Television. In 1940, Madison Square Garden tried an internal broadcast; a decade later, television had so invaded the cultural consciousness of the continent that the Chicago Black Hawks became the first team to try out weekend matinee games in the 1952 season, fearing that hockey couldn't compete with weekend night TV.

The CBC decided to create the best of both worlds by putting hockey on television on Saturday nights, and the tradition of *Hockey Night in Canada* was born. The network's first hockey telecast took place in Toronto on March 21, 1951, but only six people saw a show transmitted to a TV in the radio control room of Maple Leaf Gardens. Foster Hewitt did the first period play-by-play, then resumed his radio broadcast. The first CBC network telecast took place in Montreal on October 11, 1952, when Gilbert Renaud, a 24-year-old newspaper sports editor who hadn't even seen TV, produced a hockey game between Montreal and Toronto. He was given the assignment by McLaren Advertising, the original producers of *Hockey Night in Canada*. It was no accident that an advertising firm was in on the ground floor, for television's power made radio look scrawny.

Though Canadian NHL clubs earned vaults of money through television rights, they refused to share them with their brethren in the

United States until 1962, by which time the Canadian clubs were pulling in more than $1 million annually from broadcast revenue. In 1963, when the U.S. network CBS planned to broadcast hockey on weekend afternoons after the football games had ended, the NHL opposed them, arguing that this would create too many travel and scheduling problems. The real reason was that it might create media stars out of lowly puck-chasers who would start demanding their fair share of hockey's superlative revenues.

The NHL's owners not only maintained that they didn't make any money from TV, they told the players that they didn't make money from anything. Indeed, they sang from the same page of the hymn book as the owners of a half-century earlier, claiming they were just struggling to keep the rinks lit and heated so that their boys could keep playing the game they loved. Lindsay, and his fellow Pension Society members, suspected otherwise.

At the beginning of the 1956 season, Lindsay approached the Montreal Canadiens' defensive star and hard-rock Doug Harvey during a warm-up skate at the Forum. It was an act of singular courage, for not only was inter-team fraternization forbidden by the NHL, the six-team league forced clubs to become sufficiently familiar with each other that the contempt bred was often unspeakably violent.

Harvey and Lindsay had seen their share of mutually spilled blood on the ice, but they had also served together on the Pension Society. Now Harvey agreed to the idea of a hockey players' association, and soon the duo had representatives from all six teams. When they held a press conference just four months later in New York on February 12, 1957 to announce the birth of their association, they had signed up every player in the NHL save for Toronto's Ted Kennedy, who was retiring.

Though Lindsay and the players reps were careful to present their new association as a cooperative venture between themselves and the owners, the feudal NHL owners saw it as communist union, run, as Conn Smythe called it, by "New York Jews" who were about to kill the golden goose. The owners went into a scorched-earth mode, threatening the uppity players with demotion and benchings. The owners were scared.

Jack Adams, who could manipulate his players the way he once used to manoeuvre the puck, went on the attack. Though Adams had dropped his coach's hat in 1946, no one was in any doubt that the Norris family team was really run by Jack Adams. The devout, teetotaller Adams (common to men of his era, who'd grown up with a strong temperance movement, often accented with hard-drinking relatives) had already shown his methods. He would send operatives to spy on the Wings when they went out socially, to see who was having one beer too many. When Gordie and his wife had their first child, Adams called Colleen Howe's doctor and told him to keep her in the hospital as long as possible to avoid distracting Gordie's home life, and so, his game. He would tell rookies that "every spot on the team was open," meaning that future Hall of Famers Howe, Lindsay, Abel, and Kelly were, in his mind, disposable. Adams would even walk around the Wings dressing room with train tickets to Omaha visible in his pocket, letting everyone know that one slip-up could have them riding the rails to Detroit's minor league team.

Now, in the face of Lindsay's mad act of war, Adams put the fear of destitution into his team if they continued. But Lindsay held firm. Adams responded by demonizing Lindsay, stripping him of his captaincy and slapping it onto Red Kelly, who, to his credit, refused Adams twice. Adams degraded Lindsay's performance while at the same time inflating Lindsay's salary to tame Detroit reporters, at the same time exaggerating Lindsay's small business income, to make him look like a greedy ingrate.

Adams also browbeat Lindsay's teammates into submission, putting the biggest bulls-eye on Gordie Howe. Adams, his jowls red and trembling, would strut from player to player in the Detroit dressing room, asking them the same question: "Do *you* want this?" Adams would then pause in front of Howe, knowing that he was insecure about his lack of education and would rather avoid this kind of fight. "I know you're not for this, I don't even have to ask," Adams said to Howe, who would look down at his skates, saying nothing. Then Adams glowered at Lindsay and promised, "Time will take care of him."

Time and Jack Adams, who sent Lindsay packing to the basement in Chicago, along with fellow subversive Glenn Hall. Adams put a "he made me do it" spin on Lindsay's exile for the media, pleading that Lindsay was a good kid who got distracted from hockey by "the players' association." On the other hand, hockey, the thing that brought him up from the mining country to NHL glory, was the thing that "he'd forgotten." In case the lines to read between were too subtle, Adams added, "there's always a reason to trade a player — maybe he's a clubhouse lawyer."

It was a chilling message to the others, for if such punishment could happen to a star like Lindsay, the average player could be wiped from the face of the league. Indeed, the Wings had already seen Lindsay's friend Marty Pavelich airbrushed from the photos and sent to the minors just for supporting the players' association.

Lindsay, true to form, held his own press conference, setting the record straight about his salary and businesses. Then he went to Chicago and pulled on the Black Hawks' jersey while outraged Detroit fans vilified Red Wings' management. Lindsay continued his mission from Chicago, and while the league portrayed him as self-interested villain out to ruin hockey, he persisted with an anti-trust suit filed in the United States in October 1957, one aimed against the NHL owners' monopoly of pro hockey.

The owners fought back, and it was Detroit that saved the day. In a brilliantly manipulative counter-attack, Bruce Norris slow-marched into the Wings dressing room, the team's ledger books under his arm. With tears in his eyes, he dared any player who didn't believe his pleas of poverty to open the ledgers and see for himself. Even if any player had taken the dare, it's a safe bet that the doctored ink in the ledgers would have been as red as the Wings' sweaters.

Led by Gordie Howe and Red Kelly, the Wings decided they had been bamboozled by firebrands like Lindsay, and had come dangerously close to ruining the Norris family. So they resigned from Lindsay's mad tilt at the windmill, and less than a year later, the players' association was dead.

Ted Lindsay would come back to the Red Wings for one last season in 1964, and in a grand irony of revenge, became the team's general manager in 1977. Yet years later he remained rightfully bitter about the failure of the players' association, and the shroud around the players' pension fund. Had Lindsay won his war in 1957, there would have been no need for the man who revived the players' association a decade after it expired, and would use the players and their pension fund to his own criminal purpose — Alan Eagleson.

Late in the 1959–60 season, Jack Adams went to work on Red Kelly, who had been his second-favourite player after Howe. After leading the charge against Lindsay's players' association, Kelly had nevertheless led the way in getting legal advice for the Wings' players. Suddenly, he wasn't Adams' second-best boy anymore. The Wings had lost three games in a row, and Sawchuk, now back in the Wings' cage, was hurt. So Adams asked Kelly to suit up six days after suffering a broken ankle, even though his ankle was in plaster.

Reporters weren't told about the injury and thought Kelly was over the hill when they witnessed his agonized play. Coach Sid Abel even said his veterans "weren't producing" and fined them $100. Kelly kept quiet but let the truth out early in 1960 in an interview with Toronto sportswriter Trent Frayne, who asked if Kelly was finished because of his struggling play. Kelly, his foot now healed, figured no opposing player could use the information to hurt him. So he told Frayne that he'd had a broken foot, that management had asked him to play, and he said he would try.

The *Detroit Free Press,* in that catchy paraphrasing beloved of head-line writers, asked, "Was Red Kelly forced to play on a broken foot?" Kelly had said nothing about being "forced" to do anything, but that was enough for Jack Adams, who traded him to New York.

Astonishingly, Kelly said he would think about it. This wasn't the kind of answer that Adams or Bruce Norris would tolerate, but the 32-year-old Kelly went home, secured full-time employment, and announced he was retiring. Adams threatened to suspend his former captain, and league president Clarence Campbell intervened. Kelly held tough, saying he had nothing against New York but would not serve. He felt that Adams had blamed him for the Red Wings' last place finish the season before, and he would have nothing to do with this culmination of their betrayal.

In the end, Kelly was saved by King Clancy and the Leafs, who offered him a job in Toronto, where he had once starred for St. Mike's. Jack Adams agreed to take the comparatively unknown Marc Reaume in exchange for his All-Star, Norris, and Byng Trophy winner. Reaume would play 47 games for the Wings, then spend the rest of his career, barring short stints with Montreal and Vancouver, in the minors. Kelly would win another Lady Byng Trophy and make four more All-Star appearances en route to four more Stanley Cups.

In 1962, the sword swung the other way. The Wings had finished in second-last place, and Bruce Norris saw the 66-year-old Adams as ready for the glue factory. Adams, who had been with the club in its various incarnations since 1927, was moved downstairs to become president of the Central Professional League. Sid Abel, now coach of the Wings, was promoted. It was the end of Adams's extraordinary era, and the end of Detroit.

Jack Adams's tyrannical smarts and James Norris's endless cash had conspired for nearly 30 years to build them into a dynasty; Jack Adams's paranoid power plays and Bruce Norris's louche ways undid them in five. The Wings, who had been mightiest of them all in the early 1950s, would not win another Stanley Cup until 1997 — 42 years after their 1955 triumph over the Canadiens.

Gordie Howe, the ultimate franchise player, soldiered on, winning the last of his six Art Ross and Hart Trophies in 1963, and being awarded the Lester Patrick Trophy in 1967 for his service to hockey in the United States. Howe finally hung up the red-and-white sweater in 1971, when he was a stately 43 years old, disappointed in a season where he'd missed 15 games due to injury but still managed 23 goals and 29 assists.

Though he would come back to play in the NHL again as a 51 year old (after six seasons in the WHA), Howe, ever-deferential to authority, believed the Red Wings when they offered him jobs as vice-president of the Wings as well as one of Bruce Norris's insurance companies on his retirement from the club he had symbolized for 25 seasons. Howe soon discovered that his job description was just another Red Wing shell game, for he had nothing to do except receive the once-mighty Wings "mushroom treatment." The one that kept people in the dark and threw manure on them. But that manure wouldn't make anything grow, for the team that had so dominated league play for nearly three two decades was finished, derided now as the Detroit "Dead Things."

7

LES GLORIEUX

"To you from failing hands we throw / The torch; be yours to hold it high." These are the lines painted on their dressing-room wall, words from Major John McRae's First World War poem "In Flanders Fields." First put there in 1940 by coach Dick Irvin, they have inspired generations of hockey players to charge on to glory, though McRae was exhorting his fellow soldiers to kill more Germans, not the Toronto Maple Leafs.

The players who have looked up at those lines and carried the torch form one of the most successful sports franchises in history, the men in the *bleu, blanc, et rouge* who hail from hockey's temple and make miracles on ice. To heretics, they're known as "The Yankees of Hockey," but true believers know that the Yankees are really just the "Montreal Canadiens of Baseball." With 24 Stanley Cup banners hanging above their regal heads, the Canadiens represent hockey's ideal of class, poise, and success, destined from birth to be a cut above the other teams both on and off the ice.

For years, the Habs — short for the French "habitants," or residents — have served up hockey stars to make their constellation the brightest on the ice. Georges Vezina; Newsy Lalonde; Aurele Joliat; Howie Morenz; "Toe" Blake; Elmer Lach; *les frères* Richard, Maurice and Henri; Doug Harvey; Jacques Plante; Jean Béliveau; Yvan Cournoyer; Guy Lafleur; Ken Dryden; and Patrick Roy. All are at the pinnacle of pro hockey's honour roll, and all of them made their reputations as Montreal Canadiens. Most would never play for anyone else.

Even so, part of the brilliance of the Canadiens' success is in the creation and careful preservation of their own mystique. To those who love them, the Canadiens were born great and stayed that way, but the truth is far more interesting. As is the case with many other aristocratic lines, there were some foul and unusual deeds done in that dark long-ago to put the princes on their throne.

The great Montreal Canadiens franchise was created out of revenge. In December of 1909, Senator Michael O'Brien couldn't get his posh Renfrew team a place in the new Canadian Hockey League, from which the Montreal Wanderers had just been excluded. So the wealthy O'Brien and his rich cronies formed the National Hockey Association, gave the Wanderers a spot, and created a team for French Canada: the Montreal Canadiens.

The idea seemed to be one whose time was long overdue, but again hockey's myth collides with the reality. Though Montreal was the prime mover in hockey's development as a game and as a pro sport, French Canadians (as they were then called) didn't start to play hockey with any degree of seriousness until the mid-1890s. Hockey was an English, and Scottish and Irish game, and it took religion to let the francophones into the rink.

Montreal's Irish and French, being Catholic, educated their sons at bilingual colleges, where they would study separately in their mother tongue but play together on the fields. The Irish boys taught their French mates how to play and supported the efforts of francophone hockey clubs to join the "English" leagues.

That enlightened event didn't happen until 1904, when a club called Le National was admitted to the Federal Amateur Hockey League. In 1906–07, a francophone team called Le Montagnard wanted to cap their fabulous season with a challenge the Montreal Wanderers for the Stanley Cup. The Montagnard had cause to feel resentment when the league responded like some playground sore loser: they took two of the Montagnard's victories away, and so knocked the team out of the running for the Jug.

For the next two seasons, there were no French Canadian teams in hockey league play, until a group of English worthies decided to change things and add a neglected fan base to their fledgling National Hockey Association. It came down to the bottom line: it would be good for business.

The plan had always been eventually to turn the Canadiens over to the francophone community, but the change of ownership came in a most unusual way, and once again, the francophones were around in name only. George Kendall, a professional wrestler who also called himself "George Kennedy" managed a sports club called *Club Athlétique Canadien* and now claimed rights to the name which the hockey team also used.

Kennedy's strategy to get the hockey team was simple: a lawsuit if the National Hockey Association didn't have the good judgment to admit him to the league. That logic was good enough for the NHA, and they turned Les Canadiens over to Kendall for the 1911 season.

Finally, the Grim Reaper intervened to help put the Canadiens in the hands of the francophone community, but even then, they had to work for it — with some good old-fashioned cash, and despite opposition from the NHL's iron-fisted boss, Frank Calder. When George Kendall / Kennedy died in 1921, the Canadiens were not left to any favourite nephew in his will. No, the team was going to be returned to the public through that vulture-like post-mortem known as the "estate" auction, where a punter could show up and buy George's old furniture and dishes and hockey team.

There were many suitors for the Canadiens, but a colourful Montreal trio known as the "Three Musketeers" had the means to do it. The fabled promoter "Monsieur Leo" Dandurand was as French Canadian as anyone could be who spent his first 16 years in Bourbonnais, Illinois. Joe Cattarinich was a Montrealer who had once been the Canadiens' goalie, a position he surrendered to Georges Vezina upon discovering the great Chicoutimi Cucumber in a barnstorming match. The *bon vivant* Leo Letourneau was a real live French Canadian who made his mark as an amateur sportsman and his money in business deals with the other two, including the joint-ownership of a thoroughbred racetrack in Cleveland.

Yet on the day of the Kennedy estate auction, the Musketeers were so eager to capture the *Club Athlétique Canadien* for the tribe that they weren't even at the auction — they were at the races, in Cleveland. Instead they sent a future Canadiens Cup-winning coach, Cecil Hart, to bid as high as he had to.

Hart had some competition, for two other groups wanted to buy the team, with Ottawa's interests represented by none other than NHL

President Frank Calder. While today's NHL executives wouldn't dream of touting in public for a potential franchisee, Calder's participation nakedly reveals the degree of so-called impartiality at the league's highest executive level.

Frank Calder was also on a tight leash. When bidding opened at $8,000, Cecil Hart raised it by $500, and Calder asked for an adjournment to get permission to go higher. Permission took a week, and once again Hart was back in the fight. After the other Montreal interest raised the bid to $10,000 — theatrically, by laying out the 10 bills on the table — Hart called Cleveland, told the Musketeers the score, and bought the team for $11,000.

Dandurand and his fellow swordsmen wanted to create a brand of product from which they could make money, and the Canadiens' trademark "Firewagon Hockey" of speed, skill, and punishing brawn was what they set out to create — though their own methods were often heavy on the brawn. Dandurand let the charter-member "Flying Frenchman" Newsy Lalonde go and made the proudly violent butt-end artist Sprague Cleghorn team leader. Along with his brother Odie, the Cleghorns cleared the ice with muscle and mayhem, making room for the reluctant young wizard Howie Morenz, who with Aurele Joliat, led the team to its second Stanley Cup in 1923–24.

Under the tutelage of coach Cecil Hart, the Canadiens would win back-to-back Cups in 1930 and '31, but after that there would be no more silverware for the Habs until 1944, when, as the knock on them went, most of the real men were off fighting the Nazis, and the Cup was easier to win.

This is not to say that Montreal hockey wasn't exciting during the Depression years, especially with the rivalry between the Canadiens and the Maroons, who carried the torch for Montreal's English community. The Maroons had come in to the NHL in 1924 courtesy of Leo Dandurand, who knew that Montreal always had room in its divided heart for an English team and French team duking it out on ice. So Dandurand sold his territorial rights for a paltry $15,000, figuring it was good for business.

And it was. From the get-go, the Maroons and Canadiens developed the kind of mutual antagonism that further entrenched the Habs' reputation for élan. The Maroons were big and tough, led by the ill-tempered "S Line" of Babe Seibert, Nels Stewart, and Hooley Smith.

The Canadiens were small and fast, led by the speedy Joliat, Morenz, and Billy Boucher. It was the Plains of Abraham all over again, and the Canadiens were often on the losing end of it. The Maroons won their first Jug in 1926, lost to the Rangers in 1928, and then swept Toronto in 1935, under the acumen of coach T. P. "Tommy" Gorman, who had coached Chicago to a Cup the season before.

The Depression took its toll on hockey everywhere, and despite its holy reputation in Montreal, the '30s were bad times for the Canadiens. Drawing less than 2,000 people into a Montreal Forum mortgaged to the hilt, the Canadiens were on thin ice. But in September 1935 the team was sold to a syndicate with links to the Canadian Arena Company — which owned the Montreal Forum as well as the Montreal Maroons.

Now there was another problem. The town wasn't big enough for both teams anymore, but there was no way that the team "created for French Canadians" was going to be allowed to die in a city that was three-quarters francophone. The Maroons had to go.

But that was no so easily done. Tommy Gorman and the Maroons had screwed up the plan by winning the Stanley Cup, and the new owners couldn't just ship the Cup champs off to St. Louis. So they let the Maroons slide, and by August 1938, the team was no more, with some of its players blended into the Canadiens, some divvied up with the rest of the NHL.

The Canadiens responded to this reprieve by finishing last or second last until 1942–43, when they finished third last. Then as now, it wouldn't help the NHL's cultural balance-book to lose another Canadian team, so the plan to rescue them was devised by the masterful Lester Patrick in New York.

Patrick would send some of his players along with brother Frank up to change the Habs fortunes. Frank Patrick touted former Rangers star Bun Cook as coach, and Cook responded by showing up at his job interview so drunk that it seemed as if he'd emptied the Stanley Cup's bowl of champagne all by himself. The plan was abandoned.

Enter Tommy Gorman. Known as "Tay Pay" (the French pronunciation of his initials), Gorman's hockey pedigree was legendary. In 1910, Gorman was the cub reporter in Ottawa who was standing around when Cyclone Taylor had made his famous boast about scoring a goal while skating backward. In 1917, as co-owner of the Ottawa

Senators, Gorman was one of the founding members of the NHL, and over the next seven seasons he watched his Senators win another three Stanley Cups.

Gorman then hooked up with Bill Dwyer and Tex Rickard and helped broker the deal for the transfer of the rebellious Hamilton Tigers to New York. He headed south to Tijuana, Mexico, helping to run the new Agua Caliente horse racetrack, which served Southern Californians who were prohibited from playing the ponies at home by their state laws. Gorman even won the right to take the magnificent Australian thoroughbred Phar Lap on his North American tour, but the horse died an untimely and suspicious death. Gorman prudently went back to hockey.

When he walked into the Montreal Canadiens organization, Gorman was appalled at what he found. In addition to their woes on ice, the Habs had serious financial troubles. Their owners, Senator Donat Raymond and his pals, had shown their business heads to be soft by signing away all the concessions and advertising to their friends, and the Canadiens' revenue stream was pathetic. Gorman knew that he could fix the money if he fixed the team, so, with the kind of dramatic gesture that fans would love to see today, he put the whole team on waivers, with the exception of Toe Blake. No other team took a single Canadien.

Gorman recruited Dick Irvin from Toronto and together they built a winner: cultivating young players; bolstering the Quebec Senior League and letting them play in the Montreal Forum; adding to the building's coffers with professional wrestling shows. He also exploited a loophole in the wartime draft regulations that said any men in essential industries were exempted from military service. Gorman got his players jobs in munitions factories, which kept them wearing the Canadiens sweaters and not khaki.

In 1943, Irvin and Gorman received the kind of luck that you can't plan for: the advent of a hot-eyed young messiah, one who would carry out his singular and frequently bloody ministry until 1960, redefining what it meant to pull on that red, white, and blue sweater and play hockey in Montreal. The messiah's name was Maurice Richard, and life was about to get a lot better for the Canadiens.

When coach Dick Irvin put the anglophone Elmer Lach and bilingual Toe Blake with French-speaking Maurice Richard in the 1943 season, another of pro hockey's magical lines was born. Though in hindsight this move seems to be an obvious one, it was by no means so when the rookie Richard joined the Canadiens in 1942.

Felled by a broken ankle, Richard had been stung by the public musings of coach Irvin and manager Gorman, who suggested that he might be a little too fragile to play in the NHL. In the psychology of the era, the duo hoped to make Richard less prone to injury by questioning his manhood.

Their lack of confidence sent the sensitive 21 year old into a depression, but it had the desired effect. It humiliated the proud, competitive Richard, and it made him angry. As he would do for the rest of his career, Richard decided to get even and showed his gifts so convincingly that Irvin had no choice but to create the "Punch Line."

Though Richard's English was at first limited to "yes" and "no," or about the same amount of French spoken by manager Tommy Gorman and coach Dick Irvin (reflecting the reality of English as the language of rule for *les habitants* in the 1940s), both Richard and Irvin spoke the language of winning. Irvin, who had seen the best of hockey talent when playing against Cyclone Taylor and when coaching against Howie Morenz and Aurele Joliat, had to recalibrate his tough standard of excellence when he saw the Punch Line at work. He called them "thrill producers," a trio who could have the crowd on their feet as soon as they hit the ice.

As the second-eldest of a working-class family of seven kids in North Montreal, Richard began playing league hockey when he was 11. After a cup of coffee with the Verdun Junior Maple Leafs, he joined the Senior Royals, and the first Canadiens' game Richard ever saw was the one he played in. Though ankle and wrist fractures kept him out of most of his last two seasons of minor hockey and his first as a pro, Richard showed his pedigree during his second season.

In 1943–44, the Montreal Canadiens won 38 games, tied seven, and lost only five. The team had doubled their number of wins from the previous season and finished first with 83 points out of a possible 100 — an extraordinary accomplishment. Despite missing a chunk of the early season with a shoulder injury, Richard caught fire. With his new nickname "Rocket" and his new jersey Number 9 (changed from

15), Richard scored 23 goals in the last 22 games, to bring his total to 32, joining Joe Malone, Newsy Lalonde, and Howie Morenz as the only Canadiens to score 30 or more goals in a season.

It was in the Stanley Cup playoffs that the "Rocket" would take off on a mission to the stars. After losing their first game 3–1 to their natural enemies, the Toronto Maple Leafs, Richard shouldered the responsibility for the next game in a dramatically literal fashion.

On March 23, 1944, the "Rocket" scored his first two goals 17 seconds apart in the first two minutes of the game, then made it a natural hat trick — or three goals in a row — before the period was out. After a scoreless second period, the "Punch Line" sent the Rocket into orbit again, and he scored twice more to tie Newsy Lalonde's 1919 record of five Stanley Cup goals in one game.

With the final score the Maple Leafs 1 and Rocket Richard 5, Foster Hewitt picked out the three stars announced to the delirious Montreal Forum: "Maurice Richard, Maurice Richard, and Maurice Richard." Richard later said of his five-goal record, "I only had six or seven shots on net and each goal was scored a different way. The funny thing is when we beat the Leafs 11–0 [to win that series], I only scored two goals."

On April 4, the Canadiens completed their sweep of the Chicago Black Hawks to win their first Stanley Cup in 13 years. Rocket Richard had scored 12 goals in nine playoff games. Montreal had another Stanley Cup, and the people had a new symbol for their hopes and dreams.

Richard was unusual in that though he played right wing he shot left-handed, and he would use this to his advantage to cut into the middle of the ice, shooting hard, low, and often. Indeed, he would shoot from anywhere on the ice, and long after he retired, he gave a quick, short lesson to New York Rangers rookie Rod Gilbert, who dared to approach Richard in a New York coffee shop and ask him for some tips.

Richard laced on his skates, grabbed a stick, filled a bucket with pucks, then took the rookie out onto the ice at Madison Square Garden. He dumped the pucks all over the ice, then started firing them at the net from wherever they lay, using his forehand, backhand, wrist, and shoulders to put almost every puck into the goal. He then gave the awestruck Gilbert a piece of his devastatingly simple philosophy: "If you want to play hockey, you have to know where the net is." Then he skated off.

Though just five-foot-ten and 160 pounds, Richard was so strong that he often sped in on goal with an opposing defensemen or two hanging off him like locker-room towels. When Detroit coach Jack Adams lit into his defenseman Earl Seibert for letting Richard beat him, the six-foot-two Seibert replied, "Any man who can carry me on his back from the blue line deserves to score."

The 1944–45 season saw the Rocket soar, his black eyes glowing with the afterburn, scaring teammates and goalies alike. Three days after Christmas 1944, Richard spent the day moving furniture — including a piano — into his new house. That night he showed up in the Montreal dressing room and sprawled out on the training table. He was too tired to play; the Canadiens were on their own. But no, if Richard had breath, he would lace up his skates, and so he did, scoring five goals and setting up three more as the Habs walloped Detroit 9–1. In a nine-game stretch Richard fired in 15 goals, and players who tried to slow him up with an elbow to the face or a stick to the gut found themselves laid out on the ice by a ferocious punch.

As the season wound down, the Rocket had one more goal to accomplish, and it was a literal one: he needed to put the puck in the net just one more time to tally the impossible total of 50 goals in 50 games. It looked as if he might never do it. When Richard beat ex-Canadien Joe Malone's record of 45 goals (set in 1918, over 22 games) he still had eight games to reach 50. But he couldn't get past 49.

Everyone wanted to stop him; no one wanted to be remembered as the team that gave up the impossible record to Rocket Richard. So shadowed, badgered, tripped, hooked, and challenged, Richard went hungry and hunting for the magical goal. In the last period of the Canadiens' last home game of the season, Richard was all alone in front of the Chicago net when he was cut down by a Black Hawk defenseman. The referee gave the Rocket a penalty shot. Here was number 50: just he and the goalie, like two ancient duelists. The electricity of anticipation in the sold-out Montreal Forum crackled off Richard's stick, but the Chicago goalie, Mike Karakas, stopped him. If the Rocket was going to make history, he would have one last chance to do it on the road.

With just over two minutes left in the third period of the last game of the season, Richard scooped up a pass from Elmer Lach and fired it into Boston's net. The record that they said could never be set was one that would stand for more than three decades. The Nobel laureate American novelist William Faulkner, said, as a Southerner might, that the Rocket possessed "the passionate glittering fatal alien quality of snakes." He was from another magical planet.

Still, there was nasty talk that the Rocket was a little too human. He had flown so high, said the critics, because all those Canadian (i.e., English) players who could otherwise have stopped him had gone to fight for their country. The Rocket had indeed tried to enlist, and was twice rejected because of his broken — and fragile — bones. The army thought that his ravaged ankles would never survive the rigours of route marching.

In Rick Salutin's classic 1977 play *Les Canadiens,* a group of actors dressed like Toronto Maple Leafs circle Richard as he moves toward the goal, and Richard hotly addresses their charges of cowardice. "I volunteered for your war," he says. "They turned me down because my bones break. That season I scored 50 goals. I'm not fragile. I'm reckless. I'm not accident prone. I'm obsessed . . ."

Indeed, his obsession was organic. Marshall McLuhan wrote in *Understanding Media* that Richard was so keenly sensitive to his working environment that he "used to comment on the poor acoustics of some arenas. He felt that the puck on his stick rode on the roar of the crowd."

On February 1, 1945, Conn Smythe, only recently on his feet after suffering wounds in his latest war, celebrated his fiftieth birthday by going to his first NHL game in three years. The major was keen to see if this French Rocket that had so lit up the hockey world (while Nazi artillery lit up Smythe's) was for real. Smythe, not easily impressed, was so taken by Richard that he wanted him to ride on the roar of his crowd at Maple Leaf Gardens.

It was an astonishing testament. Smythe had never had a French Canadian player on his team, and he distrusted francophones almost much as he distrusted Catholics, once beginning a speech in Montreal with the salutation "Ladies, Gentlemen, and Frenchmen." The Rocket's flame had scorched Smythe's bigotry, and the major offered the Canadiens $25,000 for Richard, and another $1,000 to anyone who could swing the deal. No one could. Richard knew that his was a particular vocation, and while he might regularly dazzle the crowds in other temples, a change of vestments would be sacrilege. In Montreal he was more than a player; he was a symbol of an entire culture. If he went to Toronto, it would be in the kind of servitude from which his Montreal presence represented freedom. The Rocket would serve himself and his tribe, but he would not serve Conn Smythe. Conn Smythe would never forget it.

——⁓——

An act of revenge would lead to the next Canadiens' dynasty, one of the greatest in sports history, and Conn Smythe would have a hand in that, too. In the summer of 1946, the war had been won, and Canada was on the edge of a boom, where its exports would rebuild Europe, its university graduates would have jobs thrust upon them, and people could buy a decent house for $13,000, get a fixed-rate 25-year mortgage at 4 percent, and not have to worry about locking their doors. For rural Maritimers, Quebeckers, women, immigrants, "minorities," the handicapped, and blue-collar workers, though, the good times still kept them far enough down the economic scale to do no damage.

Frank Selke belonged to none of these downtrodden groups. Frank Selke's problem was that he belonged to Conn Smythe — and in the summer of '46, Selke, Smythe's mild-mannered lieutenant whose idea of bliss was raising exotic chickens for exhibition, had finally had enough.

Selke and coach Hap Day had run Smythe's beloved Leafs while the major was off fighting the Hun again in the Second World War. The duo had done well, keeping the team competitive despite Smythe's gutting of it for his soldier battalion, even winning the Cup in 1942 and 1945. When Smythe returned from the war and saw that things were fine without him, his response was typically generous: he took all credit for the Leafs' success while he was away, and now he wanted Selke's backing to elevate himself from managing director of Maple Leaf Gardens into the president's chair.

At 53, Selke had two years on his boss, who still listed him as the publicity man in the Leaf directory, who badmouthed him to the press, and who now demanded Selke's support for Smythe-as-President. Selke had no cause to engage in a political fight with the directors of the Gardens, and backing Smythe would do him no good. Smythe derided his old friend's loyalty as being worth the price of a cup of coffee, but then, the Protestant firebrand Smythe had never completely trusted the Catholic Selke. Now his prophecy had become self-fulfilling.

When Selke returned from lunch one day, he found a memo from the major ordering him not to leave the Gardens without his permission. Selke responded with an angry memo of his own: "Lincoln freed the slaves in 1865. Goodbye, I quit." Thus scorned and humiliated, he went to Montreal with revenge on his mind.

Frank Selke was the son of an immigrant Polish farmer and had grown up the hard way in the hockey hotbed of Berlin (Kitchener), Ontario. Selke was precocious, coaching teams when he was in his early teens and winning the OHA junior league title as 20-year-old coach of a team of Polish and German kids whom the other teams disdained. Selke would lose the overall championship to the Toronto Varsity Juniors, whose captain was Conn Smythe, but Smythe had taken notice.

When the First World War broke out, Selke, like Smythe, joined the army, and he, too, was asked to form a troop hockey team, which played in the intermediate leagues. Hockey was spared when Selke's progress to the slaughterhouse was halted by a medical discharge, and so he married, became an electrician, and moved to Toronto, where he wound up coaching the Marlboros in 1924. When Smythe invented the Maple Leafs in 1927, the Marlies pumped players into the Leafs, and a partnership was born.

Like Smythe, Selke was a bantamweight, standing five-foot-seven and weighing perhaps 130 pounds in his shoes. With his round glasses and polite, shrewd demeanour, the devoutly Catholic Selke looked like a priest in civvies, and one of his nicknames was the gently mocking "Father Frank." Another, edgier handle was "Little Rollo," after the sanctimoniously perfect character in the Katzenjammer Kids cartoon strip, a sobriquet Selke earned from the iconoclastic Toronto sportswriter Ralph Allen after publicly reprimanding Allen in the Leafs' game program for not being a homer.

Whether "Father Frank" or "Little Rollo," the one thing Selke had beneath his grave demeanour was a first-class brain. When he arrived in Montreal in July of 1946, the situation was felicitous, for Canadiens' owner Senator Donat Raymond had just rid himself of

Tommy Gorman. Raymond had always felt inferior to Gorman's hockey and business acumen, and once the Habs had won the 1945 Cup, and with money coming in, the two clashed. Gorman didn't need the grief, so he walked, leaving the door wide open for Frank Selke.

Senator Raymond was in an expansive mood. Where he had tried to block Gorman at every turn, he gave Selke the keys to the palace and told him to do what needed to be done. Despite Selke's long career in hockey, this was the first time he had been at the helm. Though the Canadiens would be his masterpiece, they weren't even a masterpiece-in-waiting when he took over. "I'll never forget that day in '46 when I walked into the Forum," Selke later told a reporter. "The place was filthy and the smell of urine was enough to knock you over when you walked in the front door."

The Forum had been Montreal's premier hockey venue since November 29, 1924, when the Canadiens and the Toronto St. Pats opened the $1.5-million, 9,300-seat ice chateau at St. Catherine and Atwater. With its peaked stone facade and elegant arches framing huge glass windows, the Forum was what the Montreal *Gazette* called "palatial quarters" for the city's beloved Canadiens.

The irony, of course, is that the Forum, so called because it was built on the site of the Forum (roller-skating) Rink, had been built by the English community as the showcase for their brand new team, the Montreal Maroons. The Canadiens, on the other hand, played in the Mount Royal Arena, which was dependent on fickle Ma Nature for its ice. Since the Mount Royal was still being fitted with artificial ice that November, and the Maroons were scheduled to begin their NHL life on the road in Boston, the Canadiens were guest hosts in the building that would eventually become their shrine.

When Frank Selke took over, the shrine was a shell. Selke went around the shabby Forum an introduced himself to every worker in the joint, from the cleaners and carpenters to the ushers and secretaries, treating them as he wished to be treated, and making them feel part of something — a something he was going to make great.

But not quite yet. Though Senator Raymond was satisfied with the $13,000 the club pulled in on game nights, the gate receipts never tallied with the number of people at the game. Selke hired private detectives to watch the turnstiles, and they caught 2,300 people sneaking in for free. He also raised ticket prices in the "Millionaires'

Section" at the north end of the arena, where the 4,000 seats still cost 50 cents — the same as they had in the Depression. Selke also got rid of the chain link fence surrounding the Millionaires' bleachers, a barrier that had been designed to keep the higher-paying customers from lowering the tone in the cheap seats.

With some of the new revenue, Selke put the painters to work, obliterating the boring and dirty brown paint on the Forum walls with the red, white, and blue of the Canadiens, making the place fit for a dynasty. Then he went out and built one.

As he had done for Toronto, Selke reorganized the Canadiens' farm system. Montreal's junior teams were in bad shape, playing fewer games than other junior teams and often late at night in the Forum, when fans — and players — were nodding off during play. Selke spent money to make the junior teams attractive to budding young French Canadian stars, and he spent lavishly to establish a nationwide farm system to develop the best players in the country, at one point spending $300,000 alone on amateur hockey in Edmonton.

He also rewarded smarts and loyalty. A strategically brilliant young Montreal hockey man was recommended to Selke as coach of the Junior Canadiens, but the junior club's honorary president protested. He thought the job should go to a local amateur hockey star, now rising in the banking world. Selke's response was simple: one man had chosen hockey and the other banking. So he hired 22-year-old Sam Pollock, the man who would himself become a builder of blue-chip teams.

Even though Selke wanted to catch the best and the brightest of Quebec junior talent, there were some who got away not because of how they played, but because of their skin colour. The Quebec Senior Hockey League featured Herb Carnegie, who, with his brother Ossie and Manny McIntyre, starred for the Sherbrooke Rand team shortly after the war on the first all-black line to be integrated into a white professional hockey team.

Centre Herb Carnegie was a magical stickhandler whose ability to control the puck made him not only a champion penalty killer but also an expert playmaker. His crisp, seeing-eye passes to McIntyre and brother Ossie made the line the best in the league.

Sponsored by the Ingersoll-Rand company, the team gave the players money and jobs, and life as a Sherbrooke Rand job was much more secure than one playing for an NHL team. Yet Herb Carnegie was so good that he easily could have played in the premier pro league, and the NHL could have beaten baseball into the twentieth century by breaking the colour barrier.

But they did not, blocked by their own bigotry. "I would pay $10,000," Conn Smythe allegedly said, "to the man who can turn Herb Carnegie white." What the Canadiens thought on the matter is best expressed by the fact they did nothing.

On the ice, Frank Selke's Canadiens wouldn't do anything either for six more seasons, but Gorman had left Selke with some of the greatest names in hockey to build on.

In goal the Canadiens had "Big" Bill Durnan, a 28-year-old "rookie" when NHL vacancies created by the war liberated him to the big leagues in 1943. Durnan was no grateful puppy and refused to sign his contract until a few minutes before the first game of the 1943–44 season. Once Durnan had put down his pen, a sweating Tommy Gorman told him to suit up — he was starting the game.

Durnan held the Bruins to a 2–2 tie, captivating fans and frustrating opponents with his unique goaltending style. An ambidextrous summertime baseball player, Durnan transferred this skill to the ice, wearing a catching-mitt/stick-glove combo on each hand to take advantage of his two-handed catching ability. Bill Durnan would win six Vezina Trophies between the pipes for the Habs, four of them consecutive.

While Durnan kept pucks out of the net, Montreal's "Punch Line" of Toe Blake, Elmer Lach, and Maurice Richard put them in. The veteran Blake had won the Hart Trophy in 1939 and bore the nickname "The Lamplighter" for his ability to turn on the goal light. Elegant centreman Elmer Lach, called the "Nokomis Flash" after his Saskatchewan birthplace, was one of the greatest playmakers hockey has known, and he was someone that Selke already knew all too well.

Toronto had recruited Lach from the wilds of Saskatchewan for St. Michael's College — or St. Mike's to the hockey world — a Catholic school whose hockey excellence Conn Smythe was forced to swallow. St. Mike's and the Toronto Marlboros supplied the Leafs with young talent, and Smythe underwrote both of them. Elmer Lach could never see himself as a Leaf and headed out west to play for Moose Jaw, thus escaping the Leafs' jurisdiction. He would sign with Montreal and wind up winning the Hart Trophy in 1945.

The Punch Line had finished one-two-three in scoring in 1944–45, with Lach notching 80 points, Richard 73, and Blake 63. Frank Selke knew that he couldn't count on their knock-out scoring punch forever, so he cultivated an extraordinary crop of talent through a vast Canadiens' farm system that would see some of hockey's greatest players in the *bleu, blanc, et rouge* between 1950 and 1969.

Doug Harvey had come up to the big club in 1948 as a 24-year-old veteran of the Montreal Royals, and by 1955 he was on top of the league, winning the first of his seven Norris Trophies within the space of eight seasons. Pundits who compile lists of "Hockey's All-Time Great Players" are near-unanimous in choosing Doug Harvey as one of the two greatest defensemen to ever patrol the blue line. Harvey was the Habs' general, directing play, controlling pace, passing with uncanny accuracy, and busting the head of anyone who got in the way of him or his teammates. He even attacked a group of U.S. Marines at the Detroit Olympia because they were razzing him.

He was also nasty, once spearing the New York Rangers' "Red" Sullivan so viciously that he ruptured Sullivan's spleen. "Red" Storey, the superb football-player-turned-hockey-referee, had been officiating that game. He recalled that when New York reporters descended upon the Canadiens' dressing room after the game to tell Harvey about the seriousness of Sullivan's injury, Harvey replied, "I hope the son-of-a-bitch dies. Put that in your papers."

Harvey was not the only Hab who terrorized the opposition. Midway through the 1952 season, Dickie Moore, a feisty right winger, came up to the Habs from the Montreal Royals. He was switched to left wing on a line with Lach and Richard and won the Art Ross Trophy in 1958 as the league's leading scorer.

In 1953, Bernie "Boom-Boom" Geoffrion won full-time promotion to the big club, giving goalies terror with his full-swing shot which we know as the slapshot. As the first player to hone the shot into a weapon, it helped win him both his nickname and the 1953 Calder Trophy as Rookie of the Year.

In Bernie Geoffrion's 1950 debut game with the Canadiens (he'd only stay for 18 that season), another young prospect also made his first appearance. No one had to look up his name in the program, for Jean Beliveau was famous throughout Quebec as the star centre of the Quebec Citadels. Nicknamed *"Le Gros Bill"* because of his six-foot-three, 205-pound frame and consequent resemblance to an heroic character in a French Canadian folk song, Beliveau beggared super-latives. Known as one of the most graceful and gallant players the game has ever known, he was much more than that.

The young Beliveau lived for hockey. After serving as an altar boy at Sunday Mass, he would run next door to the family home in Victoriaville, Quebec, to play on the backyard rink. So eager were the kids to shoot and score in the hour before lunch that they played in their boots, using a tennis ball for a puck. Beliveau didn't play "organ-ized" hockey until he was 12, and he joined the Quebec Citadels at 18. During his stellar junior career, Beliveau rejected the Canadiens' pleas for him to join them, saying that Quebec City felt closer to home, and that he liked the team's owner, Frank Byrne, a powerful figure in Quebec's pulp and paper industry.

When Beliveau again rejected the Canadiens and signed with the Quebec Aces, a senior pro team, Frank Selke and the Montreal Canadiens were frustrated to desperation. The people of Quebec, how-ever, loved their big, handsome centre and showered him with gifts. Merchants gave him suits and hats and shirts and free steak lunches every time he scored three goals. In 1952, the Aces — a snappier diminutive of their owner's name, the Anglo-Canadian Pulp and Paper Company — gave the 21-year-old Beliveau a $20,000-a-year contract and two cars, one of them a stylish convertible with the license plate "2B." Quebec's godlike premier, Maurice Duplessis, had the license plate "1B."

Since the Canadiens owned Beliveau's NHL rights, they exercised their option to call him up for a three-game "lend lease." Beliveau scored five goals in those three games, including a hat trick against the Rangers. Frank Selke offered Beliveau a contract in the same realm as that of Rocket Richard: $53,000 over three years. Beliveau, already making more in Quebec, said "thanks, but no thanks" and went back to the Aces.

Though the Canadiens had won the 1953 Stanley Cup, the club's owner, Senator Raymond, had seen enough. He bought the entire Quebec Senior Hockey League, thus turning it — and Beliveau — into the property of the Montreal Canadiens. The senator then told Frank Selke to put Beliveau in a Canadiens' jersey once and for all, and damn the cost. Beliveau had made the same decision himself, after his 1953 summer wedding to Elise Couture, who, until she met Beliveau, had never seen a hockey game. It was now time to try out the big time.

In October of 1953, Beliveau signed his new contract while coach Dick Irvin flashed the V for victory sign. Frank Selke smiled like a man whose prize thoroughbred (which he also raised, in addition to chickens) was about to go to the races. When asked how he'd finally put Beliveau into harness, Selke was modest. "It was really simple. All I did was open the Forum vault and say, 'help yourself, Jean.'" Beliveau's contract weighed in at a guaranteed $110,000 over five years, the largest in the Canadiens' history.

Beliveau played on a line with Rocket Richard and Bert Olmstead, a six-foot-one left winger whose spirited hitting and relentless work in the corners made him the perfect linemate for the driven Richard and the elegant Beliveau. Olmstead was also a terror in the dressing room, showing absolutely no fear as he berated the temperamental Richard for not passing the puck. While other players waited for Richard to punch Olmstead in the nose, the Rocket just listened, then passed the puck more often.

Even with all their talent, the Canadiens would lose the 1954 Stanley Cup to Detroit in an overtime heartbreaker in the last game of the series. Indeed, it was one of those goals that make hockey players on the losing team think the fates were just toying with them all along. As Detroit's Tony Leswick was skating to the bench, he flipped the puck into the Montreal zone. Doug Harvey tried to catch it with his glove, but ended up tipping it past Habs goalie Gerry McNeil.

The novelist Hugh MacLennan once said that Montreal coach Dick Irvin felt about losing the same way John Knox felt about sin. After this fluke goal had cost his boys the Cup, Dick Irvin refused to let his team shake hands with Detroit, saying that any show of good sportsmanship on his part would not have been heartfelt, and he refused to be hypocritical. But real hypocrisy was just a year away, and at the centre of it would be the glory of *Les Glorieux*, Rocket Richard.

—◦◦◦—

In the 1954–55 season, the Canadiens came back from their Cup loss to Detroit with bloody revenge on their minds. *Le Gros Bill*, Boom-Boom, and Rocket were a scoring machine, averaging just over a point per game — each. Yet 1955 is remembered less for its magnificence than for how it ended for the Montreal Canadiens, and for Rocket Richard.

Rocket Richard was as clean a hockey player as one could hope for — unless provoked — and provoked he often was. The man who believed he was put on Earth just to score goals suffered all kinds of indignities and injustices to stop him from doing so. When angered, Richard would become a solo wrecking unit, carrying opponents on his back, his eyes blazing in fury as he steamed in on another spooked goalie to take revenge with a goal.

While Richard hardly — if ever — started a fight, he was involved in many, often at the provocation of his own coach. Dick Irvin would goad the Rocket into violence by telling him that people would think he was coward if he didn't bash his tormentors. It was the same strategy the Canadiens had used to fire up their injured rookie in 1942: question his manhood.

By March of 1955, Richard had already been punished by the NHL head office with $2,500 in fines — more than any player so far — and several game misconducts for his rampages, which weren't confined to the ice. Richard once attacked referee Hugh McLean in the lobby of a New York hotel, grabbing the startled official by his lapels before being restrained by his teammates.

With only four games to go in the 1955 season, Richard, Geoffrion, and Beliveau were 1–2–3 in the race to win the Art Ross Trophy. Richard had never won the award as the league's leading point-getter, and he wanted both the Ross and the $1,000 that went with it. Richard played harder, and his opponents tried to stop him with spearing, tripping, holding, and jabbering.

In March, Richard was already hot from an earlier incident when he retaliated to a hard check from Toronto's Bob Bailey by smacking the Leaf in the mouth with his stick. During the melee, referee "Red" Storey and his linesman George Hayes took Richard's stick away, but five times Richard came back with new ones. It wasn't until referee Storey looked at the game film that he figured out how the Rocket kept re-arming himself with sticks: his coach, Dick Irvin, kept supplying them from the bench.

Though difficult to imagine in today's micromanaged game, and though Richard had slapped Hayes and face-washed Storey with his glove, the officials pulled their punches in the report to the NHL, knowing the kind of torment Richard was under. The Rocket got off with $250 fine and the warning from NHL President Clarence Campbell that, the next time, he would be suspended from play.

"Next time" came on Sunday, March 13, 1955, when Boston's Hal Laycoe nailed Richard in the face with a high stick. The Rocket went berserk, charging Laycoe and hitting him in the face with *his* stick. Richard escaped from the restraining officials, and twice more launched a stick attack against Laycoe. The rookie linesman Cliff Thompson — who had once been a defenseman for the Bruins — finally tackled Richard, and the blindly furious Rocket punched him twice in the face, later saying that Thompson was holding him down so Laycoe could sucker punch him.

On Wednesday, March 16, league president Clarence Campbell pronounced. It was one thing to take a swing at an opponent, but to strike an official was to strike the league itself. The great Rocket Richard was not above the law, and Campbell suspended him for the remainder of the season. And for all of the playoffs.

To francophone Quebeckers, Richard had shared their struggles, fought their battles, and won their victories. He was more than a symbol: he was their flag — a flag that had just been trampled into the mud by an arrogant English lord.

"*La punition jugée trop forte* [The punishment judged too strong]," read Montreal's *La Presse* newspaper headline for March 17, 1955, restrained, under the circumstances. People jammed radio station switchboards to complain about this latest Anglo injustice and wrote angry letters to Campbell suggesting that if Richard had been named "Richardson," he'd still be playing. One Montreal weekly newspaper published a cartoon showing Campbell's head on a platter, captioned "This is how we'd like to see him."

A Rhodes Scholar, former NHL referee, and a lawyer, Campbell had won the Order of the British Empire for his work as a prosecutor with the Canadian War Crimes Commissions in Germany after the Second World War. Upon his return to Canada, the NHL appointed him assistant to interim president "Red" Dutton in June, and three months later Dutton recommended Campbell as league president.

In Campbell, the NHL Governors had a loyal, industrious team player who would work hard and late, even taking calls from drunken fans in bars asking him to settle hockey arguments and bets. Yet for all his complex mix of Oxbridge pedigree, arrogant paternalism to the players, and beer-hall populism to the fans, Campbell was really just an underling who himself was at the mercy of his NHL masters, a perfect "second-in-command" as Conn Smythe saw it. Smythe's son, Stafford, was more forthcoming about what it meant — and means — to be the president of a pro sports league. "Where else," he asked, "would you find another Rhodes Scholar, graduate lawyer, decorated war hero, and former prosecutor at the Nuremberg trials, who will do as he is told?"

And this time, Campbell was told to break Richard and the Canadiens. Two days before his hearing with Richard, Campbell flew to New York for a secret meeting with the NHL owners and laid out his plans for the Rocket. Conn Smythe and the Detroit Red Wings were delighted. The Wings were in a tight race against the Habs for the league championship, while the Leafs were in third place, but a long way back. Still, Conn Smythe never forgot Richard's snubbing of him 10 years earlier, when he wanted to clothe Richard in blue and white. The Wings just wanted Richard out of the way so they could win the Stanley Cup relatively unencumbered. That was fine with Conn Smythe, so he and the other owners told Clarence Campbell to bring the hammer down, and Campbell had done it.

On the night of March 17, 1955, the Wings came to the Montreal Forum to finish their handiwork. Despite warnings from Montreal police, as well as from Mayor Jean Drapeau, Clarence Campbell attended the game and sat in his usual spot with his secretary Phyllis King (whom he would later marry) and two of her young female friends.

Before the game, enraged crowds milled outside the Forum, chanting and throwing bottles. Inside the rink, the Canadiens were moving sluggishly, as if in mourning. When Campbell showed up, late, the Canadiens were down 2-1. The crowd stirred at this arrogant late arrival, and began to chant "On veut Richard—à bas Campbell!" ("We want Richard, down with Campbell.") By the time the first period was sputtering to its close, there was no Richard, and the Wings were up 4–1.

Suddenly, a man who had talked his way into Campbell's section 7 started hitting the president, landing several punches before the police hauled the assailant away. Play resumed, but when the period ended, another young fan attacked Campbell, squashing two tomatoes against his chest. In moments, Campbell's box was surrounded by angry fans.

Novelist Hugh MacLennan, who was sitting a few rows in front of Campbell said, "I remember knowing with very frightening and distinct certainty that with the mood of the mob, absolutely anything could happen. It was like a Roman circus."

Suddenly, a tear gas bomb exploded near Campbell, and the screaming, coughing crowd began to rush for the exits as the Forum organist sardonically played "My Heart Cries Out for You."

No one knows who threw the tear gas, but one investigation showed it to be of the type owned by the Montreal police department, another, that it was of the "chemistry set in the basement" variety. Even so, Campbell had seen the effects of tear gas in the Second World War and headed for the first-aid centre, where he consulted with the Montreal fire chief before sending Detroit a note. "Jack Adams: The game has been forfeited to Detroit. You are entitled to take your team on your way any time now. Mr. Selke agrees to the decision as the Fire Department has ordered the building closed. Signed Clarence S. Campbell."

Red Storey was in the referee's room when the tear-gas smoke started to pour in, and he ran out to look for his wife, Helen. A man started yelling at him in angry French, and Storey yelled back that he was frantic to find his wife. Another man intervened and interpreted for the agitated referee: the man yelling at him was a cop, and he was saying that he was going to shoot Storey if he didn't get out of there.

The Forum crowd spilled onto St. Catherine Street, where they ran into the *other* crowd that had been protesting Richard's suspension. With only 250 police to contain 10,000 people, the crowd became a mob, smashing windows, rocking trolleys, setting fire to a newsstand, overturning cars, and looting shops until 3 o'clock in the morning.

Those police who had managed to round up prisoners would often have to release them when overpowered by the mob, and in the end, arrested only 100 people. The rioters had inflicted over $100,000 worth of damage to Montreal, and the day after the riot, French and English Canada showed the width of their divide.

"Mob Rule Wrecks Forum, Game," scolded the Anglo *Gazette*, making a sweeping historical analogy to find the actions of the hockey mob "just as shocking and just as violent as the hordes who screamed their defiance [in Berlin] at the close of the Second World War ..." The francophone papers, however, blamed Campbell for antagonizing the crowd, and Montreal's mayor Drapeau agreed, saying however inexcusable the riot was, *"le fracas a été provoqué par le présence de M. Campbell au Forum* [the fracas was provoked by Mr. Campbell's presence in the Forum ...].

There were fears that the mob would assemble again the next night, to pick up where they left off, so Rocket Richard, under pressure to calm the mob, went on the radio shortly after 7 P.M. on the night of March 18. He explained that he did not agree with the degree of his punishment, but he added, "I will take my punishment and come back next year. So that no further harm will be done, I would like to ask everyone to get behind the team and help the boys to win from Rangers and Detroit." Such was Richard's power that the mob gritted their teeth and obeyed.

Though he missed the last three games of the 1955 season, the suspended Rocket Richard lost the league scoring title by just one assist. Just two days after "The Richard Riot," teammate Bernie Geoffrion's point total passed that of Quebec's latest martyr, and the gregarious, big-hearted Boom-Boom, who idolized Richard, won the Art Ross Trophy with 38 goals and 37 assists. The fans at the Montreal Forum booed him.

After the riot, Montreal coach Dick Irvin slapped a city waking from its nightmare by saying that while he had seen the Rocket fill many rinks, he had never seen him empty one. That was the last straw for the Canadiens' management, and Irvin packed his bags for Chicago to coach the Black Hawks, a team for which he had once played and had said he wanted to rejoin. A little over a year later, Irvin was dead of bone cancer, an excruciating, cruel disease from which he'd been suffering while coaching with Montreal. No one had known.

Some cultural observers have called *l'affair Richard* the flashpoint for Quebec's "Quiet Revolution," manifested in the "masters in our own house" policies of Quebec governments in the 1960s as a response to 200 years of English Canadian and American domination. The "Quiet Revolution" would change the nature of the continent: from the creation of official Canadian biculturalism, to the not-so-quiet terrorism of the FLQ, to the long and costly battle between Canadian federalists and Quebec *indépendantistes* to decide what a nation really means.

Francophones had tolerated many indignities at the hands of the English, but the railroading of Richard had attacked them in their hearts and homes. It was personal. In taking up arms against this assault on their essence, they sent a signal to the English community that the rules of the game had just changed. Neither they, nor Rocket Richard, would ever be the same again.

—~~~—

The glories of yesterday are often diminished through the prism of today's discontent, with contemporary commentators remembering *that* championship season of yore as the zenith of the game, one which the money-grubbing princes of today's game can scarcely see through the fog of their own egos. However, it is not too much to say that the Montreal Canadiens of 1955–56 were the most glorious in the history of the franchise, and they had a championship season that is the stuff of legend.

"Toe" Blake, the former digger of the great "Punch Line," stepped into the breach behind the bench. Rocket Richard had played with Blake and young Beliveau had idolized him, but the "Old Lamplighter" soon put sentimentality in its place, running practices so tough that Red Storey would later describe a punishing Mike Keenan or Pat Burns practice as a day at the beach compared to one of Blake's.

The new coach's philosophy was simple: hockey is a two-way game in which players skate from their zone in a V formation, then invert to converge on the opponent. The quick, fluid "transition game" was the essence of Blake's vision, and his players had to keep moving, heads up, sticks on the ice. Jean Beliveau used to laugh when hockey experts bowed down before the Russian and European teams of the 1980s, for these so-called great innovators were playing the type of game the Canadiens used to play in the 1950s.

The Habs won their first game of the magical season with a 2–0 shutout of Toronto. Then they blanked Boston 2–0, and beat them again 5–2. On October 15, their fourth game of the season, the Canadiens beat the Rangers 4–1 at the Forum, and Rocket Richard — who was playing as cleanly and brilliantly as he ever had — scored two goals. His rookie kid brother, Henri, scored his first NHL goal and received a standing ovation as the shape of things to come.

Henri Richard was six years old when big brother Maurice started playing for the Canadiens. Yet Maurice was still an animating and inescapable presence for a boy with ambition. Young Henri used to rise on cold, dark winter mornings to practise hockey outside the walls of the Bordeaux jail in Montreal's North End, but it was never too cold for him. It was only by being out here in the great freezing alone that he would hone by practise what his brother had been given by God.

And then, maybe then, he would join the Canadiens, and his secret would be revealed. "I always told people that I wanted to be a brick-layer," he later confessed to James Quig in a *Weekend Magazine* interview. "I was too shy to admit I wanted to play with Maurice. My sister used to go out with a bricklayer."

Henri was a five-foot-seven, 160-pound, 19-year-old speedster with the Junior Canadiens when word came down that Frank Selke wanted to see the kid, along with his idolized older brother. When the Richards appeared in Selke's office, the Canadiens' manager asked simply: "Is he ready, Maurice?" The Rocket replied "He's ready, Mr. Selke," and walked out.

The Habs offered Henri $7,000 for his first year and $8,000 for his second, but as he said two decades later, "I would have signed for anything to play with Maurice and the Canadiens. That was my dream, and it came true."

Young Henri's dream was not without its detractors. Some feared that the Brothers Richard would be reduced to a schoolyard act, with incendiary Maurice fighting his little brother's battles as well as his own and losing his focus. The result was quite the opposite, as the Rocket was becalmed and encouraged by Henri's presence. "It used to be that I played for myself," he said. "Now I play for the two of us."

Henri's beautiful skating featured quick acceleration, earning him the nickname "The Pocket Rocket," a handle he never liked. Despite wanting to emulate the Rocket, he also wanted to have an identity separate from his magnificent older brother. And while the comparisons came, they couldn't have been more flattering. Coach Toe Blake said the younger Richard was not "puck lucky" but smart, able to size up "how a play is going to go, and then he gets there, and the first thing you know, he's got the puck."

The highest compliment came from the man who mattered most, with a perfectly natural brotherly jibe. "Henri is a better all-round player than I ever was," said the Rocket. "He stickhandles better, controls the puck more, and skates faster. He's better in every way except in goal scoring."

When Henri arrived in the NHL, he was so quiet off the ice that a reporter asked Toe Blake if the Rocket's little brother could speak English. "Hell," said the bilingual Blake, "I'm not even sure he can speak French." Henri's on-ice eloquence was subsumed by something larger off it — the fact that he was a Montreal Canadien. Being in the dressing room of *Les Glorieux* was like being in a holy place. "It took me five years before I was able to talk in this room," said Henri, and "10 before I shaved in it. It was like a chapel for me."

In his rookie season, Henri Richard had a fellow churchgoer in Jacques Plante, who at age 26 had finally made it as the Canadiens' goalie. Montreal has always been a home for great goalies: Georges Vezina, whose excellence begat the trophy for the league's best goalie; George Hainsworth, the first winner of the Vezina Trophy 1927, which he liked so much that he won it for three straight seasons; and then Big Bill Durnan.

While Hainsworth hated to fall down to stop pucks, and Durnan was ambidextrous, neither the Canadiens nor the league had seen anything like Jacques Plante. On ice he was an extrovert, making mad dashes for the puck, yelling advice to his defensemen, and feeding forwards with nerve-wrackingly long passes.

Off the ice, after giving a brilliantly articulate bilingual post-game interview, Plante turned introvert, keeping to himself in the dressing room. On road trips, he would stay in a hotel separate from the rest of the team; for relaxation, he would knit toques, sweaters, and even his own underwear. His teammates joked that the real reason the frugal Plante liked knitting so much was because he was so cheap.

Plante's frugality was learned the hard way, and his story seems filtered through the imagination of a Quebec Dickens. As one of 11 children still living at home in Shawinigan, there was no money for a radio on which young Jacques could hear his Canadiens take flight. Still, there were comparatively rich neighbours and thin walls. "I used to lie awake at night," he said, "listening to hockey games in the ceiling coming through from the radio upstairs that some people there owned ..."

Near the end of the first period of the game between the Canadiens and the Detroit Red Wings on the night of March 17, 1955, a tear gas bomb exploded in the Montreal Forum in protest to the harsh suspension given by NHL President Clarence Campbell to Canadiens' hero Maurice "Rocket" Richard. The Forum was quickly evacuated, and the "Richard Riot" had begun. LA PRESSE

above, left: Even in repose, Montreal Canadiens' Maurice Richard shows the same intensity in his eyes as he did on the ice. "The Rocket" played 18 seasons with the Canadiens, embodying the hopes and dreams of a generation of fans in Quebec, and elsewhere. Richard was the first player to break the magical 50-goal season mark, and NHL goalie Glenn Hall once remarked that when the "Rocket" sped in on goal, "his eyes were flashing and gleaming like the lights of a pinball machine." HOCKEY HALL OF FAME

above, right: After being struck in the face by a puck, Jacques Plante defies years of prejudice by wearing a mask on November 1, 1959. Conventional wisdom held that masked goalies would go soft, but Plante's response was to add three more Vezina Trophies to the three he already owned, as well as the 1962 Hart Trophy. HOCKEY HALL OF FAME

facing page, bottom: Canadiens' captain Jean Beliveau celebrates another triumph with (left to right) The Rocket's kid brother Henri Richard, enforcer John Ferguson, and Yvon "The Roadrunner" Cournoyer. The quartet represented the essence of the Canadiens' dynasty: skill, grace, toughness, and speed. CP PICTURE ARCHIVE

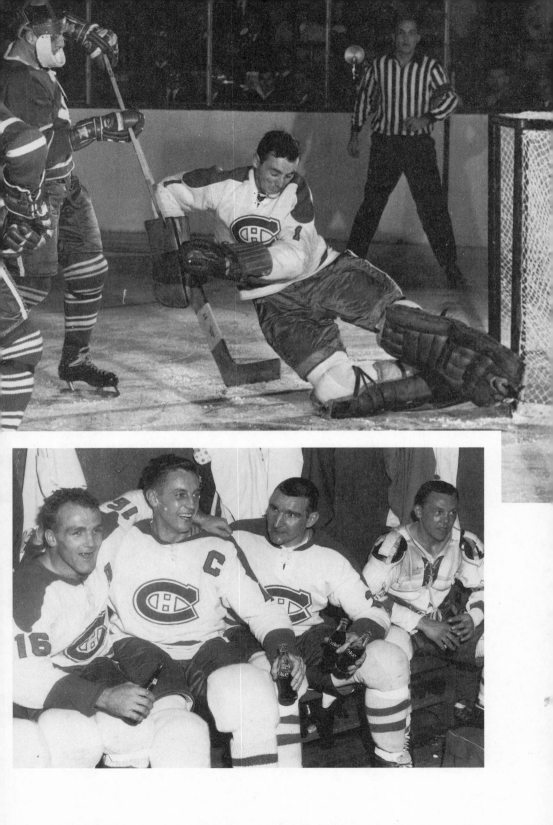

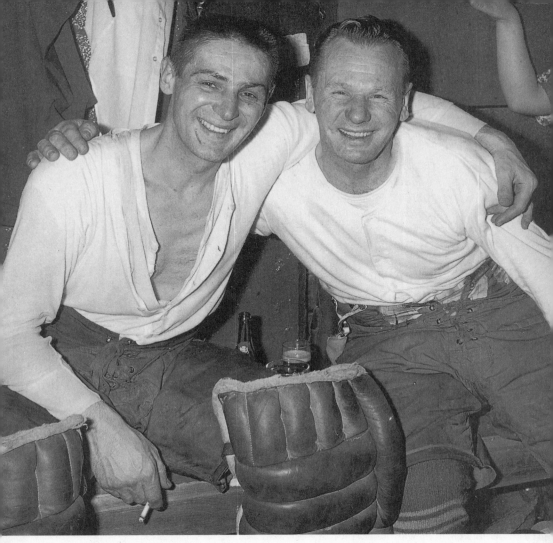

facing page, top: Major Conn Smythe swears in a recruit to his 30th Royal Canadian Artillery "Sportsmen's" Battery in Toronto during WWII. Arch-patriot Smythe, who had belonged to a Sportsmen's Battery in WWI persuaded some of Canada's finest athletes to take up the call to arms. Smythe and the Battery would see action in France, where Smythe was wounded. HOCKEY HALL OF FAME

facing page, bottom: Leafs captain Ted "Teeder" Kennedy embraces an old friend. Kennedy joined the Leafs for two games in 1942–43 and then stayed with the blue and white for his entire NHL career, including five Stanley Cups at the height of the Leafs' dynasty between 1945 and 1951, retiring after the 1956–57 season. HOCKEY HALL OF FAME

above: Leaf goalies Terry Sawchuk and Johnny Bower shared the 1965 Vezina Trophy as the NHL's best goaltending duo. Here they celebrate their 1967 Stanley Cup championship, where the 37-year-old Sawchuk and the 42-year-old Bower combined to help the "Over the Hill Gang" Leafs beat Montreal in six games. HOCKEY HALL OF FAME

right: Bobby Orr joined the Oshawa Generals, a junior team sponsored by the Boston Bruins, when he was just 14. Orr averaged 33 goals a season—while playing defence—with Oshawa, and further cemented his reputation as the Bruins' Saviour. HOCKEY HALL OF FAME

far right: Though Bobby Orr's threat as an offensive power was huge, winning him two Art Ross Trophies as the NHL's leading point scorer, he was first and foremost a defenseman, notching eight James Norris Trophies as the NHL's best rearguard over his injury-ravaged twelve seasons as a pro. HOCKEY HALL OF FAME

bottom: Bobby Orr flies through the air after scoring the Stanley Cup-winning goal in overtime, against St. Louis, in May 1970. It is one of the most famous and evocative images in Orr's career, and in pro hockey history: Orr as winged victory. HOCKEY HALL OF FAME

following page: Paul Henderson scores the goal that saved a nation. With just 34 seconds left in Game 8, Henderson capped a three-goal third-period Canadian rally to lead Canada to an emotional 6–5 game win and series victory. Nearly a century after James Creighton put hockey under a roof, Henderson's goal told the hockey world that the game still belonged to Canada. In the coming decades, that game would increasing belong to the world, and Henderson's goal would serve as a source of longing and nostalgia for Canadians.
FRANK LENNON

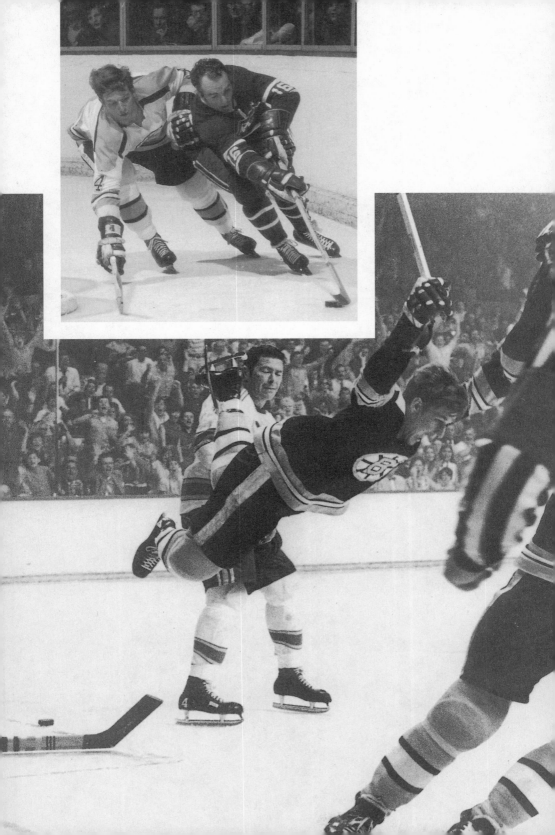

His biggest ambition in life was to play one game for his school, "then it was to play one game for the big team in my city. It's all been a dream since then ..."

It was a dream with its own sweet logic. Plante was a raw 18 year old in 1947 when Frank Selke expanded the Quebec junior hockey league from four teams to 11. When Plante was playing for Shawinigan, a Detroit scout living in Quebec City came to check out him and three other players. Plante, however, was out of action that night, so the scout signed the other three guys and went on his way. Plante was always grateful for this shrug of destiny. Detroit was rich in goalies, and with Harry Lumley in nets and Terry Sawchuk and Glenn Hall waiting in the wings, he might have been left to wither.

Plante's flamboyant style was born of necessity when he was with the Quebec Citadels, who had four bad defensemen: two were slow, one couldn't skate backward, and another couldn't make left turns. "It was a case of me having to go and get the puck when it was shot into our end because our defensemen couldn't get there fast enough," said Plante. "The more I did it, the farther I went. It seemed to be the best thing to do, so I did it and it worked."

No one who saw Plante play in the 1955–56 season would believe he was just some accident of fate. His virtuosity on ice won him comparisons to that great Canadian maestro of the keyboard, and people called Plante "the Glenn Gould of hockey," or more familiarly, "Jake the Snake," because of his lithe and quick cunning. Plante led the league with a goals-against average of 1.86 and posted seven shutouts. The kid who just wanted to play for his school team would win the first of his six Vezina Trophies that year. The Canadiens would win everything.

Jean Beliveau caught fire, scoring 47 goals — nine more than both Rocket Richard and Gordie Howe — and helped on 41 others, winning the Art Ross Trophy as the league's leading scorer, and the Hart Trophy as the NHL's most valuable player. The cantankerous genius Doug Harvey won his second straight Norris Trophy as the NHL's best defenseman. Of the six positions on the league's First All-Star team, four were filled by Canadiens: Plante in goal, Harvey on defense, Beliveau at centre, and Rocket Richard at right wing. Montreal's Tom Johnson and Bert Olmstead made the Second All-Star team.

The Habs won 45 games, lost 15, and tied 10, finishing 24 points ahead of their closest competition, Detroit. Fittingly, the Canadiens met Detroit in the Stanley Cup Final year, remembering well that the Wings had won the Jug on a fluke goal in 1954, and on a grounded Rocket in 1955.

Montreal had no love lost for Detroit and even hated their fans, getting into a fight with some of them in the third game, which the Canadiens won 3–1. Jack Adams suggested the Habs were teetering on the brink of Palookaville if they had to start donnybrooks in the stands, and sportswriters who depended on access to Adams for their livelihoods wrote that Jacques Plante was a sissy for wearing a mask in practice. Montreal responded on the ice by shutting out Detroit in the next game, then winning the Cup 3–1 at home in the Forum. It was their first of five straight Stanley Cups, a feat that had not been accomplished before, nor since. Had it not been for the fluke goal against Detroit in '54 and the loss of Richard in '55, it might have been seven straight.

The Canadiens were so good that no Stanley Cup series they played in from 1956–60 went to a seventh game, and they went to a sixth game in the Final only once — against the Boston Bruins in 1958. They finished in first place four out five seasons, being eclipsed by six points by the Red Wings in 1957. Of the 30 hard-won First Team All-Star positions available between 1956 and 1960, the Canadiens took 15 of them, and 10 of the 30 Second Team places as well.

Not content to leave the NHL's prizes for individual excellence untouched, the Canadiens won those, too. Bernie Geoffrion added to his 1952 Calder Trophy by winning the Hart Trophy in 1961; the following year Jacques Plante would be the league MVP. Dickie Moore won back-to-back Art Ross scoring titles in 1958 and 1959 and on legs so bashed up that it was a wonder he was skating at all. Boom-Boom Geoffrion won the Ross in 1955 and again in 1961. Jacques Plante owned the Vezina from 1956 through 1960, then won it again in 1962. Ralph Backstrom won the Calder Trophy as the NHL's top rookie in 1959, while Doug Harvey owned the Norris Trophy from 1955 through 1962, interrupted by his teammate Tom Johnson, who, despite being forced to play in the glare of Harvey's uncompromising brilliance, was the league's best defenseman in 1959.

On October 19, 1957, Maurice Richard made hockey history once again. At 15:32 of the first period in a game against Chicago at the

Forum, the Rocket wired a Beliveau pass through Chicago goalie Glenn Hall. It was the five hundredth time the Rocket's name had appeared on the goal scoring sheet, and fans and players alike paid homage as the Rocket accepted the puck. In a masterstroke of under-statement, the Forum organist played *"Il a gagné ses epaulettes."* [He has won his epaulettes.]

The Canadiens were so dominant that the league responded by changing the rules. In 1956–57, the NHL Governors decreed that a two-minute minor penalty would end when the team with the man advantage scored. Before this, a minor penalty had to be served in full, until the Canadiens started popping in two or three goals with each power play, with Jean Beliveau himself scoring three goals in 44 seconds during a two-man advantage in 1955.

Jacques Plante was the other reason the NHL Governors moved the goalposts. At the annual general meeting in the summer of 1959, the governors voted 5–1 in favour of a rule that would forbid the goalie from falling on the puck outside the crease. Coach Toe Blake smelled conspiracy in this attempt to thwart his boys from winning the Cup every year until the turn of the century. "I'll bet it was thought up by the Detroit Red Wings," said Blake. "They used to score a lot of goals by shooting the puck from behind the net and having a guy come in fast to grab the rebound. Plante spoiled that by coming out and grabbing the puck."

Jacques Plante was also the reason for the reprise of an innovation so long overdue that hockey people were blind to the salvation of the goalie mask. Indeed, some thought that putting your naked face and head between a careening piece of frozen rubber and the scoresheet was just part of being a man — though hardly anyone knew the mask idea first came from a woman.

In 1927, Queen's University goalie Elizabeth Graham wore a wire fencing mask to protect herself. Astonishingly, Montreal Maroons' goalie Clint Benedict had been the first pro to wear a mask in 1930, after his nose had been broken by a Howie Morenz blast from 25 feet out. Unfortunately, the nosepiece on "Praying Benny's" crude leather mask blocked his vision — already disabled by the aftershock of Morenz's shot — and he had to abandon it, then retire. "If I'd been able to perfect the mask," lamented Benedict, "I'd have been a 20 year man."

In 1955, Plante's right cheekbone was shattered by a shot from teammate Bert Olmstead, and he was out for five weeks. In 1956, a shot deflected into his face, and while recuperating, Plante mentioned in a TV interview that he'd be interested in trying out any masks suitable for goaltenders. A man in Granby heard his plea and sent him a plastic model that Plante used for three years.

In 1957, Bill Burchmore sent Plante a letter saying he'd been developing a fibreglass mask which would be moulded to fit the face, and he and Plante perfected it but for one problem: Toe Blake. As Plante recalled, his coach thought the face protector would make him complacent, and that "I wouldn't be able to play as well. So I took it off."

All of that changed in a game against the New York Rangers at Madison Square Garden on November 1, 1959 when Plante's face was on the receiving end of an Andy Bathgate slapshot. Plante refused to go back into the game unless he was armoured, so Toe Blake agreed to let him wear a mask, and Montreal promptly went on a 19-game unbeaten streak. When Plante's nose had healed, he took off the mask at Blake's urging, and the Habs lost. As Plante recalled, "Blake came to me and said that I had a chance to win a fifth straight Vezina Trophy that year, and that if the mask would help, 'do what you want.' So I put it back on." Plante won the Vezina. The Canadiens won the Stanley Cup.

At the start of the 1960 season, Maurice Richard, now a battered 39 year old, showed up a training camp for his eighteenth campaign. The Rocket's goal production had fallen from 33 in '56–57 to 19, and he had missed more than 100 games since the 1956–57 season. In his typically proud way, Richard had shown up for camp, then realized he had not lost his heart, nor his touch, but his desire. On September 15, 1960, he retired, but before he left the ice, he put four pucks past Jacques Plante in practice, to remind all those young bloods who were watching of just who it was who was hanging up his skates.

In 1964, 71-year-old Frank Selke was moved upstairs to become "special adviser" to the team he had moulded for nearly two decades. Under his guidance, the Canadiens had won six Stanley Cups and established themselves as one of the greatest dynasties ever seen on ice or turf. Selke had built on Tommy Gorman's legacy to leave the club stronger than when he came aboard, and now he passed the torch to his protégé Sam Pollock.

Fueled by Calder Trophy winners Bobby Rousseau and Jacques Laperriere — who would also win the Norris Trophy in 1966. The Canadiens of the '60s were almost as potent. With the goalscoring touch and speed of "The Roadrunner" Yvan Cournoyer, the defensive brilliance of Terry Harper and J. C. Tremblay and Serge Savard, and the goaltending prowess of Gump Worsley and Rogie Vachon, Montreal would win back-to-back Stanley Cups in 1965 and '66. They would do it again in 1968 and '69, but in the middle, they would hit a roadblock in their dynastic quest to repeat their five-star performance of the '50s. And the roadblock was just down the road, wearing blue and white and calling themselves "Canada's Team."

8

CANADA'S TEAM

Like the Montreal Canadiens, the Toronto Maple Leafs were formed out of revenge. When Conn Smythe was doubly cheated by the brand-new Rangers of New York, a team he had built and was supposed to coach, a team that was now withholding part of his fee, he created the Leafs out of pique. And some gambling money.

Smythe trashed their Irish Catholic name, the St. Patricks, and rechristened them to reflect a Canadian national symbol, one worn on the shoulder patches of soldiers in the First World War. He painted over their Irish green with the blue and white of his alma mater, the University of Toronto. Then he built them a temple at Church and Carleton Streets in the worst days of the Depression, using the help of that once-great Canadian dynasty, the Eaton family, who helped out with land.

When money ran short, Smythe's wily lieutenant, Frank Selke, used his union card in the International Brotherhood of Electrical Workers to persuade the workers to take 20-percent payment in shares. And then Smythe put in a championship crew that would win the Cup in their first year as tenants, their heroics chronicled for the country over the next four decades by Foster Hewitt, their very own Homer hanging from the rafters in his "Gondola," his crackly, excited voice ringing out in the dark of radioland.

So it's not hard to see how the Toronto Maple Leafs could advertise themselves, in all modesty, as "Canada's Team," representing the hopes and dreams of all those Canadians who didn't have an NHL hockey team in town until 1970, when the Canucks rose from the rainy winter ponds of Vancouver.

Of course, Canada did have another team, something Conn Smythe knew all too well. Since his democratic bigotry also included French Quebec, the "Canada's Team" claim not-too-subtly suggests that those who worship at the altar of the Montreal Canadiens do so in treachery.

As a member of the Holy Trinity in the so-called Golden Age of the Original Six, the Toronto Maple Leafs won 10 Stanley Cups, as did the Montreal Canadiens, with the Detroit Red Wings claiming five. While both the Leafs and the Canadiens could claim Cup equality, it was the Leafs who laid siege to Canadian hearts in the 1940s and '60s. They began in suitably mythic fashion.

In the spring of 1942, the Leafs were in the Stanley Cup Final — again. For three straight seasons from 1938 through 1940, the Buds had made it to the Final, only to lose to Chicago, Boston, and New York. Canada's Team had not won the Cup since their debut in '32. Worse, Lord Stanley's Dominion Challenge Trophy had been in Yankee hands ever since, but for a one-season kidnapping in 1935 by the now-defunct Montreal Maroons. If Canada's Team was going to seriously lay claim to this grand title, then it was time to do or die.

The Leafs certainly had some doers. "Turk" Broda, who had won the Vezina Trophy the year before, led the league with six shutouts. The son of Polish immigrants, the genial Turk won his nickname due to a reality for hockey players at the time: his summer job. Players had to work in the off-season to supplement their incomes, and Walter Broda became known as Turk because his neck went turkey-red when he toiled as a brewery truck driver in the summer sun.

The Leafs of '42 had scoring power, with Gordie Drillon, and "Sweeney" Schriner notching 20-goal seasons. A big right winger from Moncton, Drillon had won both the Lady Byng Trophy and led the league in goals, with 26, in 1938, his second season. His linemate, Sylvanus Apps, had won the first Calder Trophy in 1937, after the league's president donated a trophy to the NHL's finest rookie. Big Syl Apps would also win the 1942 Lady Byng Trophy for being the league's most sportsmanlike player.

The multitalented Apps had won the British-Empire pole-vaulting championship in 1934 and had competed for Canada at the 1936 Olympics in Berlin. When Conn Smythe first heard about Apps's athletic ability, he dismissed it with a logic not available to other mortals. "No one with the name Sylvanus," reasoned Smythe, "could possibly become a professional hockey player." Yet when Smythe saw Apps play football, he was so impressed he offered him a hockey contract with the Leafs. Conn Smythe at least had no shame about being wrong.

So in the spring of '42, Canada's Team sharpened their sticks for the Detroit Red Wings, and it looked like Toronto had lucked into an opponent it could easily handle to take the Cup. The Wings had finished 15 points back of the Leafs and had lost five times to Toronto during the season. The men from Motor City had other ideas.

The Wings had perfected a "new" style of hockey, one that Jack Adams had retrieved from the good old days: they dumped the puck into the opposition zone, then crashed their way through the opposing defense to retrieve it and fire it home.

Detroit's line of Don Grosso, Eddie Wares, and the silky left winger Sid Abel combined for six of the Wings' 12 goals in the first three games — games that the written-off Wings won. Four seasons earlier, that would have been enough to take the Cup, but in 1939, the NHL had made the Stanley Cup Final a seven-game affair. The Wings had to win just one more game and Canada's Team would be finished.

It looked like they already were, and blame was placed fast. Gordie Drillon, often a lightning-rod for malcontent Leafs fans, was again a target. Experts felt Drillon didn't use his six-foot, 185-pound heft with the same banging style as the man he had replaced, the irreplaceable Charlie "The Big Bomber" Conacher. Now it was Drillon's fault that the mighty Leafs were about to be swept off the ice. So coach Hap Day benched him, along with "Bucko" McDonald.

But even the unusual logic of benching a star to shake up his team wasn't enough, so Day turned to an unlikely source of inspiration to bring his team back to life: a 14-year-old girl named Doris Klein. Though she lived in Detroit, Doris Klein showed her feelings of adolescent displacement with an unyielding devotion to the Leafs. She sent Coach Day a letter begging her team to do something no team had ever done — win four straight Stanley Cup Final games and dig themselves out of the grave.

Day read his team the letter in the locker room. The Leafs listened, and, while the scene seems inconceivable in today's "it's just a business" world of rarefied athletes, they were moved. So Canada's Team responded to this American girl's plea by scoring two goals in the third period to win Game 4. And took a step out of the grave.

Detroit's "Jolly Jack" Adams smelled conspiracy. The Wings had been penalized an average of nine minutes a game during the season; in this series, they were riding the pine for an astonishing 135 minutes a game. Clearly Adams's sworn enemy, Conn Smythe, and the cabal of Toronto newspapers were accomplices to a crime.

Indeed, an alarmingly high number of low-paid Toronto reporters were in Smythe's pocket, accepting his money for meals, hotels, and refreshment expenses in exchange for filing their copy in blue-and-white ink. Yet Adams could hardly complain, for he was guilty of doing the same thing to get an edge, and would stand hard-up Detroit news-men drinks and dinner in exchange for a flattering word. Could it be that the Leafs were just better?

Adams's conspiracy theory exploded into war when two late penalties cost Detroit the fifth match. Portly, florid Adams, his fedora askew, joined his players to chase referee Mel Harwood off the ice. In the "consultation" between coach and ref that followed, Adams was charged with hitting the referee. The NHL suspended him indefinitely.

The incident sent the Wings into a nose-dive. After "Turk" Broda shut out Detroit in Game 6, more than 16,000 screaming Leaf fans — the largest crowd yet to watch a hockey game in Canada — crammed into the Gardens to witness the impossible. Even Major Conn Smythe, now off preparing another troop of warriors to fight in Europe, descended from his command centre at Petawawa to cheer on Canada's Team.

No sooner had Smythe arrived in his temple than he was promptly barred from the dressing room by Ed Bickle, the Leaf's executive vice-president, who wasn't going to let the ranting Smythe ruin things now. Coach Hap Day, whose pharmacy degree and sunny nickname belied a steely loyalty, cocked his fist and aimed it at Bickle's jaw, promising to deliver if Bickell didn't stand aside.

So in marched the major to pinpoint for his troops just why they were a bunch of lousy bums. The Leafs responded to Smythe's morale booster by giving up a goal to Detroit and scoring none themselves. At the end of the second period Smythe came back in the "room" and opened up with a barrage against the top line: veterans Billy Taylor and Sweeney Schriner, and young Lorne Carr. The game had slowed down, Smythe howled at the sweating, wind-sucking men, but it was perfect for old guys like Taylor and Schriner, then just cresting 30. What was the matter? Couldn't they even play like old ladies? At the end of his humiliating tirade, the amiable Schriner grinned at Smythe and said, "What ya worrying about, boss? We'll get you a couple of goals."

And Schriner did, scoring twice to lead the Leafs to a 3–1 victory, and the most unlikely Stanley Cup comeback yet seen. It was exactly the sort of do-or-die heroics the war-weary country needed. A buoyant Smythe hopped the train back to his sportsman's battalion, "feeling so good," remembered one of his soldiers, journalist Ted Reeve, that "we got away with only two hours gun drill and the route march was cut down to 10 miles." Canada's Team had come through.

⁓

Yet more was required. The war in Europe bled on, and just as they had done in the war before, many hockey players felt that the battle on ice paled to that being fought in Europe. Or they felt that way thanks to the bellicose sensibility of Conn Smythe, whose credo went, "If I don't fight for my country, who will?"

In the United States, hockey players answered the call to arms by heading to sea, or rather, to the Baltimore yard of the U.S. Coast Guard to lace on their skates as the "Cutters." Organized by the hockey-playing Michigan native Lieutenant Commander C. H. MacLean shortly after Pearl Harbor, the Cutters were slicing through opponents in the Eastern Amateur Hockey League in 1942. The New York Rangers' captain Art Coulter signed on with the Cutters, as did ace Boston netminder Frank "Mr. Zero" Brimsek, the Black Hawks' defenseman Johnny Mariucci, and Detroit centre Alex Motter, who won the Stanley Cup with the Wings in the 1943. Playing the Rangers' and Bruins' farm clubs, as well as a team from Philadelphia, the Cutters won two national U.S. amateur hockey titles in 1943 and '44, beat the Ottawa Commandos, and even played valiantly against the Detroit Red Wings in 1943, hanging on 4–3 until the third period, when the Wings opened up for four goals.

In the early days of the war, Canadian hockey players were trying not to fight for their country. Many had signed up for "home service," a sop from the federal government to Quebec, which was overwhelm- ingly opposed to "conscription"—compulsory duty in the war machine. After 30 days of basic "home service" training, the players were off the hook for the rest of the year.

Conn Smythe hated home service. He had fought in the Great War, and though 45 years old, he wasn't going to let Hitler's jackbooted thugs run roughshod over Europe. He made his 1939 Leafs take mil- itary training with the Toronto Scottish regiment, and he urged all of his players to join a militia. As the war continued, Smythe badgered the Canadian government, echoing Canadian soldiers overseas in call- ing the home service troop "zombies" and "duty dodgers."

No self-respecting hockey player wanted to be called a "zombie," but the last thing the NHL wanted was its marquee names being blown to pieces or tortured to death by the Gestapo. So the players who signed up often got safe jobs away from the fray.

Boston's brilliant "Kraut Line," of Bobby Bauer, Woody Dumart, and Milt Schmidt (sanitized as the "Kitchener Kids"), were recruited *en masse* to the Royal Canadian Air Force Flyers hockey team. New York Rangers' coach Frank Boucher saw the writing on the wall before the 1942–43 season and helped to create a Canadian Army All-Star hockey team to entertain troops, munitions workers, and everyone else.

The Ottawa Commandos included Neil and Mac Colville, and Alex Shibicky, veterans of the 1940 Stanley-Cup–winning Rangers squad. Rangers' goalie "Sugar" Jim Henry was a Commando, as were Ken Reardon of the Canadiens and his coach, Dick Irvin, who split shifts as benchman for both the Montreal Canadiens and the soldiers.

By the spring of 1944, 90 NHL players had signed up for the war. The 1943 Cup-champion Wings were ravaged, losing five frontliners, including Sid Abel. The New York Rangers, who had made the playoffs for 15 out of the past 16 seasons, finished dead last in 1944 with six wins and 39 losses. The Blueshirts had lost Clint Smith, Lynn Patrick, Alf Pike, and Dudley "Red" Garrett to the war. (Garrett had no soft job and was killed in action.) Lester Patrick was so distressed by the Rangers' slide that he wanted to take the team out of the league until the war had ended.

To lose New York was unthinkable for the other owners, a possibly fatal slap in the collective wallet if the NHL's showy, big-town franchise were to go down. Frank Boucher came out of retirement at age 42 to suit up for the Blueshirts and managed 14 points in 15 games. The Montreal Canadiens loaned the Rangers two players in exchange for Phil Watson, who, like other players whose off-ice jobs made them "essential" to the Canadian war effort, was restricted from crossing the border to play in the United States. Overtime periods were canceled to allow fans to catch the last train home before the evening "blackout" plunged the continent into darkness.

For those soldiers stationed in England, comforting, nostalgic hockey could be had courtesy of the soldier teams on the ice, or courtesy of Canada's Team. Bard Foster Hewitt's wireless accounts of their exploits on the ice back home were transmitted to Britain, and had a profound effect on Canadian morale. "I was walking past a service hostel right near the Tottenham Road tube station [in London, England] when I heard this voice — your voice — coming through the blackout curtains," one soldier wrote to Hewitt. "I ran in there and it was a hockey broadcast. I damned near cried."

Given the patriotic zeal of their creator, Conn Smythe, Canada's Team lost a third of their crew to the army, including Sweeney Schriner, Syl Apps, and ex-Leaf Gordie Drillon, now on the Toronto Daggers hockey team. The Leafs All-Star goalie Walter Broda went, too, but it was the "Turk" who ruined the party for hockey players in the army.

On the night of October 18, 1943, Broda was yanked from a Montreal-bound train by the RCMP. It seemed that Broda's military service call-up notice had expired, and Broda was now a wanted man. The problem was, he was wanted in two places.

At the time of his arrest, Broda was in the company of an Army sergeant-major from Montreal, where the Turk was heading to enlist. The fact that he had already enlisted in Toronto with the Royal Canadian Artillery caused a problem that Broda hadn't anticipated. When the Toronto major who interviewed Broda decided to make him an army truck driver on October 16, Broda saw this as an obstacle to a reunion with his mates on the Toronto Daggers. So, without violating his call-up notice but breaching his terms of enlistment, he decided to take his chances in Montreal with a different regiment.

His arrest caused much braying in the House of Commons and in the papers. Montreal *Gazette* conspiracy theorists suggested that Conn Smythe was behind the whole plot to keep Broda from playing for Montreal Army, where he had been offered $2,400 above his military pay. The *Calgary Herald* came out swinging on October 20, echoing the mood of many by calling it a national disgrace that hockey players who had enlisted one or two years earlier were still in Canada playing hockey. The Army and Air Force responded to this outcry with alacrity, and within months the military hockey teams were disbanded and their players sent on for advanced training in preparation for war.

After a stint guarding Tofino, B.C., from a feared Japanese invasion that never materialized, Major Conn Smythe, commander of the 30th Battery of the 7th Toronto Regiment, shipped out for Europe with his hockey player warriors. Indeed, Smythe had turned his troop into a unit of golden sporting heroes, signing up the starting line-up of the Mimico Mountaineers, winners of lacrosse's Mann Cup, several Ontario baseball stars, a Toronto Argonaut, and two of Canada's best golfers, Jim Boekh and Clare Chinery. Even a couple of Toronto sportswriters joined Smythe's gunners: Ted Reeve of the *Telegram* and Ralph Allen of the *Globe & Mail*, with Allen going on to become a war correspondent for *Maclean's* two years later.

Three weeks after D-Day, Conn Smythe and his battery shipped out from England to Normandy, and a month after that, Smythe was nearly killed again when German fighter planes attacked his encampment at Caen with gunfire and fragmentation bombs.

As parachute flares lit up the hot summer night, Smythe did something odd, and ran to pull on his heavy trenchcoat — a First World War reflex, when thick trenchcoats had been known to save men from flying bullets and steel shards. A bomb came hurtling to earth, and Smith dove for cover. When he tried to get up, he was paralysed from the waist down — a jagged piece of metal having pierced his colon and bladder, its lethal progress halted by the trenchcoat. The war Smythe fought so hard to get into would now be fought from a hospital bed.

Doubting that he would ever walk again, Smythe turned his battle homeward. He and others were appalled at the slaughterhouse effect of sending poorly trained volunteer troops to the Front — some of whom didn't even know what a Bren gun was. Smythe wanted to put another spur into his arch-enemy, Prime Minister Mackenzie King, so he alleged that the Canadian government was killing its own soldiers.

The prime minister was still playing a delicate political game with Quebec and responded to Smythe's charges by attempting to court-martial the bed-ridden major. The scrappy Smythe was delighted, informing King's emissary that he would retaliate by publishing the names of every soldier who had supported his stand. It would be an embarrassment the government couldn't afford.

There would be no court-martial. After Canada's defense minister went to Europe and saw that what Smythe said was true, the government changed its troop-training methods. In a very direct way, a hockey man had materially influenced the outcome of war by embarrassing the government to action, saving lives in the process.

Even though Smythe was often vilified — and rightly so — as a hypocritical martinet, he wasn't afraid to support his words with deeds. By confronting the realities of the war, and by bringing hockey to the frontlines, he had further enshrined the Leafs' patriotic mystique into the Canadian psyche, while at the same time taking a shot at the Montreal Canadiens and their pusillanimous, anti-conscription supporters. Buoyed by their blooding, the Leafs were now keen to prove that they were indeed Canada's Team.

—◆—

Though they had won the 1945 Stanley Cup, Canada's Team hit the beach flailing in 1946, even if everything said they shouldn't have. Core players Syl Apps, Gaye Stewart, Bob Goldham, Billy Taylor, Don Metz, and Ernie Dickens were back safe and sound, as was Turk Broda, with a flashy new set of teeth after taking a puck in the mouth during practice with the Canadian Forces team in the Netherlands.

The Leafs also had a wonderful young centre in Ted Kennedy, who had led the rag-tag Leafs in 1945 with 29 goals. They were lucky to have him. As a shy 16 year old in 1942, Kennedy was so overwhelmed by the bright lights and foreign tongues of Montreal that he fled the Canadiens training camp for his home in Humberstone, Ontario. He hoped his career wasn't ruined.

The following year, while Smythe was away preparing for war, his loyal lieutenant Frank Selke and coach Hap Day traded away a hot young defenseman named Frankie Edolls to get Kennedy. Smythe's fury calmed once he saw the strapping Irish Protestant lad, whom he said he could watch play "forever."

The hard-working Kennedy was a clutch player who would win the big face-off or score the winning goal. The fans loved him, and a Leaf apostle named John Arnett would shout "Come on Teed-er, come on" whenever he felt Ted Kennedy needed to save the day.

Despite Kennedy's heroics and the return of the warriors, the Leafs spent 1945–46 hovering above the cursed, cellar-dwelling Rangers and missed the playoffs completely. Indeed, Canada's Team showed a far more disturbing crack in their heroic Maple Leaf armour at the end of January 1946. NHL President "Red" Dutton made the shocking announcement that Leaf defenseman Walter "Babe" Pratt had been expelled from professional hockey — for betting on hockey.

Betting on hockey was as old as the professional game and had once been exuberantly reported in the papers as a source of pride. "The Big Train" Lionel Conacher came to Pratt's defense, saying the old Montreal Maroons would have been thrown out of the league *as a whole team* had the same law been applied to them. President Red Dutton had bet on the horses himself, hoping to help the Brooklyn Americans. His former boss "Bootlegger" Bill Dwyer used to make Dutton and the other players run a gauntlet of some of New York's finest mobsters when the team came to the Forrest Hotel to collect their paycheques.

Indeed, betting was the very thing Conn Smythe had done to build the Leafs in 1927, and Toronto was still rife with hockey betting two decades later. Not surprisingly, Maple Leaf Gardens was Toronto betting's head office, where punters would congregate in the "bull ring." This gambling area on the Church Street mezzanine was hardly a secret, and many were wondering why Pratt was singled out.

The NHL's official version was that Pratt had defied their warnings about gambling. Other NHL teams professed shock that gambling was going on in Toronto, but every NHL city had its bull rings, and the owners knew it.

Pratt had been targeted because his outspoken, impulsive *bon-homie* made him a problem for disciplinarian Conn Smythe. The problem became outright damnation when Pratt didn't run to answer Smythe's call of battle in the war. This *non serviam* linked up with the rumour that the Leafs had crashed after winning the 1945

Cup because the team was riddled with players betting against themselves.

Indeed, Ted Kennedy was one of the Leafs' star gamblers, and he and Pratt and other Leafs would lay off bets at a newsstand at the corner of Yonge and Carlton, a block away from the Gardens. Ted Kennedy hated losing bets as much as he hated losing hockey games, and the Leafs of '45 would regularly be blistered by his scorching tirades between periods about how much money their sloppy play was costing him.

Kennedy was a more valuable star than Pratt, having led the Leafs in points during their Stanley Cup season the year before. Though Pratt had set a scoring record for defensemen with 57 points that won him the 1944 Hart Trophy as league MVP, he was more expendable. The old warrior Smythe thought he would shoot Pratt *pour encourager les autres,* so when Pratt was seen giving a $20 bill to a newsboy who offered him odds that he *wouldn't* score that night, the jig was up.

The NHL court martial had picked on the wrong man, for Pratt was popular, and even hard-bitten sportswriters weighed in on his behalf. Red Dutton allowed Pratt to appeal, and the candid Babe showed up before the NHL Governors with an irresistible confession, saying he "never bet on any team except the Maple Leafs." One NHL supremo responded that he wished he had 25 players who bet on themselves every time they played.

Pratt was duly reinstated, but the fun-loving Babe's zest for the game was crushed. In March 1946 he was arrested for drunk driving, and in July he was sold to the Boston Bruins for an undisclosed amount of cash and the rights to 17-year-old Eric Pogue, "scoring ace of the Oshawa Generals." Pratt retired from the NHL the next year; Pogue never played an NHL game.

Conn Smythe later said that he regretted Pratt's "decision," as the big former railwayman had been "the best all-round defenseman the Leafs ever had," but in his contrary way, the commandant of Canada's Team had set up the fall he was now lamenting. And the Leafs rolled on.

Smythe and Hap Day had made them tougher, adding four strapping rookie defensemen to guard the blueline, including Bill Barilko, whom he'd called in from Hollywood of the Pacific Coast league. With his dark good looks and rugged play that earned him the nickname "Bashin' Bill," the fan favourite would soon add his name to Leaf mythology.

As would right winger Howie Meeker, a twice-wounded, 22-year-old war veteran who scored five goals in one game on his way to winning the 1948 Calder Trophy as the league's finest rookie.

When Montreal goaltending wizard Bill Durnan told Conn Smythe that the best centre in the league was Max Bentley, the major went out and got him in a blockbuster trade. Bentley had beat Rocket Richard the year before by one point to win his second straight scoring championship with 72 points, and his "Pony Line" in Chicago galloped through the opposition to rack up a league-leading 179 points. Bentley was a perfect fit in Toronto, and with "Teeder" Kennedy finished one-two in the playoff scoring, combining for 12 of Toronto's 38 goals.

Turk Broda led the league's goalies in both the regular season and the playoffs to win his second Vezina Trophy. The easygoing, tubby backstopper, called "The Fabulous Fatman" by his teammates, was such a clutch goalie come springtime they said he "could catch lint in a hurricane." Broda was typically self-effacing, saying he "always needed the money from the playoffs" but was probably "too dumb to realize how serious it was" to let the pressure get to him.

Toronto's Jekyll and Hyde were "Gentleman" Syl Apps and "Wild" Bill Ezinicki. Ezinicki, a five-foot-ten, 170-pound bundle of muscle, dished out unforgiving bodychecks, often following up with his fists. Opposing fans loathed him, and once in New York when Ezinicki leaned over to take a face-off, a female spectator reached over the boards and stabbed him in the buttocks with her hat-pin.

The Leafs' 33-year-old captain Syl Apps was a nobleman for whom the spoils of hockey life were as foreign as dirty play. At team parties Apps could still be one of the boys without the aid of booze or smokes. "I know they won't do me any good, but they may do me some harm," he'd laugh, and the other players would laugh back, believing him a superior being by nature. In 10 years of play, Apps had racked up a scarcely credible 56 minutes in penalties.

Syl Apps had always said he wanted to get 200 goals and then retire, but with time running out on the 1948 season, Apps was a few goals short, and Conn Smythe teased him that he'd have to play into his dotage. Apps advised his gambling boss — with a good deal of

irony, considering Babe Pratt's fate — not to put money on it, then
went out and scored nearly a goal a game.

On the final weekend of the season Apps was sitting at 198 goals, so
he scored a hat trick against the Red Wings to notch 201. The Leafs
then downed Boston in five games and swept Detroit in four to win the
1948 Stanley Cup — with Apps scoring his last of four playoff goals
in his last game. Smythe and Hap Day thought the 1947–48 Leafs
the best team ever assembled. Though Apps was gone, they weren't
finished yet.

———〰———

Toronto would win the Cup again in 1949, lose it in overtime of the
seventh game in the first round to Detroit in 1950, and be back in the
Finals in 1951. Yet there were one or two curious events en route.
"Apparently we are running a fat man's team," the dictatorial Smythe
told *The Toronto Telegram* in November of 1949. "Broda weighs 197
pounds ... I'm taking him out of the nets and he's not going back until
he shows some common sense. I am also telling four others that they'll
get the same treatment if they don't show some interest."

The real reason for Smythe's ploy was a five-game Leaf losing skid,
and he was looking for a little distraction. The postwar diet craze gave
him one, and the sporting Broda went along with it, allowing himself
to be photographed riding a sweatbike, while his perplexed wife Betty
told the *Star*, "the girls and I eat more than he does ... I think Walter is
one of those persons who is naturally inclined to be stout." Broda eventually lost the weight and made it back between the pipes for the rest
of the season, but it was one more example of Smythe's overbearing,
regimental attitude toward the man who had won the Vezina Trophy
the year before. By 1951 Broda would be sharing the net with Al
Rollins; the following season he would retire.

"Gentleman" Joe Primeau, the physical and spiritual centre of
Toronto's great "Kid Line" became the Leafs' coach, guiding them to a
second-place finish behind Detroit. Earlier in that 1951 season, the
Leafs were down 2–1 against Wings when Max Bentley got into an
astonishing conversation with a season-ticket holder named
Hemstead who sat right next to the Leaf bench. "'Max,' he said, 'if you
score a goal on the next shift, tie the game up, I'll give you a race

horse,'" Bentley recalled. "'Go on,' I said. 'I will so,' he said. Well, I scored right away and Mr. Hemstead came jumping up at the boards. 'You got the horse!' he hollered."

Bentley was the Leafs leading scorer and third in the NHL with 62 points when Toronto faced archrival Montreal Canadiens in the Stanley Cup Final. Montreal's GM Frank Selke badly wanted to bloody his tyrannical old boss Conn Smythe, and the series lived up to it, complete with glorious heroes, impossible plays, and dramatic last-second comebacks.

At the start of Game 5, Toronto was up three games to one, in a series in which every previous game had been won in overtime. Now, down 2–1 with less than a minute to go, Joe Primeau pulled the Leafs Al Rollins from goal. The Gardens was as tense as an alcoholic trying to find a drink in Hogtown on Sunday night when, with 32 seconds left, Tod Sloan scored his second goal of the game, and the fifth game went into overtime, too.

At two minutes, 53 seconds of sudden death, with the Leafs pressing in the Montreal zone, Toronto's 24-year-old defenseman Bill Barilko stretched to keep Howie Meeker's pass from sliding over the blueline. Off balance and about to go airborne, Barilko fired the puck high, right into the Canadiens' net to give Toronto its fourth Stanley Cup in five years. The crowd of 14,447 erupted as if they were hot-blooded Spaniards at the *corrida,* and Barilko's jubilant mother ran on the ice to kiss her heroic son. Frank Selke wasn't so devastated that he lost his wit. "I hate that Barilko so much," he said, "But I sure wish we had him with the Canadiens."

Four months after his overtime goal, and with the stardust just beginning to sparkle on his jersey, Bill Barilko flew with a dentist friend, Dr. Henry Hudson, to a Northern Ontario fishing vacation. They never made it. Despite a massive search for the small plane and its occupants, nothing was found.

Rumours, full of hope and fantasy, abounded. One had Barilko surviving the crash and living in the wilderness. Another had him in the Soviet Union, where he had secretly flown to pay homage to his Russian parents by coaching the Soviet hockey team. In the superstitious hockey world, people took note of the fact the Toronto Maple Leafs' did not win another Stanley Cup for 11 seasons.

It wasn't until one year after the Leafs defeated Chicago to win the world's championship and begin their next dynasty that the shroud lifted from Barilko's tomb in Northern Ontario. Investigators found a metaphor for many a hockey team in the reason for the crash: the plane had been on course for its destination; it had simply run out of fuel.

—⁓—

Canada's Team would surge in the early 1960s to challenge the Montreal Canadiens record of five consecutive Stanley Cup titles, though the next blue-and-white dynasty began with a shabby incident in the spring of 1957. When the Leafs finished just 10 points ahead of the basement-dwelling Black Hawks in March of 1957, Conn Smythe flew from his winter retreat in Florida to New York to give the hockey media his opinion. Even though the Leaf system might be "out of date," said the major, he hadn't lost confidence in his general manager Hap Day, who would be asked if he was "available" to carry on.

Day, floored by this sandbagging from his longtime friend, said it was strange after 30 years to be asked if he was "available," but "since I have been asked, I don't want the job any more." Day had been with Toronto since 1927, playing defense and forward for the team in winter, and working in Smythe's sand-and-gravel pit in summer. It was Day who advised Smythe on the building of the team and Maple Leaf Gardens; it was Day who won his first Stanley Cup with the team in 1932 as a player and five more as the Leafs' coach. He would have been "available" until his last breath, and Smythe knew it. The fearless warrior just didn't have the courage to dismiss the loyal Day in person.

Smythe's randy, boozy son Stafford took over as interim general manager. The libidinal drive of Smythe the Younger was so strong that at NHL board meetings, while owners might be using their break to have a coffee, or in Detroit's Jim Norris's case, a martini, Stafford Smythe would be lifting the skirts of some accommodating woman.

Given the old man's treachery to Day, divine justice of sorts struck the Leafs in 1958. Billy Reay, who had been a decent centre for the star-studded Canadiens in the late 1940s and early '50s, took over as the Leafs' coach, steering Canada's Team into last place with 53 points in 50 games, their worst finish since 1946. So Stafford Smythe, thinking with his brain for once, picked 40-year-old George Imlach as general manager. Imlach, who had coached Jean Beliveau's old Quebec Aces to

championships soon fired Reay to put on the coaching hat himself —
one that would manifest on Imlach's bald dome as his lucky fedora.

Splenetic, epically profane, and superstitious, Imlach had played as
a young man in Toronto's Bank leagues, then moved up to the seniors.
While playing for the Toronto Goodyears in a game at Windsor,
Imlach was leveled by a foot-and-elbow combo, whacking his head on
the ice. He came to fighting mad and swinging at his own trainer, but
his teammates managed to haul him into the dressing room, where
the manager offered him a tonic. "I didn't know what the heck it was
at the time, but it was good shot of Scotch," he recalled in his memoir
Hockey Is a Battle. "I'd never had a drink of any kind up until then.
Apparently this shot sort of fixed me up. Anyway, I'm told I got up and
went back out on the ice."

Concussed, Imlach played the third period as if he were on the
moon. After the game, and inspired by the whisky, Imlach and some
teammates went across the river to Detroit's Cork Town Tavern. They
wound up sitting next to the stage, where a slightly tipsy couple was
slow-dancing. The couple lost their balance and fell onto Imlach's
table, and, like some improbable fiction, the force of their crash
brought him back to full consciousness.

The *Toronto Telegram*'s Bunny Morganstern wrote that Imlach
had been "Punch Drunk," and kept referring to him as "Punchy
Imlach" in the paper "until some kindly old typesetter got fed up
with putting the last letter on and just left it 'Punch', which it has been
ever since."

Imlach injected life to the drooping Leafs, first signing 21-year-old
defenseman Carl Brewer. King Clancy thought the fast and gifted
stickhandler would have made a fine forward, but Imlach paired the
stormy Brewer with the tough blueliner Bobby Baun, who had come
up through Toronto's farm system two years earlier. Together, Brewer
and Baun owned the middle of the ice.

Imlach then traded Jim Morrison to Boston for 10-year NHL veteran Allan Stanley, a smooth, rushing defenseman who was known for
his heavy but clean bodychecks. Imlach paired Stanley with 29-year-
old Myles Gilbert Horton, another excellent rushing defenseman who
had been known as "Timmy" ever since boyhood, but how now went
by the more muscular "Tim," befitting his status as one of the strongest
men in the NHL.

Horton was another product of the Basilian Fathers' hockey seminary at Toronto's St. Michael's College, and the year after joining Toronto for the 1953 season, Horton made the second All-Star Team. At the end of the 1955 season, Horton badly broke his right leg and jaw in a Bill Gadsby bodycheck. Though the doctors said he was finished, Horton disagreed and became the cornerstone of the Leaf dynasty Imlach that was building.

From Montreal, Imlach bought the big left winger Bert Olmstead, who knew how to win, and in the 1960 season he got "Red" Kelly, the Norris and Lady Byng Trophy winner who had fallen out of favour with the tyrannical Jack Adams in Detroit. In an inspired move, Imlach moved Kelly from defense to centre, and the following year Kelly's 20 goals and 50 assists made him the NHL's seventh highest scorer — two points back of Gordie Howe.

In 1961, St. Michael's College sent the Leafs Dave Keon, a fast and elusive pin-wheel who, at five-foot-nine and 165 pounds, was dismissed as too fragile for the Goliaths of the NHL. Like the Little Men of Iron and Aurele Joliat before him, Keon proved that it's hard to hit a moving target, scoring 20 goals his first season while winning the Calder Trophy — and the $1,000 bonus that went with it.

In addition to his trades and his rookies, Imlach inherited a package of talent. Goalie Johnny Bower was a Billy Reay prospect dragooned into service by the Leafs from the minor leagues. In a dark irony which points up the insecurities faced by NHLers in the so-called glory days of "the Original Six," Reay was scouting Toronto's former Vezina Trophy winner Al Rollins when he found Bower. Rollins had won the Hart Trophy in 1954 with the appalling Chicago Black Hawks and had then sunk into the minors, weighed down by stress. On the night Reay was watching him, Rollins was dreadful, but his replacement was brilliant. At age 34, Johnny Bower would get his second shot in the NHL — though he didn't really want it.

Johnny Bower had cracked the NHL with the New York Rangers in the 1953–54 season, playing all 70 games for a team that finished second from the basement. Then he went back into the minor leagues, which was a more financially secure place for a guy who had grown up the hard way.

Like other backstoppers before and after him, Bower became a goalie because of circumstance: his family couldn't afford to buy him skates, so the other kids let him play in his boots. The young Bower would follow horses around in frigid Saskatchewan winters, waiting for the horse to raise its tail and turn its breakfast into a puck. Black poplar and jackpine were carved into sticks; Eaton's catalogues were rolled up for shin pads; and a friend of Bower's figured out how to make goalie pads from an old mattress and an inner tube.

Like many a poor Prairie boy, Bower lied about his age to enlist in the adventure army in 1940. He went overseas, and when he was discharged in 1944 he returned to junior hockey. The other teams complained that anyone who had spent four years in the army was too old to play junior, but since no one could find Bower's birth certificate, he played. In fact, Bower was born on November 8, 1924, and would have been approaching 20, which was junior enough.

In 1945, Bower turned pro with Cleveland and won the American League's Most Valuable Player award; he was named that league's top goalie three times and judged the best in the Western Hockey League when he spent a year in Vancouver. When Toronto "rescued" the immensely popular Bower in the minor league draft in the spring of 1958, he told them he couldn't help them. He knew his livelihood could be over with a few bad games in the unforgiving NHL.

Since each NHL team carried roughly two dozen players, there were about 140 jobs in the NHL. In a year like 1958, when Bower came up to the Leafs, there were 30 teams in the minor pro leagues just a step below the NHL. Each of those carried 23 players, making 690 minor league jobs. Add the minor pros to the NHL, and suddenly there more than 800 players after fewer than 150 jobs. Not only did this mean that a player had to be good to make it to the NHL; you also didn't have to be bad to get bounced. Coaches routinely used fear and intimidation to make players conform, and the NHL often seemed more like a despotic army than it did a hockey league. As former junior player, NHL coach, and current hockey broadcaster Harry Neale recalls, "When I was growing up in the Leaf organization, if you were a wing for the Leafs and had three forwards coming down and you got caught not being in front of one of them, you were sent to Pittsburgh."

The Leafs responded to Bower's reluctance to play for them with that time-honoured piece of hockey diplomacy: they threatened to suspend him if he didn't report. So Bower reported, and he did help the team, winning the Vezina Trophy in 1961, and sharing it with fellow Leaf Terry Sawchuk in 1965, when Bower was Toronto's *éminence grise* at age 41. Once, when traveling to the United States on a road trip, a U.S. Customs official scoffed at Bower's claim to be a goalie, saying Bower was too old. It was the kind of respect that the grizzled and stocky Bower had to put up with as an NHL star.

A great natural leader and the man whom the taskmaster Smythe called the "best captain, as a captain, the Leafs have ever had" was 29-year-old George Armstrong, a six-foot-one right winger from Skead, in Northern Ontario. Surprisingly, Smythe's bigotry didn't seem to include aboriginal people. Or perhaps it was because Armstrong would never say die that Smythe loved him.

As a boy living with his Scottish father and part-Iroquois mother near the Falconbridge Mine, Armstrong was taunted about his native background, and he was embarrassed. "He was with my mother, who was a full Indian," said Armstong's own mother, "and while George was not aware of what he was, white, Indian, or what, he was ashamed to be seen with his grandmother because she was different. That's why he told me he works so hard, so that no matter what he is, he won't ever be ashamed."

Armstrong was affectionately nicknamed "The Chief," which was more than a sobriquet since Alberta's Stoney Indian tribe had made him honourary "Big-Chief-Shoot-the-Puck" when Armstrong's senior hockey team made a western tour after winning the 1950 Allan Cup. A great two-way player, Armstrong would captain the Leafs from 1957 to the 1968 and come to rank as one of the top five Leafs in club history in goals, assists, and points.

Left winger Frank Mahovlich, one of the greatest natural goal-scorers in Leaf history, was such an impressive junior prospect in 1953 that scouts from throughout the NHL were finding a reason to make the journey to Timmins, Ontario, to try to sign the 15-year-old son of a Croatian miner. The Chicago Black Hawks offered Frank's father, Peter Mahovlich, a five-acre fruit farm on the Niagara Peninsula if his boy would sign with them, but Peter hadn't toiled in the minefields of Canada since he stepped ashore in 1929 just so he could make money off the backs of his kids. No, young Frank would take the scholarship from St. Michael's College in Toronto, and, if everything worked out, Frank would be one day become a Leaf.

That day came in 1957, when 19-year-old Frank arrived on the Big Club directly from Junior A. His father and mother came, too, for now that Frank was making proper money, he got his dad out of the mines of Timmins and into the safety of Leaside, a suburb of Toronto.

In his first season, Frank Mahovlich scored 20 goals and showed such grace and imagination that notoriously reserved Toronto fans were pulled to their feet by the force of him romancing the puck down the ice. The darkly handsome, sensitive Mahovlich was the kind of guy that women wanted, and men wanted to be. Sportswriter Stan Houston nicknamed him "The Big M"; Hap Day just called him "Moses."

In the 1961 season, the waters parted, and the Leafs crossed over to the promised land, rising from 53 points and last place in 1958 to 90 points now — just one win out of first. Playing on a line with Red Kelly and Bob Nevin, The Big M found nothing but net with 48 goals, finishing third in the scoring race with two goals less than scoring champ Boom Boom Geoffrion. It was the highest goal total in Leaf history and remained a record until Rick Vaive broke it in 1982.

Conn Smythe was delighted with this latest incarnation of champions. The major would survey the battlefield from his special box in the Gardens — a place sportswriters nicknamed the "Berchtesgaden" after Hitler's alpine lair. When the old artillery gunner saw troop activity he didn't like, he'd send messages down to coach Hap Day, reordering the grid. With Imlach, however, he had met his match. "Before I could get the message down to him, he would have done exactly what I wanted him to do," Smythe enthused. "He was the best coach I ever saw. It was as if he were a mind reader."

The Mind Reader's charges had a magnificent season. Dave Keon won the Calder Trophy; Red Kelly, the Lady Byng; and Johnny Bower pried the Vezina loose from Jacques Plante. The Leafs finished in second place, just two points back of Montreal, and 15 up on third-place Chicago. They cruised into the playoffs with visions of another dance with Lord Stanley's Jug, but were knocked out in the first round by fourth-place Detroit. Mahovlich only had one goal.

It was a devastating dose of reality. The team couldn't win the big game, and it made Conn Smythe take stock of his place at the table. Though he wanted to go out with his reflection glinting off Lord Stanley's silverware, it had been 10 seasons since the Buds had brought home their last Jug. If this crew couldn't do it, Smythe didn't know who could. Now he felt that it was time for someone else to worry about the fate of Canada's Team.

—〜〜—

In November of 1961, 66-year-old Conn Smythe resigned his commission and sold his 50,000 shares in Maple Leaf Gardens to his son, Stafford. "The Old Warrior" hoped that Stafford would one day in turn sell his shares to his own son Tom, and so the team and their house that Smythe built would remain in the family. He couldn't have been more wrong.

Stafford Smythe turned around and sold part of his shares to Toronto sportsman Harold Ballard and *Toronto Telegram* owner John Bassett, who then announced the deal on the front page of his paper even before the documents were signed. Conn Smythe, furious, gave his son a homily on the virtues of working with people who tell the truth, but in the end, he conceded. After signing the papers, "all that was left was for me to say thanks, and walk out," he said. "Game over." The long, sometimes glorious, sometimes nasty reign of the man who built the first New York Rangers, the Leafs, and Maple Leaf Gardens was finished.

Despite Smythe's gloom about the future of the Leafs, the game was far from over for a mature crew about to embark on a new Stanley Cup dynasty over the next five years. They would be called "The Leafs of Autumn."

Chicago proved a formidable opponent in 1962, for the Hawks had interrupted the Trinity's monopoly of the Stanley Cup in 1961, and they looked to do it again. They also had Bobby Hull, who had scored 50 goals that season, and was one of the game's superstar heirs apparent.

"Hull fired a shot at me from 60 feet out that was just a black blur ... heading straight for my ear," Leafs goalie Johnny Bower remembered. "I straightened up and tried to take it on my chest but it was too fast and caromed in off my forearm. It felt like I had been seared by a branding iron."

With wrists that measured nine inches in circumference and forearms like Popeye's, Hull could put so much power into a shot that his backhand — once clocked at 96 miles per hour — was 10 miles per hour faster than an average player's forehand shot. While opponents tried to stop him by means fair and often foul, Hull never fought, though he was unafraid of pain, once playing with a frozen separated shoulder, and a nose so badly broken he could hardly see out of one eye. He scored eight goals in that playoff series, including three in one game.

In addition to the mighty scoring machine that was Hull, Chicago's Stan Mikita and Kenny Wharram were among the cream of NHL forwards; defenseman Pierre Pilote and goalie Glenn Hall had made the Second All-Star team; and Hull and Mikita had made the First. Though the Leafs went up two games to nothing, Chicago tied the series at home.

Frank Mahovlich's two goals and Bob Pulford's hat trick led the Leafs to an 8–4 blowout in the fifth game in Toronto, and the sixth was a goose egg until eight minutes into the third period, when Bobby Hull scored to lift Chicago Stadium a notch or two above its customary pandemonium. But the Leafs didn't panic. A few minutes later, Toronto's Bob Nevin tied it, and Tim Horton set up Dick Duff's winner.

In the jubilant dressing room afterwards, Frank Mahovlich kissed the Stanley Cup as if it was his one true love, while Toronto displayed its glorious heroes, as custom demanded, in front of city hall. The boys in blue-and-white had won their first Jug since 1951, the year of Bill Barilko's heroic overtime goal, the year the young defenseman had gone missing in a plane crash. Canada's Team was back on top.

Yet to show just how different the Leafs' new managerial order was to the old, a boozy gathering in a Royal York hotel suite after the All-Star game dinner in October of 1962 cast Canada's Team into a sleazier light, one that also caught the glint of gold that would soon be in the NHL players' futures.

Leaf partner Harold "Pal Hal" Ballard found himself enjoying the liquid hospitality of Jim Norris, and soon Norris was bidding upwards from $250,000 for the services of the still-unsigned Frank Mahovlich. When the figure hit $1 million, Ballard said they had a deal, and Norris peeled off 10 $100 bills as deposit.

The next morning, the Leaf brass treated the whole matter as the price of having a drink with a man like Norris, whose worth was $250 million. The laughing stopped when Chicago GM Tommy Ivan showed up at Maple Leaf Gardens with a cheque for $1 million. Stafford Smythe panicked, and said he could do nothing until he called a directors' meeting. Tommy Ivan phoned his boss at the Royal York to give him the news. Punch Imlach later said you could hear Jimmy Norris's opinion of this craven reneging all the way from Front Street to the Gardens.

Stafford Smythe laughed off Norris as a publicity stunt. "No human being is worth $1,000,000 — to buy or sell," he said, but Harold Ballard admitted he had "$1,000 in my pocket right now confirming the deal." Clarence Campbell, doubtless under the gun from other owners to shoot down this mad dog in the street, said an offer was made, but "no responsible (i.e., sober) officer of the Leafs accepted."

The players were agog, but not so far gone that they couldn't figure out what this would mean for them. "If we get him the club will be worth two and a half million dollars," joked Chicago's Pierre Pilote. "We already have our million dollar babies — Bobby Hull, Bill Hay, and Murray Balfour. I guess the rest of the team is worth $500,000." Jolly Jack Adams saw the future all too clearly, saying, "This has been bad for the sport."

While people picketed Maple Leaf Gardens with signs pleading for management not to sell Frank, some papers accused Norris of trying to get a little ink. Others suggested with tongue-in-cheek that Mahovlich should take the offer as an insult, considering $1.25 million was paid for a thoroughbred racehorse in 1955.

Mahovlich responded by finishing fourth in the scoring race — two points and one place better than the year before. The Leafs, however, finished second. Punch Imlach wanted to be first, and decided to deal with an old devil: Eddie Shore.

The riotous four-time Boston Bruin Hart Trophy winner was now the hardy 61-year-old owner of the Springfield Indians of the American League, and a man for whom Imlach had once coached. Though he unfailing addressed his colleagues as "Mister," Shore's frugality and unorthodox training methods still send shudders through players who suited up for the Indians, and his rigorous dealings both on and off the ice meant that the Leafs were not going to get away easy.

The object of Punch Imlach's affection was Kent Douglas, a 26-year-old defenseman from Cobalt, Ontario. Mr. Shore said that he would be happy to deal with Mr. Imlach — provided the Leafs sent him five players in return for Douglas. In the end, they did. Kent Douglas would win the Calder Trophy as 1963's top rookie, and the Leafs would accomplish Imlach's goal—finishing in first place, one point ahead of Chicago.

The Leafs swept through the injured Montreal Canadiens in five games, then beat Detroit in five. Johnny Bower was a 38-year-old marvel in net, posting two shutouts and allowing only 16 goals in 10 games. In the two series, Toronto got goals from practically the whole team.

Frank Mahovlich, the man whose inspired play during the season helped the team finish first, played through the finals with a bum knee and the effects of the flu. He scored no goals and managed only two assists on the Leafs 31 playoff goals, and the Toronto fans booed him. It was a turn of events that would characterize the relationship between Mahovlich and the Leafs for the next five years.

Society was emerging from its postwar neuroses, and for the first time the change was global, preaching peace and love and the dignity of the individual. Of course, not everyone heard. Carl Brewer had made First Team All-Star in 1963 and thought he deserved a raise. Punch Imlach thought not, so Brewer hired a brash, competitive, young lawyer who had grown up with him and the Leafs' Baun and Pulford in the west end of Toronto.

Alan Eagleson was keen to catch the attention of hockey players, and he advised Brewer to withhold his services and to continue his education. When the Leafs' brains trust saw a picture of the All-Star defenseman wearing a football uniform at McMaster University, Brewer's raise was forthcoming.

The following year, Tim Horton further enraged Imlach when he started a chain of donut shops to provide a source of income for his retirement—like most other players, having no faith in the NHL pension system. Imlach would berate Horton about his commitment to the game, sarcastically wondering aloud if donuts were more important than hockey. Horton responded by bringing a box of stale donuts to practice and used them as pucks.

In mid-December, 1963, The Big M had scored only two goals in three weeks. Punch Imlach loudly condemned Mahovlich while praising his former protégé, Jean Beliveau. Punch Imlach had long been riding Mahovlich, mispronouncing his sensitive star's name as "Ma-hal-o-vich." Imlach believed the way to cure inconsistent genius was to pummel it into submission, making The Big M practise after everyone else had gone home, along with all the other pressures that twice put his complicated star in hospital with depression, something Imlach thought was just weakness.

Even so, Imlach needed to get his star player back to form, and in February 1964, he acquired the Rangers star Andy Bathgate, thinking this might be the spark to fire up Mahovlich. Imlach put Bathgate on a line with Mahovlich and Kelly, then moved The Big M to centre. Finally, on March 8, 1964, Mahovlich ended a 12-game drought with two goals against Chicago. When the season was over, Bathgate finished fourth in the scoring race and Mahovlich fourteenth.

Toronto finished solidly in third place — five points ahead of Detroit — but it was the Leafs and the Wings who made it to the 1964 Stanley Cup Final. Detroit coach Sid Abel relaxed his team by taking them to Toronto's Fort Erie Race Track on their off day; Punch Imlach worked his players hard, even though veterans like Stanley, Armstrong, and Kelly were in their mid-to-late 30s, and Johnny Bower was nearly 40.

Imlach's methods paid off, as Detroit's big line of Gordie Howe, Norm Ullman, and Alex Delvecchio was held to four goals in seven games. The sixth game, however, was the one that would catapult the Leafs' Bob Baun into hockey lore. The Leafs were down three games to two and trailing by the same score in Game 6 when Leaf centre Bill Harris tied it. After a scoreless third period, the teams headed into overtime.

Baun had been taken to the dressing room with a possible broken ankle, but he refused to have it x-rayed. The ankle was frozen. Baun was out there on the second shift of overtime. Bob Pulford controlled the puck in the Detroit end and passed it back to Baun on the blueline. Baun shot the puck at the net, and Terry Sawchuk adjusted his angle.

Just then, Detroit defenseman Bill Gadsby got between the puck and Sawchuk, and it banked in off his skate. Baun's goal had saved the Leafs, and they blanked Detroit 4–0 at home to win their third straight Stanley Cup. Bob Baun then had his ankle x-rayed. It was broken.

———

Though the maple leaf would officially become Canada's symbol on the new national flag in 1965, it did not augur well for Toronto, as the

Leafs were eliminated in six games by their archrival Montreal Canadiens in the first round of the 1965 Stanley Cup Finals. The following year, the Canadiens would again bounce the Leafs in round one, sweeping "The Leafs of Autumn" in four games. It looked as if time had finally been called on Canada's Team.

Ironically, the apparent death knell came when Canada was celebrating her hundredth birthday in 1967. Despite the old hostilities between French and English, the nation was in the mood for a party. Expo '67 was about to open in Montreal; "centennial projects" abounded; and Canadians were feeling confident about what their big rich country could accomplish in its next 100 years. After all, Canada's Prime Minister Wilfrid Laurier had in 1910 famously said that "the twentieth century belongs to Canada." Maybe his prediction was going to come true at last.

Predictions of the Leafs' demise had not come true, as the Buds were back in the hunt for silver. For hockey fans, the 1967 Stanley Cup Final was too good to be true, a national birthday present for all those who loved Canada's Team, and for those who loved Canada's Other Team. Toronto had eliminated Chicago in six games; Montreal was in an even greater hurry to meet the Leafs, dispatching New York in four straight.

Not much had been expected of the Leafs in the 1967 Stanley Cup final, and with Bower and Stanley now over 40, and Kelly, Armstrong, Sawchuk, and Horton on the wrong side of 35, newspapers called the team "The Over the Hill Gang," or "The Old Folks Athletic Club." Leaf rookie Mike Walton told Bower that his father had a picture of him at home. Bower thought that it was nice of the rookie's father to be such a devoted fan, until Walton reminded him that his father and Bower had been teammates in Cleveland in the 1940s.

After Montreal won the first game 6–2 against an unusually generous Terry Sawchuk, it looked like the skeptics were right. Yet Johnny Bower — who had shared the Vezina with teammate Terry Sawchuk two seasons earlier — was not going to let anything get past him, and Toronto won the second game 3–0. They came home to a glum Toronto, who suspected that this ancient cohort were about to go down valiantly, but the Leafs had other plans. The third game was a goalies' battle, with the Habs' young Rogie Vachon stopping 62 shots, and Bower, 54, before Bob Pulford won it for Toronto eight minutes into the second overtime period.

A cruel bolt of time struck down Bower in Game 4 when he injured his groin in the pre-game warm-up. Terry Sawchuk went in as his replacement and had a bad game. The Canadiens won 6–2. After Sawchuk's drubbing, a fan sent him a telegram asking "How much did you get?"

Sawchuk, profoundly hurt by the fan's cruelty, responded with the form that had made him a four-time Vezina winner. Toronto beat Montreal 4–1 and went home ahead three games to two. They could now win the prize that no one expected them to win — at Maple Leaf Gardens.

George Armstrong and Allan Stanley felt confident of the Leafs' chances, knowing that if the old boys could survive Imlach's regular season practices, they could survive to win the Cup. For youngsters like Ron Ellis, the dressing room was electric when "Punch" Imlach came in bearing a box of money, which represented the team's playoff bonuses. "This is what you're playing for," said Imlach, which was both true and a kick to their pride as players. They were playing to win.

And winning they were, up 2–1 with less than a minute left in the game. The Canadiens pulled Vachon and sent out an extra man for a face-off in the Toronto zone. When Foster Hewitt, then in his forty-fourth year of hockey broadcasting, called out that George Armstrong had scored into an empty net, the country — and the Maple Leafs — knew they had won the Stanley Cup, their fourth in six seasons.

The Leafs had never been able to equal Montreal's superlative five consecutive Stanley Cups, but they had put together a pair of three-straight runs, and added another four Cup wins between 1942 and 1967. The centennial victory was the end of their dynastic reign. It was also the end of the "Original Six" and "The Trinity."

The NHL had its sights on the United States once again, and a whole new era of expansion would open up the league. No more would three teams be able to dominate the way Toronto, Montreal, and Detroit had done. Now, there would be more teams and more players and much, much more money competing for Lord Stanley's prize. It would be the beginning of hockey's modern era. And of hockey's own nostalgia for an innocence it only imagined that it had lost.

9

THE AGE OF ORR

He would change everything. The way hockey was played, the way it was paid, the way it was beautiful, and the way it was sad. The story of Orr is not only the tale of a magnificent player, but the story of professional hockey entering its "modern era." Technicians will say modernity happened when the redline came to be in the 1940s, but those who look at the long arc of the game know that it really happened when Bobby Orr met Alan Eagleson and began the professional relationship that would re-cast the hockey world on and off the ice into something much bigger, and gilded, and in the end, tarnished. But when it all began, Bobby Orr was about glorious promise, and there were many who were counting on him to keep it.

Bobby Orr was heralded by desperate hockey fans throughout New England before he'd even worn a Bruins jersey. Between Boston's 1941 Cup win and 1970, the Bruins had appeared in the Cup Final only five times, with their last tilt at the Jug coming in 1958. From 1960 through 1967, Boston finished dead last in the standings six out of eight times. The two years they weren't at the absolute bottom, they were second last. But in the mid-1960s there was a nascent joy in the land because a saviour was on the way.

Such was Bobby Orr's stature that he was famous when he was just eight years old. An opposing coach once tried to fire up his charges by brandishing a piece of paper bearing Orr's spidery childish signature. "How can anyone who signs his name like this play hockey?" thundered the coach to a bunch of Grade Two's, who probably saw Orr's handwriting as completely normal. Then they stepped out on the ice to confront a player who wasn't normal at all.

In 1960, Bruins' GM Lynn Patrick, along with Wren Blair, a coach for their minor league affiliate in Kingston, had been scouting two 14-year-old players at an All-Ontario bantam tournament when they saw a five-foot-two, 110-pound, 12-year-old peewee who was skating rings around the older boys. They couldn't take their eyes off this kid who owned the ice, and Blair ran down to rinkside to find out two things: the miracle kid's name, and whether or not any NHL team "owned" his rights.

To the Bruins' delight, Robert Gordon Orr was free, and they would make him theirs. "There were players in the NHL who couldn't feather a pass the way Orr did that night," Patrick recalled in Orr's autobiography *Bobby Orr: My Game*. Those who saw Orr play believed the kid could have led Boston right then and there.

Boston, despite its years in the wilderness, knows its hockey, and any lippy Detroit Red Wing had better wear armour before saying that he hailed from Hockeytown while in Boston. Variations of the game had long been played in New England, with newspaper references to embryonic forms of the game going back to the eighteenth century. When the NHL moved into the United States in 1924, its first stop was Boston, long a championship home to amateur hockey.

After millionaire Charles Adams saw — who else? — Howie Morenz and his Canadiens play the Calgary Tigers for the 1924 Stanley Cup, he had stars in his eyes, and Boston got a franchise. Soon the stars were on ice, as the Bruins lit up the 1920s and '30s with a "who's who" of the era: in goal, the stingy "Tiny" Thompson and equally miserly Frank "Mr. Zero" Brimsek; on defense, showman Eddie Shore and big Lionel Hitchman; at forward, the "Dynamite Line" of Aubrey "Dit" Clapper, Ralph "Cooney" Weiland, Norman "Dutch" Gainor, and the "Kraut Line" of Milt Schmidt, Woody Dumart, and Bobby Bauer. Guided by the managerial gifts of Art Ross, himself one of early hockey's pioneer stars, the Bruins had finished first in either their division or the league nine times en route to their three Stanley Cups in 1928, 1939, and 1941. Boston was a town that had seen glory before.

And couldn't see it soon enough again. The Bruins quickly befriended Orr's family in Parry Sound, Ontario, half-way up the eastern edge of Georgian Bay. Boston came in noble altruism, wanting only to protect the Orrs from other teams, or rather, from the fanged predators who ruthlessly wanted to exploit the hockey genius of Mr. and Mrs. Orr's son.

So, in 1962, Bobby Orr signed a "C" form — a standard contract that gave Boston his hockey rights for life. While any other player then signing a "C" form would have received a $100 bonus, the Orr family wrung $2,800 out of the Bruins, including $900 worth of new stucco to the family home. The deal also included a second-hand car — which Bobby was still too young to drive — and the promise of a new wardrobe, about which Boston later forgot. It was a memory lapse that would later prove very expensive.

The year after Orr signed with the Bruins, a young Toronto lawyer and member of the provincial parliament came to speak at a sports banquet near Parry Sound. Orr's father, remembering the Bruins' failed promise to give Bobby a wardrobe, saw a potential protector in this lawyer. So he gave Alan Eagleson a test, asking him if he could get his son a $10 living expense raise from his Oshawa junior team. Eagleson failed the test, but he wore failure as easily as he might wear a necklace of cement. Eagleson wanted to win for Bobby Orr. And the relationship that would revolutionize pro hockey had begun.

Bobby Orr skated rings around his junior hockey colleagues, averaging 33 goals a season — an astonishing total for a defenseman. Such was his promise that he even appeared on the cover of *Maclean's*, a national Canadian newsmagazine, as a 17 year old. But Orr was no swaggering teenage star. While billeted in Oshawa, 125 miles southeast of Parry Sound, Orr would cry with homesickness. In summers he would hurry back north to top up his meagre living allowance by working for the local butcher, or in a clothing store, or as a bellhop.

Meanwhile, the Boston papers and the Bruins themselves hailed him as Moses, the man who would lead the Bruins to the promised land. When Orr turned 18 in 1966, his father announced he would be turning professional. He would not be going alone, for Alan Eagleson would now get another chance to do the thing he liked best: win.

Eagleson's meddling was sacrilege to Boston, for the Bruins, sniffed the team's general manager "Hap" Emms, were not prepared to meet with any "lawyer." Alan Eagleson was not just any lawyer, but a cross between the smarts and fearlessness of a Ted Lindsay and a Doug

Harvey, along with the knavery of every horse-trading, underhanded owner who had every existed.

Underneath Hap Emms's superior dismissal of the lawyer lurked genuine fear, for Eagleson's reputation was already making owners quake. For decades, the NHL owners had treated the players like idiot servants, who should know enough to be grateful for their bounty. Indeed, the players are still blamed for their own servitude, and Gordie Howe, and to a lesser extent Maurice Richard, are the immortals accused of keeping hockey salaries in the Golden Age of the Original Six a little less than golden. Because they were seen as "the best" in the league, no other player would dare to ask for more money than the Rocket or Mr. Hockey.

Then again, most players didn't even know how much money Howe and Richard took home because both the NHL and its clubs were obsessed with keeping salaries secret. Today, kids trading hockey cards in the schoolyard know the salaries of the players they're trading. In Cyclone Taylor's time, newspapers crowed over the salary battles and triumphs of the game's early stars. But during hockey's "golden years," money was a forbidden subject, for the owners knew that they were sitting on a gold mine, and if the players ever found out, there could be serious unrest among the miners.

Players were made to think of their salaries in the way they thought of their conjugal intimacies — as no one's business but their own. While you might tell your best mate on the team about a night of magic with your wife, you certainly wouldn't broadcast it around the locker room, and you would never, ever mouth off about it to the enemy. It would be a treason for which they hadn't yet devised punishment.

So each season, Gordie Howe would accept his $1,000 raise and take comfort in the fact that the rest of the Wings were only getting a quarter of that. Since he was four times as good, it made the world order seem just. Until one day in 1968, when Bob Baun, a players' association activist, was traded to Detroit. Howe asked Baun how much he thought Mr. Hockey was making. Baun's answer "$49,500" startled Howe, because it was presciently close to the true amount. When Baun then told Howe that he, just an All-Star defenseman, was pulling in $67,000, Howe was stunned.

So Baun gave him a pep talk, reminding Howe that as the best player in the league, he was worth at least $150,000. Howe, inspired, angry, went to see Bruce Norris, and all of his old insecurities about being the class dummy came flooding back. So Howe only asked for $100,000 — and Norris gave it to him. Howe, now triply shocked, asked Norris a question. Why, after 22 seasons, was he was agreeing to this huge raise? "Gordie," said Norris, speaking for his brethren of owners, "you never asked for anything more. I'm a businessman."

Bob Baun was an old hand at shaking up the established order, for it was he and fellow Toronto Maple Leafs Carl Brewer and Bob Pulford who had first hired their childhood friend Eagleson to help negotiate their contracts. The players soon learned that they had just opened the vault — but it would be years before anyone realized the vault was Pandora's box.

As hockey's latest young messiah, Bobby Orr was going to be Alan Eagleson's ticket to paradise, and the lawyer wasn't about to let the sensitivities of NHL GMs ruin his trip. Eagleson didn't stand on subtlety, himself being an incendiary mix of contradictions: more profane than a sailor's parrot, more competitive than the professional athletes he represented, and still, the Toronto lawyer wore a suit and tie and spoke respectfully to the NHL Board of Governors. It was a ruse that belied little of his inner fury, or his credo that if you hit an opponent (who might not even know he was an opponent) with everything you had on the first blow, the battle would be won.

There are hundreds of nasty Eagleson stories, but one from his college days reveals the essence of his tactics. When Eagleson was a University of Toronto law student, he took up lacrosse. One day, a basketball team showed no hurry to surrender the gym to let Eagleson's lacrosse team practice, so he loudly told the "faggot" basketball players to make a move. When a ball-player asked Eagleson if he had a practice permit, Eagleson decked him with a punch, and said, "There's my permit."

Eagleson's reputation as a big league dragon-slayer began in 1966 when he triumphed, appropriately, over the former Boston Bruin legend Eddie Shore. The sport's first "Mr. Hockey" had transformed the eccentric ferocity of his playing days into a part-genius, part-monster role as owner of the Springfield Indians, and NHL coaches used the threat of sending a troublesome player to Springfield as a behaviour modification tool.

Shore was a well-meaning despot. He would perform self-taught chiropractics on players, often injuring them with some hare-brained stab at spinal manipulation. He would make his teams practise in the dark to save electricity. He would forbid them strength-sapping sex with their women. He'd tie goalies' heads to the crossbar of the goal net so they wouldn't "flop." Once, he even traded a player for a hockey net, then complained that the net was "used."

Shore could indeed be a tyrant, but Eagleson's role as the emancipator of the hockey serfs has been raised to mythic proportions. Even though Shore's teams had won three straight American League championships from 1959 through 1962, and former players credited him with being the best hockey teacher they ever had, by the mid-1960s Shore had suffered his fourth heart attack and his relationship with his players became harsh and arbitrary. The players, cheered by the job prospects of NHL expansion in 1967, told Shore they wanted a raise, or they would withhold their services.

Shore kicked them out of his office, and his team went on strike. Shore brought in replacement players and threatened to sue his own team for breach of contract. So Brian Kilrea, the striking players' go-between, called Alan Eagleson.

Eagleson made the players swear affidavits about their sufferings under Shore, then presented them to Springfield's manager Jack Butterfield — who also happened to be Eddie Shore's nephew. As interim president of the American Hockey League, Butterfield put on his two hats and went to reason with his uncle.

Shore, furious, threatened to fire his nephew, but Butterfield stood firm. Clearly worried about his uncle's health, Butterfield went back to Eagleson and stressed Eddie Shore's delicate physical condition. Then, to Butterfield's astonishment, Eddie Shore stepped down as Springfield boss without ever talking to Eagleson. But the legend of Al Eagleson was born.

So it was as conqueror of the Beast of Springfield that the 33-year-old Eagleson was seen by the NHL owners. Or rather, a typically Canadian conqueror, a seemingly polite, University of Toronto law grad who could — and would — easily mix with the owners at their country clubs, unlike the fractious union fixers "destroying" baseball and football in the United States.

By the time Alan Eagleson had the golden boy Orr as his bargaining ace, the Bruins' had another problem: the success of their own propaganda. They had been promising the coming salvational glory of Orr for years, and the natives were more than restless.

When Hap Emms dared to offer Orr $10,250 over two seasons, Eagleson treated this as 40 acres and a mule. With no small contempt he reminded Emms that the New York Jets had signed football rookie Joe Namath for *$400,000* over three years in 1965. Warming to his kill, Eagleson merrily ventured that Orr didn't *have* to play for Boston right now — he could finish school. Or play for the Canadian National Team. Or, follow the zeitgeist and join an ashram if he wanted. Orr had time, but the Bruins did not.

Eagleson's belligerent strategy worked. In September 1966, the young god and his demon-buster lounged aboard Hap Emms's yacht, signing the largest rookie contract yet seen in the NHL. Bobby Orr would receive a $80,000 over two years, including a $25,000 signing bonus. Hap Emms, made distinctly unlike his nickname by the precedent he had just set, refused to pose in the celebratory picture. Bobby Orr didn't care: he knew that Emms would be smiling before too long.

In his first NHL season, Bobby Orr scored 13 goals and added 28 assists to win the Calder Trophy as rookie of the year, and he was voted to the Second All-Star Team. New York's 36 year-old Harry Howell, the 1967 Norris Trophy winner as the NHL's best defenseman, saw the future with great clarity. "I'm glad I won [the Norris] now," said Howell, "because it's going to belong to Orr from now on."

Indeed, the Norris Trophy belonged to Orr for the next eight seasons, but he owned much more than that. He owned the ice. The Montreal Canadiens' ace Jean Beliveau said that when Orr debuted as an 18 year old, he had "maturity and hockey sense" far beyond his years. Indeed, Orr's first NHL goal came against the Habs one October Thursday night when Orr lasered a slapshot from the blueline into the Montreal net. The faithful in the Boston Garden stood in ovation at the messiah's first miracle. Canadiens' coach Toe Blake, once a flashy goalscorer himself, just said, "I ain't ever seen anything like it."

While Bobby Orr changed the business of hockey, his greatest impact came in how he changed the game. There had been rushing defensemen before him, necessitated by the "no forward pass" rule that had dominated hockey until 1918–19, when the blueline was widely adopted. With the addition of the redline in 1943–44, defensemen would headman the puck up to streaking forwards, then hang back to protect their zone.

Bobby's Orr gift—like that of Cyclone Taylor and Howie Morenz and Pavel Bure—was speed. He could do everything well, and he could do it fast, rushing up from his own blueline, stickhandling through traffic, then laying off a beautiful pass, or making a glorious deke and shooting the puck himself. Opponents had to react faster, and the one who reacts is always under more pressure because he's also trying to anticipate.

But it's hard to anticipate genius. Even Jacques Plante, a genius himself who wasn't given to hyperbole, saw Orr as a marvel. "You say about each of the great players: he's a good skater, or a particularly good stickhandler, or he has a great shot, but something is always missing" said Plante. "Bobby Orr has it all. He is the best I've seen. Ever."

Teams playing against Orr had to learn to do things differently. They had to get a man out to the point faster on face-offs in their own end, to cover Orr. When forechecking, teams used to send two men deep to pressure the defense and keep a third man at the blueline to cut off a pass. Because Orr was so fast, the two-man forecheck would frequently get trapped as Number 4 stickhandled past them to lead the rush the other way, with the Bruins now outnumbering the opposition.

If he wanted to, Bobby Orr could simply pull deeper into his own zone and draw the forecheckers in, then send one of his seeing-eye passes up the ice to an unmarked teammate. And those tough-guys who thought they'd pound a little fear into Orr soon learned that his hands were fast outside his gloves, too. In his rookie season, Orr thumped noted Rangers' pugilists Vic Hadfield and Reggie Fleming, and Montreal's Ted Harris. He indeed had it all, and when a frustrated Gordie Howe was asked what Orr's best move was, Howe looked at his questioner with incredulity and said, "Just putting on his fucking skates."

The Orr Effect dominated all, including Orr, whose own talent transcended team boundaries. Once, in a game against the Washington Capitals, Bobby Orr was watching the Caps get into position for a face-off. The Washington centre directed a rookie defenseman to move farther to his right, and the player moved. Then he caught Bobby Orr's eye, and Orr shook his head: the kid had been correct the first time, and Orr motioned him to move left. Astonishingly, the young Washington player believed his opponent, such was Orr's integrity. And when Washington won the face-off, the puck popped back to the Cap's rookie, just as Orr knew it would.

The generation that knew Bobby Orr thrilled to his mercurial ice-long rushes toward the enemy goal, rising to their feet as he cut through the gap between the boards and opposing defenseman the way a kid cuts through a hedge. The hedge, however, is not 200 pounds of whipcord muscle trying to atomize the moving target, and people soon learned that Bobby Orr was not invincible.

In his rookie season, Orr's poetry-in-motion was pinned to the boards by Detroit defenseman Marcel Pronovost, and he went down hard. His first knee operation — to scrape away bone chips and bits of cartilage — came in August 1968, and two months later came his second, again to clean out ravaged cartilage and bone. Even now, at the beginning of his professional glory, the shadows on 20-year-old Bobby Orr's brilliant career were growing longer.

—⁓—

Bobby Orr's celestial talents pulled the Bruins upward, from last place in 1967 with 44 points to second in the East Division in 1969, with 100. Orr's 1968 contract renewal sent NHL salaries rocketing upward. When shocked newspapers reported that Eagleson had negotiated $400,000 over three years for Orr, other players started to think in fractions, calculating themselves two-fifths or half as good as Orr, and demanding appropriate raises.

Even though Orr's new deal was actually closer to $200,000, the damage had been done. Bobby Hull went on strike at the beginning of the 1969 season until Chicago hauled an estimated $100,000 out of the vault to sign him.

As in pro hockey's earlier years, the revolution couldn't have happened without the United States, and a god that it now served called TV. Television had at once shrunk and exploded the global village, bringing war and suffering into the dinner hour and galvanizing public opinion like nothing before it ever had. The tube also made us long for escape and diversion with programs like the *Tommy Hunter Show,* and *Laugh-In,* and *Hockey Night in Canada.*

The TV networks' scramble to capture the time and money of North America's sports fans grew dizzying. The NHL's old guard of Governors had opposed expansion throughout the early 1960s — convinced that additional teams would ruinously deplete the talent pool, create an insane travel schedule, and be unprofitable to boot.

Their thinking changed radically when the American Football League — the National Football League's *arriviste* competitor — struck a five-year, $35 million deal with NBC. American TV executives baldly announced the Western Hockey League had as good a chance of getting a television contract as the NHL did, unless the National Hockey League became something more than a regional pro sport.

So the NHL gave itself a fiftieth birthday present in 1967 by launching the largest expansion it had yet seen in order to catch hold of some of that TV money. League president Clarence Campbell announced that the "Original Six" would now take to the ice against a whole new division of teams from Minnesota, Pittsburgh, Philadelphia, St. Louis, Los Angeles, and Oakland in a "truly North American" league — without any new Canadian teams.

Since the newcomer teams were all in the same division, the much-vaunted "parity" that the NHL sought to create was a relative thing. So, too, was NHL hockey's new labour force, for expansion had doubled the number of hockey jobs to around 240. Of these puck-chasers, Alan Eagleson represented 180, mainly by default, since he had no competition.

He did, however, have opposition all around the league. The parochial and conservative world of hockey was kicking and screaming at the revolution within. Toronto's Punch Imlach, who hated the idea of unions, had refused to talk to Eagleson in contract negotiations because Eagleson wasn't a hockey player. It's safe to bet that Imlach would have changed his mind had Bobby Orr wanted to play closer to home, in Toronto.

By the turn of the decade that would be known, not always seriously, as the "Heavenly Seventies," the Boys from Beantown were a rising powerhouse built around the best hockey player in the game. Because of Orr's offensive gifts, Boston created the "four-man attack," which was a forward line, plus Orr. One of his "linemates" was Johnny

Bucyk, who had come to Bruins in the 1958 season. Boston coach Milt Schmidt had put Bucyk on the left wing of fellow Ukrainian-Canadians Vic Stasiuk and Bronco Horvath, and the "Uke Line" led Boston to the 1958 Stanley Cup Finals before the roof caved in and left the Bruins in ruins.

Nicknamed "The Chief" by a Boston cartoonist who thought his face truer to Alberta's badlands than to the steppes of the Ukraine, Bucyk made the best of the Bruins' eight-year hibernation by averaging more than 20 goals a year, and twice finishing among the top 10 goalscorers. By the time Bobby Orr arrived, Bucyk was ready, and in the first half of the 1967–68 season he helped generate a scoring run that shot the Bruins from last place to first. Though they would finish in third at the end of that season, there was cause for hope.

That hope was nudged by an astonishing trade that gave Orr even more talent from which to feed his own: Chicago sent over one Phil Esposito, a 25-year-old centre who had scored 71 goals in his three full seasons with the Hawks, but who was accused of "choking" in the 1967 playoffs. After finishing the season in seventh place in the scoring race, Esposito didn't notch a single point in six playoff games.

Esposito had learned about his trade in a rather shabby fashion when the Hawks' press officer called the news to Esposito's wife, who then phoned him. Esposito was so stunned he had to call her back. Then, white with shock, he called CJIC-TV in his hometown of Sault Ste. Marie, Ontario, to give them the scoop.

When viewers tuned in, they were appalled not only to hear of the trade, but to hear it from the source: "Hi sports fans, this is Phil Esposito. Yours truly has been traded to Boston with Ken Hodge and Fred Stanfield for Gilles Marotte, Pit Martin, and Jack Morris. This is no hoax." When the man whom Esposito had helped to set a goalscoring record heard the news, he was inconsolable. "I lost my right arm," Bobby Hull lamented. "My right arm."

At six-foot-one and 215 pounds, Esposito would park his hulking frame 20 feet out from the net in the goalscorer's brief kingdom called "the slot" and wait for the puck. He would shrug off the burly defensemen who tried to move him as if they were bantam shinny players. There, he'd stay put until the puck found his stick, and then its way into the net. Bobby Orr joked that Esposito rented the slot from the Boston Garden.

With Orr blasting pucks from the blue line, and Wayne Cashman and Ken Hodge digging them out of the corner, Esposito would take the pucks that came his way and flick his wrist in a "snap shot." In his first season with the Bruins, "Espo" scored 35 times, while assisting on another 49.

The following year, Esposito became the first player to crack the hitherto unattainable 100-point barrier, scoring 49 goals and 77 assists to win the Hart Trophy as MVP and the Art Ross Trophy with 126 points — the highest the NHL had ever seen.

Esposito was also a cut-up, keeping teammates loose with his banter and blue-collar wit, once joking that if hockey hadn't got in his way, he'd have driven a truck, as he did in the summers when he played for Chicago. "I had to," he said, "given the money the Black Hawks were paying me."

When it came to superstition, Esposito was the most serious man in the league. On entering the Bruins' dressing room, he'd wink at a red horn hanging above his stall, a gift from his Neapolitan granny to ward off *malocchio* — the evil eye. He'd put his black T-shirt on inside-out and backward, then pin a St. Christopher medal to his suspenders. Boston's trainer would sprinkle baby powder on the blade of his stick, while Phil scanned the room for any crossed sticks, a sure sign of doom. And then he would go out and score goals.

The NHL expansion had created jobs for players, and in Boston and Philadelphia, especially, it had created jobs for players who were big and tough. The defending Cup champions, the Canadiens, were neither, and in 1969–70, Montreal finished tied with New York for the fourth playoff spot, each with 38 wins, 22 losses, and 16 ties. The Rangers, however, would advance, and the mighty Habs would have an early spring for the first time in 22 years. With the last-place finish of the Toronto Maple Leafs, there would be no Canadian team in the playoffs for the first time in Stanley Cup history.

Expansion had changed the format of the Stanley Cup playoffs, where the champions of each division would now meet in the Final, giving the new teams a quick chance for glory. The Bruins had entered the 1970 playoffs in a hurry, and none more so than Orr, who, with 87 assists and 33 goals, had broken Esposito's record for assists and his own record for goals by a defenseman.

After mauling their way through New York and Chicago, Boston had the St. Louis Blues down three games to nothing in the Stanley Cup Final, with the fourth game going into overtime on Mother's Day, 1970.

The Boston Garden was a greenhouse, with steam rising off the ice in 90-degree humidity. The players were sapped, and, as with all athletes facing sudden death, they wanted to end it quickly. The clock had not ticked off a minute of overtime when Bobby Orr blocked a clearing pass deep in the St. Louis zone, then slid the puck to Derek Sanderson in a give-and-go.

If television had not been around to record and replay the moment, it is tempting to wonder how we would remember one of the most famous goals in Stanley Cup history: Orr speeding toward the net, Sanderson whipping the puck onto his stick, and Orr snapping the twine a heartbeat before he trips courtesy of St. Louis defenseman Noel Picard and goes airborne.

"The Goal" has stuck in the popular hockey imagination in a way that it never could have done had it come down to the world through radio or a still photograph in a newspaper. Though nothing out of the ordinary in its execution but for Orr's spectacular post-goal launch, the image of Orr flying through the air with his arms raised in triumph becomes more worthy of any Greek hero-god every time it gets replayed on television.

Orr's goal was spectacular, though, as the culmination of a season in which he had rewritten the NHL record books. Winner of the Art Ross scoring title with 120 points, the Hart Trophy, the Norris Trophy, and the Conn Smythe Trophy as the most valuable post-season player, Bobby Orr had become the first man to win all four trophies in the same year. And he was 22 years old.

As others had been before him, Orr was now the most exalted player in the game. Everyone wanted to touch the hem of his jersey, and Eagleson had snagged endorsement deals for his young client with General Motors, Yardley of London, General Foods, Bic Pens, Munro Games, Crestliner Boats, and Labatt's. Yet Bobby wouldn't be swigging down Blue in between periods the way Didier Pitre used to revive himself with champagne — he would be making personal appearances for Labatt's. His presence at corporate events was money in the bank.

Alan Eagleson swore his client would be a millionaire by the time he was 30, though he said the insouciant Orr "couldn't care less." Bobby

Orr cared all right, but he showed it in his surprise visits to sick children and in his anonymous donations to charity. He just didn't care much for the corporate image-makers.

Orr saw himself as a jumped-up bondman who had more in common with the guy fixing his Cadillac than he did with the guy buying one. "I was only 14 when I was sold into servitude to Boston, so really, playing hockey is the only thing I've ever done," he said. "Everyone is telling me about how I've changed the game ... Everyone is asking me about money. Hell, I'm just one of the Bruins. I just try to do a job. I'm no different from a mechanic."

A mechanic who was dominating the NHL, perhaps. After following their 1970 Stanley Cup triumph with a first-place finish of a staggering 121 points over a 78-game schedule — the highest point total in NHL history — the Bruins went into the playoffs with a easy confidence. Some critics said that it wasn't confidence at all but complacency coming from a "country club" atmosphere around a team that had forgotten the recent lean years.

The Bruins looked to knock off the Canadiens in the opening round, hoping to intimidate the Habs' rookie goalie, Ken Dryden, a tall, thoughtful law student who leaned on his stick during play stoppages like Rodin's *The Thinker* on skates. As the series progressed, Dryden showed that being intimidated wasn't his strong suit, and the mighty Bruins went down in seven games.

Even so, the smart money in 1972 again had their bets on the Boston Bruins as the team to beat, for they had once again topped the league with 119 points. Phil Esposito again won the Art Ross Trophy; Bobby Orr again won the Norris and Hart Trophies. And in goal they had the solid Eddie Johnston and the irrepressible Gerry Cheevers, who had set an NHL record by playing 33 consecutive games without a loss, and had broken another record in the Bruins' 1970 Stanley Cup triumph with 10 straight wins.

Cheevers was also an original: a gregarious, scrambling goalie who loved to play the horses and had a wit as quick as his glove hand. When a reporter once asked him what a puck looked like when Bobby Hull shot it at him, Cheevers replied, "How would I know? When he shoots I always close my eyes."

Cheevers was famous for his mask, painted with stitches where pucks had hit him — an innovation that came from sloth. One day, while trying to exit early from practice, Cheevers took a shot on his mask that couldn't have broken a beer glass. Staggering off the ice, he was recovering with a Coke in the dressing room when coach Harry Sinden arrived to see the miracle, and ordered him back in net. Cheevers offended, told the trainer to paint a 30-stitch gash on the mask. "Then I went out and told Harry, 'See how bad it is?'"

Cheevers began his goaltending career with a Catholic youth organization team in St. Catharine's, Ontario, when the real goalie failed to show for a game. Cheever's father was coaching, and his son recalled that he "didn't have the nerve to ask anybody else to play goal, so he put me in there. I got beat 17–0."

Cheevers recovered from the experience to win a scholarship to Toronto's St. Michael's College, where he was coached by the legendary Father David Bauer. The priest showed a deep understanding of the pressures on young teenagers and tried to make their passage through the Basilian fathers' hockey academy as balanced as it could be when a star player was spending half his waking time on the ice.

Cheevers backstopped St. Mike's to a Memorial Cup championship in 1961, then did the same for the Rochester Americans, who won the Calder Cup in 1965. That same year Cheevers nearly became a Toronto Maple Leaf, but Punch Imlach decided to go with the age and experience of Johnny Bower and Terry Sawchuk, well aware that he might be making "a terrible mistake" in letting Cheevers go in order to "protect the two best goalies in the world."

Nicknamed "Cheesie" by his teammates, the relaxed goalie wouldn't blame teammates when their defensive lapses hurt his goals-against average, and he also knew the best watering holes in the NHL cities in which to let bygones be just that.

When Cheevers and Orr and Esposito met the Rangers in the 1972 Cup final, the Blueshirts were getting good odds themselves in the sports bars around the continent. With the second-best record in the NHL—10 points back of the Bruins—the Rangers were still trying to shake the Stanley Cup curse of 1940. Indeed, they boasted a superb collection of talent, a crew whom critics said would have easily been the cream of the NHL, were it not for the existence of the Boston Bruins.

Eddie "Go-Go" Giacomin, nicknamed for his bold sorties out of the net, had shared the 1971 Vezina Trophy with teammate Gilles Villemure. With Giacomin's eight shutouts and Villemure's four, the duo had backstopped the Rangers to a 109-point finish, shattering all team records. After enduring the boos of the unsentimental in Madison Square Garden fans who disapproved of his roaming style, Go-Go won over the Monster, whose refrain became "Ehh-deee, Ehh-deee" every time he made a big save.

New York's star defenseman Brad Park had been buoyed — and weighed down — with the praise that he was "Bobby Orr in a Rangers jersey" when the Rangers brought him up from the minors in December of 1968. Three weeks later, in a 9–0 rout against the Bruins, Park scored his first NHL goal and, in his leap of joy, fell flat on his face. It was one of the few embarrassments that he would ever experience on ice.

With a shot clocked at 120 miles an hour, pinpoint-passing skills, and a gift for hipchecking, Park had made the First All-Star Team that season with Bobby Orr. Unlike Orr, Park was not part of a rough and tumble crew who as often as not liked to intimidate opponents with their fists. The Rangers who met the Bruins in the 1972 Final were a finesse team who relied on speed and playmaking, especially that of the GAG Line — an acronym for the goal-a-game trio of Vic Hadfield, Jean Ratelle, and Rod Gilbert, who had combined for 139 of New York's 317 goals that season.

New York wanted to taste Stanley Cup champagne for the first time in 32 years, and they came out charging against the Bruins. The crisis point came in the sixth game, with Boston leading the series 3–2, poised to reclaim the Jug. Once again, Bobby Orr saved the day, breaking a scoreless tie with a graceful pirouette, the puck seemingly magnetized to his stick. Then he came out of the spin and launched the puck onto that elevated plane of reality called a "Bobby Orr goal." It would break the Rangers' will, and though the Bruins took the game 3–0, Orr's goal was the winner. "We played them pretty even," said Vic Hadfield, "but they had Bobby Orr, and we didn't."

While the "Age of Orr" was to be the eternally Golden Age of Boston, coach Harry Sinden, who said that Bobby Orr had been a star since they started playing the national anthem in his first game, now worried that he had a team with one great line, a defenseman, and a goalie. Soon enough, the Bruins didn't even have that.

In the 1972–73 season, Gerry Cheevers jumped to the brand-new World Hockey Association, as did Derek Sanderson and defenseman Ted Green. The Bruins finished in second with an impressive 107 points, but they crumbled in the playoffs. Even though the team would finish first or second in its division for the next three seasons, the Bruins made it to the Cup Final just once.

Around Boston, people had begun to expect more Stanley Cup lustre more often, and the team looked for a solution, as teams are wont to do, in a shake-up. Early in the 1976 season, the Bruins traded the highest scorer the club had ever known to New York in a move that shocked no one more than Phil Esposito.

Bobby Orr had notched 46 goals in the 1974–75 season, his highest total yet. Just as he seem poised to raise himself even higher, his left knee gave out. The next season, injuries allowed Orr to pull on the black and gold for just 10 games, spending the rest of his time under the surgeon's knife, or recovering from it. Orr said, "If I were a horse, they'd probably shoot me."

Instead of shooting their thoroughbred, the Bruins went out and got another. On November 7, 1975, a trade sent Esposito and Carol Vadnais to New York in return for Jean Ratelle, Joe Zanussi, and 26-year-old defensive prodigy Brad Park, who had laboured all his professional career in the shadow of Bobby Orr. Four times between his 1968-69 sophomore season and 1973-74, Park was runner-up to Orr in the Norris Trophy voting. Like Orr, Park could dictate the pace of a game, he could score goals, and he could make teams pay on the power-play. He even had ravaged knees. Now, the man who had tried to carve out his own identity was on the same team as his nemesis, and for a handful of games during the 1975–76 season, Orr and Park patrolled the blueline together: faded glory and shadowed glory joined in chorus for Orr's last hurrah.

Orr could only manage 10 games that season, and the Bruins responded to their star player's trauma by subjecting "The Franchise" to a long contract dispute, which hurt Orr as much as his knees did. So, when a free-agent offer came from Chicago in the 1976 off-season, the man who had built Boston became a Blackhawk.

Or so the story goes. When Orr signed with Chicago on June 9, Alan

Eagleson had made a very public accusation that the Bruins had stopped negotiating with Orr the previous December, when he had re-injured his knee. In fact, the Bruins had been so desperate to sign Orr that, in January of 1976, they had gone so far as to offer The Franchise 18.5 percent of the team. If Orr had taken the offer, it would have made him a "millionaire by the time he was 30," the boast that Eagleson made when Orr signed a "guaranteed $3 million" contract with Chicago.

The reason that Orr didn't accept the Bruins' largesse was because he didn't know about it. Alan Eagleson never told him about the offer because he had cooked up the Chicago deal himself with the Hawks' owner, Bill Wirtz. While accusations of tampering flew that Eagleson, as director of the NHLPA, and Wirtz, an NHL Governor, had offered Orr a contract before his Boston one expired, the deal stood up. So it was with great reluctance that Bobby Orr went to Chicago.

Things didn't change once he was there, for Orr and his family missed Boston. It was the city in which he became both a man and a superstar, and he liked its blue-collar anonymity. In Chicago, he was the prize thoroughbred with the limp, and he hated it.

Orr's final glory came in the 1976 Canada Cup international tournament, where his heart and his head did what his knees could not. Orr was named the Canada Cup's MVP, but aside from the valedictory 1979 Lester Patrick Trophy for services to hockey in the United States, it would be his last award. In 1977 he had his sixth knee operation, then he sat out the entire 1978 season. When he tried to come back, the knee would lock as he started a rush from his own zone, or when he walked to his car after a game.

At his press conference announcing his retirement, the 31-year-old Orr wept and said that his knees couldn't handle the strain of the game anymore. It was a poignant last stand, with Orr still trying to separate his force of will from the force of pain. Orr's knees had long been unable to "handle the strain," but only now Orr was conceding that he and the knees were on the same team. It is the curse of the great athlete, who can only know the crippling irony of being destroyed by the very thing that had once made you great.

Orr's life after hockey was filled with friction, and after a series of failed jobs as an assistant coach for the Hawks, a broadcaster, and an NHL executive, Orr seemed to be one of those athletes who would never adjust to life away from the light and heat of playing the game. Oddly enough, Orr found his way after a very public breach with the man who had helped to bring him fame and fortune.

One of Orr's bitter retirement presents in 1978 was to learn how little he was really worth. Alan Eagleson liked to joke that he and Orr split what Bobby made "90-10" then pause before delivering the punchline: "Orr lives very well on the 10 percent." It turned out to be no joke at all.

Orr had become so dependent on the agent who had guided him through hostile waters that he believed and trusted everything Eagleson told him. It was in his nature, and while hindsight can make anyone seem foolish, Orr was not. He was just duped by a man who duped people for a living.

Orr learned that the tax structure that Eagleson had set up for him was disallowed both by Revenue Canada and the IRS in the United States, something Eagleson knew might happen when he set it up. Orr had to pay much more tax than he had planned for. He also had to take the Blackhawks and their owner Bill Wirtz to court to get the monies owed to him on his so-called guaranteed contract.

In 1980, Orr formally severed his relationship with Alan Eagleson, signing a document saying that his affairs had been handled in a competent manner. Orr signed because he was ruined: he had assets of $454,000, and legal bills and taxes alone of $469,000. In subsequent years, Orr's sale of "Bobby Orr Enterprises'" assets (to Eagleson) and his settlement with the Hawks still barely covered his debt.

It wasn't until 1990 that Orr could bring himself to speak publicly about Alan Eagleson's hand in his ruin, and true to belligerent form, Eagleson told the press Orr had done himself in with profligate living. In the coming years the man who had changed hockey's salary and power structure would be exposed in a crusading investigation spearheaded by Russ Conway, a reporter with the Lawrence, Massachusetts, *Eagle-Tribune*. Eagleson would eventually receive a jail sentence and public humiliation, while the man who had made him would rebuild his life with lucrative endorsements and investments. In the greatest irony of all, Bobby Orr would also add his talents to the world of hockey as the very thing that had made him and nearly destroyed him. He became a player agent.

10

OUR GAME

"I say the best Canadian poet is Phil Esposito, and that is not a joke." So said the famous Russian poet Yevgeny Yevtushenko in the late summer of 1972, and he wasn't speaking about what the Boston marksman was rhyming off between goals. No, the Russian was admiring Espo's emotion in battle, for Canada and the U.S.S.R. were at war on ice. As far as the Canadians were concerned, it was going to be a slaughter.

For nearly a century since James Creighton staged the world's first indoor hockey match in Montreal, Canada had told itself that not only had it given the world hockey, but also it had the world's best players. Hockey was encoded in the genes of those who had survived a couple of centuries' worth of insanely cold winters north of the 49th Parallel and had learned how to play in them. Hockey was our game. What we didn't tell ourselves is that it was our game to lose.

Behind the Iron Curtain of Communist Eastern Europe, other nations had fallen for hockey, too, and thought it was *their* game. The Soviets had seen their first glimpse of Canadian-style hockey in 1932, when a German trade-union team played an exhibition series in Moscow against the Central Red Army Sports Club and the Moscow Selects.

The Soviets easily beat the Germans, and state sports magazines derided this "Canadian" hockey as being too individualistic and primitive compared to *their* game. Canadian hockey didn't allow forward passing the way the Soviets were used to in "bandy"—the field hockey on ice that the Russians had played since the 1890s. Indeed, bandy relied much more on the kind of precise, creative passing for which the Russians would become renowned. This "new" Canadian hockey was seen as "bourgeois," because it encouraged individualism, not teamwork.

Nevertheless, the Soviets knew that hockey was popular in northwestern Europe, and especially popular in their capitalist stronghold of Canada and the United States. In 1939, the Soviet authorities decided that world communism would be easier to impose if they knew how to play the enemy's game. So, hockey was introduced as part of the regimen at Moscow's Physical Culture Institute, where youths selected to bring future athletic glory to the Soviet experiment were tutored in their athletic specialty.

In 1954, just 22 years after they first clapped eyes on the "Canadian" game, the Soviets made their first appearance at the World Ice Hockey Championships — and beat the Canadians 7–2 to win the gold medal. Our game, indeed.

In the summer of 1972, however, Canadians were confident that the blips of history were going to be corrected by Team Canada, the country's mighty professional emissary sent to reclaim national honour in the "Summit Series." It was to be an extraordinary event: professional hockey players from the corrupt West were going to play the finest Soviet amateurs for the heavyweight title of the world. That it was happening at all was due to the fact that a Canadian diplomat could read Russian.

The dark prince Alan Eagleson had been cussing out and backslapping the Soviets since 1969, trying to arrange the eight-game 1972 series, but it was the efforts of Gary Smith, a Russian-speaking second-secretary in Canada's Moscow embassy, who discovered that the Soviets might be willing to face Canada in the game to which they both laid passionate claim.

In the winter of 1971–72, Smith read a piece in the state newspaper *Izvestia* venturing that the Soviet hockey team needed stronger competition. Smith knew nothing so sensitive would appear under the by-line of Boris Fedosov, the sports editor, without approval from on high. Smith called Fedosov, vodka distillers were subsidized, and so began Canadian and Soviet diplomatic efforts to bring the two countries together — at the highest level of international play they had ever known.

While the Soviets had made an international splash after the Second World War with their hockey teams, Canada's international hockey pedigree was older and mightier, befitting its status as the sport's founding tribe. Even so, it wasn't until 1920 that Canada joined the International Ice Hockey Federation, begun in 1908 by Belgium, Great Britain, France, and Switzerland.

Appropriately, Canada took its place at the international party with proprietary zest. The Winnipeg Falcons, winners of the Allan Cup, amateur hockey's Holy Grail, also won an invitation to play on behalf of Canada in the 1920 Olympic Games in Antwerp, Belgium — the first games since 1912. With big Frank Frederickson, a violin-playing First World War pilot, centring the squad, the Falcons outscored their opposition by a combined total of 28–1 to win the gold medal. "We didn't know it, but one of the Americans was sure they'd beat us and offered a good sized bet," Frederickson said later. "Our treasurer never told us, but he took him up on that wager."

The Canadians beat the United States 2–0, and the delighted treasurer presented each Falcon with a new suit of clothes. The Canadian Olympic program's head found out, and was furious. With a puritanical amateurism that seems surreal in comparison to today's "shamateur" games, he wanted to strip the team of their gold medal.

He needn't have worried, for five years later the International Olympic Committee decided that the winter games would be "official" only from 1924 onward. Frederickson's gold medal no longer counted anyway. Still, Canada had indisputably won the first "World Championship."

A robust group of male amateurs carried the banner for Canada at the 1924 Winter Games at Chamonix, France. The Toronto Granites, back-to-back Allan Cup winners, represented Canada under the snowcapped peaks of Mont Blanc, playing their first game on January 28, 1924. Cheered on by W. A. Hewitt, sports editor of the *Toronto Star* and father of nascent broadcaster Foster, as well as coach Frank Rankin, who had starred in the Eaton's department store hockey league in Toronto, the Canadians made short work of Czechoslovakia. Led by Reginald "Hooley" Smith, who would later star with the Montreal Maroons, and Harry "Moose" Watson, a devout amateur and one of the greatest left wingers of his day, the Canadians gave the stunned Czechs a pasting.

A reporter filed his account of the game in a cable back to Canada: "After the face-off, Watson dashed down the rink, passing to McCaffery, who scored. A few seconds later, Watson scored again ... 'Hooley' Smith tallied the next point. Watson and Smith combined splendidly and were responsible for the next two goals." The reporter stopped his transmission there, having figured the folks at home had grasped the general idea of Canada's 30–0 win.

The next day the Canadians beat Sweden 20–0, and on the third day of tournament they embarrassed the Swiss 33–0, with "Moose" Watson scoring 14 goals. In the team's gold medal match against the United States, Harry Watson was knocked out cold just 20 seconds after the opening face-off but came back to score a hat trick in the Canadians' 6–1 triumph.

By the end of the carnage, Canada had scored 110 goals in five matches, allowing only three. Even the stiff upper lip of the *London Morning Post* quivered that "the skill of the Canadian hockey team was the most distinct feature of the 1924 Olympic Winter Games."

In Paris, the victorious Canadians were wined and dined at chic Claridge's Hotel; in London on St. Valentine's Day, the grateful nation gave its hearts to the champions at a dance at British Columbia House on elegant Regent Street. The Prince of Wales himself invited them to pop by St. James Palace, just down the road, for a spot of champagne.

And onward rolled Canada, showing the world that any damn place or thing in the country could serve up a gold-medal team: the University of Toronto, the Winnipeg Hockey Team, the Royal Canadian Air Force Flyers, and the Edmonton Mercurys all proved themselves the best in the world. In the middle of the twentieth century, British Columbia took up the torch, sending teams from the orchard towns of the Okanagan and the industrial settlements of the Kootenays.

The Penticton Vees took their name from three different types of peaches that grew in the orchards around their town—Valiant, Vedette, and Veteran. The Vees had won the 1954 Allan Cup as the country's best Senior Amateur team, and in 1955 they were sent over to Kresfeld, West Germany, to teach the Russians a lesson.

The Soviets had picked up their international hockey aspirations after the Second World War, with mastermind Anatoly Tarasov having nothing less than world domination on his mind. Hockey was a means by which the Soviets could propagate their ideology to the world, and losing wasn't the best way to do this. When the Soviets gave a thrashing to a Lyndhurst, Ontario, crew in 1954 to win their first gold, the Penticton team went to the World Championships loaded for Russian bear.

Led by playing-coach Grant Warwick, a former Calder Trophy winner with the New York Rangers, the Vees were bolstered by a rugged crew of ex-pros and skilled amateurs. The valley boys pounded the life out of the Russians in the gold medal game, while Foster Hewitt relayed the unequivocal 5–0 rout to the folks back home.

The European fans loathed the Canadians' punishing, physical play, and one fan nearly beaned Warwick with an empty (of course) liquor bottle. It didn't matter at all to the Canucks, for they had restored Canada to its rightful place on top of the world. The Vees were national heroes.

Six years later, the wittily-named Trail Smoke Eaters (reflecting that city's industrial cachet as a smelter town) went to the World Championships, where they beat the Soviets 5–1. And in between, another intrepid bunch from the land of orchards actually went *through* the Iron Curtain to take on the Soviets on their own ice.

In November 1958, the Kelowna Packers became the very first Canadian team to play inside Russia, preceded only by a British team the year before. As Okanagan Senior Hockey champs, the Packers had earned their trip the hard way and had impressed amateur hockey's powers-that-be by making it to the Allan Cup finals despite having five of their best players out with injuries.

The wounded Packers fought all the way to the seventh game of that series only to lose to the Belleville McFarlanes. When the Canadian Amateur Hockey Association chose the valiant losers to make the historic trip to the U.S.S.R., the cries coming from Ontario were dire indeed. "All Canada [knows] we aren't sending our best team," said Whitby Dunlops coach Wren Blair. Foster Hewitt, who had seen the wounded Packers' play with tough spirit, now wouldn't even encourage them, saying their chances of winning even a single game in Russia were "fearful."

And dangerous. The boys from Kelowna landed in the middle of a reheated Cold War. Though Soviet Communist leader Nikita Krushchev had announced a de-Stalinization process after the death of the tyrant Josef Stalin in 1953, the detente had come to a violent end in 1956 when Soviet troops brutally crushed an uprising in Hungary. Krushchev was now premier, and the Soviets were not going to tolerate any destructive capitalist ideas. They made sure the team from Kelowna was in no doubt about it.

Upon landing in Moscow, the Kelowna team's plane was at once filled with menacing soldiers. Foreshadowing the diplomatic tribulations of Team Canada in 1972, the Canadian embassy told the Packers their hotel rooms were bugged. Series MVP Bill "Bugs" Jones recalled that the team "slept with the lights on ... we were afraid to turn them off."

Worse, Soviet law could hold any son or daughter of Russian nationals, regardless of their current citizenship. No one in Canada had told the Packers anything about this "law," and now players Greg Jablonski and Russ Kowalchuk — of Ukrainian parentage, and who spoke good Russian — might be locked up behind the Iron Curtain forever. The Soviets confiscated the Canadian duo's passports, and they played the entire series fearing they would never see Canada again.

The Packers were shadowed by KGB agents everywhere they went. Fraternization with their hockey opponents was forbidden, while contact with curious Muscovites was out of the question. To relieve the tension, the team's practical joker Bugs Jones led the Packers into a Moscow music shop, and with the air of virtuoso, picked up an expensive violin and held it to his chin.

Customers crowded in hushed expectation as this burly capitalist product milked the moment, adjusting the tilt of the fiddle, pausing the bow above the strings like Haifetz himself. Then he sniffed the air and shook his head: the winds weren't right. So he calmly put the violin back in its place as his teammates collapsed in laughter.

There wasn't much to laugh about in Moscow, a bleak, concrete monolith whose wide streets were so empty of traffic that they looked more like airport runways. The five-game series, however, had given the hockey-crazed U.S.S.R. something to be excited about, and it had been sold out for weeks.

The first two games were played at the brand new 15,000-seat Lenin Sports Palace, while the players braved a 60,000-seat outdoor soccer stadium to play their last. Soviet coach Anatoly Tarasov was keen to learn from the Packers' boss Jack O'Reilly, and the two men would exhaust their interpreters talking hockey for hours. The Soviets even filmed the Canadian practices, and players like Mo Young suspected the Russians had set their sights higher, recalling "they were getting ready to take on the NHL even back then. We all knew it."

The Packers opened the tour against the Red Army team, who overcame a 3–2 deficit to beat the Canadians. Jack O'Reilly's hot Irish temper blistered the ears of the fans in the Lenin rink as he watched his boys go down, and he promised better things to come. The second game against "Wings of the Soviet" was a tough 1–1 tie, featuring a standout performance from Packers' goalie Dave Gatherum. The third game also ended in a draw, with Moscow Dynamo matching the Canadians' two goals with the help of some familiar "reinforcements"— Soviet players whom the Packers had already seen in the first two games.

Frontliner Mike Durban recalled that the Russians were all in great shape, fast players who played the game "as if it was all designed on a blackboard. But when we knocked one of their guys down, the whole thing fell apart." While the Soviet fans came to appreciate the Canadians' robust, thumping style of play, the "Youths of the Soviet" team — again aided by some balding, thirtysomething "youths"— did not. Though they fought hard against the Canadians, they became the first Soviet team to lose to the visitors, and the Packers' 4–3 victory literally had people dancing in the streets of Kelowna.

Duly inspired, the Packers handed the best team in the Soviet Union, the Moscow Selects, a 5–1 drubbing in the fifth and final game. All Anatoly Tarasov could say afterward was that "the Canadians are magnificent hockey players."

At the end of the last game, the Packers threw their sticks into the crowd and skated around the ice to a standing ovation. The Soviet players would have been grateful for the Canadian sticks. Team captain Jim Middleton, who had also been MVP for the Penticton Vees champs, recalled that when he went to congratulate the "good, hard-nosed, sportsmanlike" Soviet teams in their dressing rooms, he was startled to see how little they had to work with. "Their equipment wasn't the best," he remembered, "and some of the players even had dress shirts on under their uniform sweaters."

The Moscow Selects were not invited to the final banquet honouring the Canadians, but in the middle of the festivities Middleton and

Mo Young received a message from a waiter that the Selects' captain Solegubov was outside in his car. The two Packers slipped out to meet the man, who spoke as much English as they did Russian. So they spoke "vodka" and sat in Solegubov's car, drinking in comradeship. It was the only time the Canadians had off-ice contact with a Russian player, and if Solegubov had been caught, he would likely have been banished from the team. Or worse.

When the Packers left Moscow, they were each stuck with thousands of rubles in expense money they couldn't take out of the country. So, being good Canadian boys, they gave the cash to their chambermaid. "She got down on her knees and kissed our hands," recalled Bugs Jones. "I guess it was like five years' wages and she was an old lady. She cried."

—⁓—

By 1972, Canada's international hockey performances had often caused tears, but they weren't the joyful kind. The national team, under Father David Bauer, had struggled against international competition, managing only three bronze medals between their debut in 1964 and their demise in 1969. There were flutterings of doubt in the Canadian breast about losing a grip on the birthright. After all, said the worriers, the NHL was really just a bunch of Canadians playing each other, and maybe the robotic foreigners really were that good. Now, with the Summit Series showdown, Canada had a chance to send its very best pro players to take on the Russians, and to knock them into the darkest gulag.

However, when Alan Eagleson, executive director of the NHL Players' Association, decreed that the Canadian team would be made up entirely of NHL players, it meant that the squad would be lacking one mightily talented Canadian player who had betrayed his brothers and now would pay for it.

In the summer of 1972, when hockey people weren't talking about the upcoming "Summit Series" they were talking about the World Hockey Association, the domain in which Bobby Hull had committed his unspeakable betrayal of the NHL. Dreamed up by Gary Davidson and Dennis Murphy, two Californians who had also created the American Basketball Association, the World Hockey Association had been formed to give the NHL — after nearly 50 years of being the only game in town—some real competition.

Untroubled by the fact they had no background in hockey and no farm system from which to draw players, the WHA's inventors were simply going to offer current and future NHLers the same thing players had responded to 70 years earlier — a choice. And a lot of money.

The Winnipeg Jets owner Ben Hatskin lured 33-year-old Bobby Hull away from the Chicago Black Hawks with a $2.75-million contract over 10 years to coach and play for Winnipeg. The Golden Jet joined the WHA on June 27, 1972, accepting a cheque for $1 million as his advance. By spending a fortune to put one of the game's brightest lights in its marquee, the WHA had given notice that it would take the fast route to respectability: money.

Superstars and journeymen alike jumped to new teams in Winnipeg, Houston, Los Angeles, Alberta, Minnesota, Chicago, New York, Quebec, Ottawa, Philadelphia, Cleveland, and New England. The NHL responded in the courts, invoking the restrictive "NHL reserve" clause, which had existed since 1917 and made NHL players the league's property for as long as they drew breath. To prove its point, the NHL forbade Bobby Hull to play for Team Canada.

The Canadian public mobilized as if for war. To leave Bobby Hull off the team because he had offended the NHL with his free enterprise was tantamount to treason. The *Toronto Sun* parodied James Bond's *To Russia with Love* with a "To Russia With Hull" billboard campaign and published a message in their paper that people could clip and send to NHL President Clarence Campbell to knock him off his high horse:

"Dear Mr. Campbell," went the plea, as if to God, "I want Bobby Hull to play for Canada. Please do everything you can to see that he does. We've waited for the Russia-Canada series for years, and it would be a disgrace if we don't put our very best team on the ice. There's an NHL rule that each team has to use its very best players. Shouldn't the same rule apply to Canada?"

Canada's dashing prime minister, Pierre Eliot Trudeau, sent a telegram reminding Campbell of "the intense interest which I share with millions of Canadians ... that Canada should be represented by its best hockey players, including Bobby Hull." Trudeau had deplored the lowly state of Canada's international hockey reputation while campaigning for the 1968 federal election. He promised — and initiated — a task force to change this threat to our culture, and from it came the creation of Hockey Canada. Now, in 1972, Pierre Trudeau knew that his chances in the general election that he was soon going to call wouldn't be harmed by appearing on the side of the angels.

Campbell haughtily told the prime minister he had been "misled," and suggested a meeting to "tell him the truth," but the truth was that Campbell's masters, the NHL owners, couldn't afford to let Bobby Hull aboard. The lone renegade was Toronto Maple Leafs' president Harold Ballard (about to go to jail after being convicted of fraud and securities thefts) who tried to convince them otherwise, saying, "I don't give a damn if Hull signed with a team in China. He's a Canadian and he should be on a Canadian team."

The other owners didn't buy it. To let Bobby Hull play would be sanctioning a money-grubbing contract-breaker who cared nothing about the game of hockey. If Hull were forgiven for his defection to the WHA, the NHL would effectively be authoring the demise of its monopoly, and they weren't going to do that, so they symbolically stripped him of his hockey passport in revenge. As Alan Eagleson later said, "My choice was either blow the tournament, or blow Bobby Hull."

So the team that lined up on the hallowed ice of the Montreal Forum against the Soviets on September 2, 1972, did not include Bobby Hull. It did, however, include an A-list of Canadian hockey players: Ken Dryden, Tony Esposito, Brad Park, Guy Lapointe, Serge Savard, Bobby Clarke, Yvan Cournoyer, Rod Gilbert, Vic Hadfield, Phil Esposito, Jean Ratelle, Ron Ellis, Gilbert Perreault, Paul Henderson, and Frank Mahovlich.

The Canadian pros were chest-thumpingly confident that they were the best in the world — they had just never been given a chance to prove it in international play. This arrogance touched every member of the Canadian war machine. When Team Canada scouts went to Moscow in August of 1972 to watch the Soviets train, they quickly wrote off the Soviets' 20-year-old goalie as being a Junior B sieve at best, and Rod Gilbert recalled the scouts telling Team Canada to be prepared to beat the Russians 15–0.

What the Canadian scouts didn't know was that the Soviet team had been split in two, and Vladislav Tretiak was backstopping the weaker half. This division of the kingdom had been done to trick the

Canadians, who figured they'd seen everything after two games — a hubris of classical proportions. The scouts also didn't know that Tretiak was getting married the next day and was gloriously hung over from his stag party the night before. Hockey wasn't the first thing on his mind.

Tretiak had the game in his genes, too, for mother had played bandy, and her son had begun his hockey career at the Children's Sports School of the Soviet Red Army when he was 11 years old. By 17 he was on the roster of the Central Red Army senior club, and from 1969 through 1984 Tretiak would backstop his national team to 10 world championships, three Olympic gold medals, and nine European titles.

In September of 1972, though, Tretiak was just a nervous goalie and a newly promoted lieutenant in the Red Army. Tretiak sustained the *naif* role to reporters, telling them he had honed his catching technique by catching tennis balls off a wall. "I throw them as hard as I can" he said, "and move closer to the wall."

The Canadians hadn't played with tennis balls since they were kids and fully expected to teach the shaky Russian a lesson or two about pucks. That is, if the Soviets ever showed up. At 6:40 P.M. on September 2, the Soviets had not arrived at the Montreal Forum for Game 1, which faced off in 80 minutes.

Teams are usually well into their rituals at the rink hours before game time. A bizarre rumour suggested that a Montrealer, armed with a court order, had impounded the Soviets' equipment at the eleventh hour as the *quid pro quo* for damages inflicted on his car during the 1968 Soviet invasion of Czechoslovakia. When the Soviets finally showed up, another rumour suggested that the divine Pierre Trudeau himself had freed their equipment. So the show — or slaughter — would go on.

The maw of television opened wide for this one, with cameras in place to beam the spectacle to 100 million viewers in Canada, the United States, Europe, the U.S.S.R., and Japan. The series was so huge that 70-year-old Foster Hewitt, then well into "living legend" status, came out of retirement for his last great play-by-play assignment, one guaranteed to end in gilded triumph.

Even the philosopher Pierre Trudeau, jaunty in a summer blazer, his red lapel rose not yet wilting under the oppressive heat, knew as he dropped the ceremonial puck that the logic was unassailable: the

Soviets were going to lose. He even worried that if they lost by too much it could put Canadian-Soviet relations in the deep freeze for years.

The great goalie Jacques Plante, doing colour commentary for Radio-Canada, had once taught Vladislav Tretiak in a goalie clinic, and he showed up in the Soviet dressing room before game time to wish the kid luck. Plante looked into the Russian's impossibly young, open face the way a platoon commander might do to a raw recruit about to make a suicide charge into enemy cannon. Out of pity, Plante drew some diagrams explaining the Canadians' shooting styles on the Soviet's blackboard, then commended Tretiak's spirit to fate.

Thirty seconds after the opening face-off, Plante was squirming in his seat when Frank Mahovlich set up Phil Esposito for Team Canada's first goal. When the Toronto Maple Leafs' Paul Henderson scored again six minutes later, it looked as if the Team Canada scouts' prediction of a 15–0 rout might be conservative.

Oddly enough, the Soviets thought quite the opposite. They were down two goals early. All the pressure was on Canada. And an organ, of all things, was blasting out snatches of weird music that made the fans howl and clap rhythmically like drunken peasants. So the Soviets decided to relax — they had nothing to lose. It was then that the Canadians received a 53-minute lesson in underestimating your opponent.

Dismissing the opposition was something the Soviet coaches had scrupulously avoided. Their head coach, Vsevolod Bobrov, had played on the same line as Soviet hockey's patriarch Anatoly Tarasov in the 1940s, and had as good a hockey lineage as one could get outside the NHL. Where Tarasov had been a steady grinder, Bobrov had been a high-octane dazzler who could seemingly score at will.

When the volatile Tarasov was finally dumped as the Soviet national coach for allowing his players to take $200 a man to compete in two exhibition games before the Sapporo Olympics, Bobrov and his assistant Boris Kulagin took over. They introduced a new system that was almost democratic in its embrace of free will, showcasing players' individual talents rather than breaking them.

Boris Kulagin had also spent two weeks at Maple Leaf Gardens watching every Team Canada practice and intra-squad game, while Bobrov watched films of the 1971 and '72 Stanley Cup playoffs to make book on the Canadian players. When Canada's coach Harry

Sinden and his assistant John Ferguson had pre-Series drinks with the Soviet coaches, they were astonished to discover the "enemy" knew everything about them.

Before Game 1, Bobrov told his nervous players not to panic if the Canadians got a couple of quick goals. His team could skate and pass better than the Canadians could, and if they stuck to the plan that had worked in the past, they would win.

And so they did, scoring the next four goals of the game — one of them shorthanded. The Montreal fans, always known for their loyalty to hockey, rather to a particular team, began to cheer the Soviets. The Montrealers were particularly enamoured by the line of Alexander Yakushev, Evgeny Zimin, and Vladimir Shadrin, who would criss-cross through the dizzy Canadians with blazing speed, notching two goals as they went.

Even though tenacious Bobby Clarke put Canada within one, the Soviets answered back with three, and those dullards who tuned their TVs in late thought a prankster had tampered with the scoreboard, because it read Canada 3, U.S.S.R. 7. But it was no joke.

After the game, the Canadians fled the ice, with only Ken Dryden, "Red" Berenson, and Pete Mahovlich bothering to congratulate the Soviets. The players hadn't been told to shake hands with the Soviets, and they certainly weren't in the mood to make nice. The big, black headline "WE LOST" in next day's Montreal *Sunday Express* spoke to much more than the game. It spoke to who we thought we were.

Canada's coach, Harry Sinden, was stunned. Team Canada had been his self-reclamation project, one that he hoped would show the tight-fisted hockey fraternity his true worth. After he coached Boston to their 1970 Stanley Cup victory, Boston rewarded him by refusing to raise his salary from $22,000 to $30,000. Sinden quit, then boldly lobbied for the Team Canada coaching job, one that he thought was his for the taking.

Sinden had captained the Whitby Dunlops to a 4–2 victory over the Soviet nationals at the 1958 World Championships in Oslo. He was a guy who could win at home or abroad, and the Team Canada management agreed. Now that his team had been embarrassed in the first game, NHL President Clarence Campbell was quick to turn on him. "I simply cannot understand some of Sinden's selections," he carped, while Maple Leaf boss Harold Ballard was characteristically modest, calling the loss "a national disaster."

Team Canada flailed about in humiliation. They were appalled, a little late, at the depth of their own arrogance, and by how thoroughly the Soviets had hoodwinked them. In response, the Canadians would approach Game 2 at Maple Leaf Gardens with a combustible measure of wounded pride. And just in case they weren't motivated enough, Harry Sinden fanned the flames by benching the Rangers' star Gilbert-Ratelle-Hadfield line. The GAG line had been on the ice for three of the Soviet goals in Game 1—one of them shorthanded—and the message was clear: there were no stars on the team anymore.

Only the year before the GAG line had combined for a NHL record 312 points and were at the highest level of the highest level of their sport. When Hadfield heard the trio would be watching the game from the press box, he generously remarked, "Sure I'm surprised, but this is not the time to gripe, this is the time to pull together." The line would not be seen again in the Series.

Tension was off the scale among the players, each now knowing that if the GAG line could be shot at dawn, so could they. Frank Mahovlich smoked a big cigar and wouldn't talk to anyone. Starting goalie Tony Esposito, the younger, introverted brother of Phil, paced the corridors of Maple Leaf Gardens and wouldn't talk to anyone either. In humid, flag-bedecked Maple Leaf Gardens, a nervous sell-out crowd waited to see which team would show up.

Tony Esposito gave the fans hope by making two brilliant saves early in the game, which gave his team confidence. The Canadians remembered how to backcheck, how to pass, and how to think. They also took a particular pleasure in bashing the Soviets at every turn. If the U.S.S.R. was going to win anything, they would do it spitting blood.

After a scoreless first period, Phil Esposito beat Tretiak. Yvan Cournoyer made it 2–0 on a breakaway early in the third period, and the Canadian bench perfumed itself with imminent victory. Four minutes later the Soviets scored, and when Canada followed this with a penalty, the perfume was starting to stink of panic.

The Canadian bench knew what a second loss would mean, and their stomachs churned with fear. It was the kind of classic do-or-be-done moment by which championship teams are measured, and the Canadians fought back. Less than a minute after his team took a penalty, Peter Mahovlich faked the defense and Tretiak out of their Red Army skivvies to score a shorthanded goal. Two minutes later his big brother Frank scored, and Canada had won 4–1. The nation sighed with a kind of Pyrrhic relief. One loss, one win. It proved nothing.

It also proved that the Canadian team was scared to death. They had won, to be sure, but they also done it with thuggish intimidation and stickwork that didn't involve the puck. All across the country you could hear a cracking sound as the "win-at-all-costs" advocates climbing onto the Team Canada bandwagon bumped heads with the "just-play-hockey" proponents climbing off.

On September 6, the third game in Winnipeg began with 30 seconds of silence for the 11 Israeli athletes who had just been massacred by Palestinian terrorists at the Munich Olympics. The Summit Series organizers were criticized for granting the horrible deed just a half-minute of remembrance, as if the urgency of the Canadians' mission was too great to stall further.

This third game was going to be the one to break the "Russian machine," as the popular press robotized the Soviets. One more loss, said the pundits, and the Soviets' wheels would fall off and roll around Portage and Main. It was the Canadian style, however, to dump, chase, and thump, while the Soviets would skate, precision pass, forecheck, backcheck, and look for the chance that could be translated into a goal. If there were robots on the ice, then they seemed to be wearing the home colours.

But the Canadians were winning in Winnipeg. Paul Henderson put Canada up by two goals nearly half-way into the third period, and it looked like Team Canada had found its killer instinct. The Soviets, though, had endured Hitler's Army and Stalin, and they weren't going to quit just because they were losing. Their "Kid Line" of the 21-year-olds Lebedev, Bodunov, and Anisin (sometimes called the "Headache Line" as a pun on the latter's surname), tied the game at four with less than two minutes left. The Series' momentum was up for grabs.

As far as coach Sinden was concerned, the Soviets had all the drive. Canada had run out of gas at the end of the second period, and Sinden knew his boys had nothing left to give. The scheduling of the Series, at a time when the Canadian players would ordinarilly be contemplating training camp, had actually helped the Russians, whose year-round training regimen meant they were always ready. Indeed, Anatoly

Tarasov had inhaled Canadian coach and physical fitness expert Lloyd Percival's revolutionary *The Hockey Handbook*, which argued that year-round training on ice and dry land, that precision drills, better nutrition, and a scientific approach would create winning hockey teams.

The NHL ignored him, but the Soviets did not. While the Canadians had shown up to Team Canada's training camp in their usual summer's-end, beers-at-the-beach flab, the Soviets were fighting fit. And in the third period of that Winnipeg game, the fact the Canadians managed a tie was worthy of celebration. "A tie is as exciting as kissing your sister," said Harry Sinden, afterward but "for the last 10 minutes tonight that hockey game looked like Raquel Welch to me."

Though the Soviets had chances, they couldn't finish the Canadians off, shooting the puck wide, or making one pass too many. The vaunted killer instinct of a champion was still sleeping. The Series was now even at one win, one loss, and one tie each. The only real winner that night was banished Bobby Hull, who was mobbed for autographs while watching the game he couldn't play in.

The last game to be played on Canadian soil took place in Vancouver, and the crowd's mood was belligerently skeptical in a city that traditionally shrugs and looks up at the mountains while its sports teams redirect sewage into English Bay. Even though Vancouver fans were still honeymooning with their new Canucks (blissfully unaware of the mediocrity that would come to define the franchise), the Left Coasters knew trouble when they saw it. And Team Canada heard a smattering of boos in the pre-game warm-up.

The Canadians duly responded to this lack of faith: Bill Goldsworthy, under orders to knock the Soviets around without taking any penalties, took two of them. Then Boris Mikhailov put the Soviets up 2–0 on two almost identical deflections. Just 60 years after the Patricks built their ice palace on Denman Street and introduced the pro game to the Pacific, the Vancouverites had appointed themselves keepers of the national flame. They now booed with gusto.

The young Buffalo Sabres' superstar Gilbert Perreault improved the crowd's mood by punctuating a flashy end-to-end rush with a goal to put Canada within one. Then Rod Gilbert, back in the line-up, tied the game, but the goal was disallowed on the grounds that he had kicked it in. The Soviets answered with two of their own, and that was enough. The Vancouverites mockingly cheered Ken Dryden when he made an "easy" stop, then the Soviets scored again to make it 4–1. The crowd's booing became a roar of scorn.

The Canadian players couldn't understand the booing, as if their individual skills were somehow suspect, but the fans were booing the fact that the team was losing. Bill Goldsworthy tried to atone for his penalties by scoring early in the third period, but the Soviets again responded with a goal. Dennis Hull's tally for Canada with 22 seconds left was like apologizing for failing, and the what-could-have-been only made the loss look much, much worse.

After the game, standing sweaty and wounded before Johnny Esaw's CTV microphone, Phil Esposito defended the honour of his troop. "People across Canada, we tried, we gave it our best," said Espo. "If the fans in Russia boo their players like some of the Canadian fans — I'm not saying all of them — booed us, then I'll come back and apologize to each and every one of the Canadians."

It was an emotional and bold speech that reminded the Canadian public that *their* players weren't robots, either. "Ridiculing us is unfair, but I think it's understandable," Ken Dryden philosophized to the *Toronto Sun*. "Canada had a party set up, and the Russians ruined it." The seemingly invincible Dryden had let in a shocking 12 goals in just two games, and after the trauma of the first game, Dryden character-ized the national mood as "a spasm of self-hatred." Now, if the embar-rassed crew wearing the Maple Leaf were going to win back any self-respect, they were going to do it from afar. The Summit Series was now a road trip.

—◦◦◦—

Before Team Canada faced the Red Machine on its home ice, they had a back-to-back respite with games against Sweden as part of the fifti-eth anniversary celebration of Swedish hockey. The Canadians had long been known to the Swedes as gangsters from frontier Canadian towns who rampaged into the world championships. While every-one else tried to play hockey, the Canadians mauled the Euro-peans, staining the ice with their bloody, smouldering carcasses, then trashing the civility of their host countries with their debauched vic-tory parties.

The Swedes, however, were just as annoying to the Canadians, particularly because they would commit their sneaky little crimes, especially with their sticks, then wouldn't answer to them with their fists. The Swedes would spear and butt end and take Olympic-calibre dives, but they played hockey like guerrillas: sneaking up, striking, then running for cover.

The two-game series in Stockholm was supposed to give the Canadian pros a chance to get used to a big time-zone change, and more importantly, to the larger European rink. Team Canada won its first game on an ice surface so huge that defenseman Pat Stapleton called it "Lake Erie with a roof over it." In the second game, the ice surface proved too big and the Swedish net too small until the last minute, when Phil Esposito scored the tying goal. Team Canada could now claim that, so far, they were "unbeaten" on their road trip.

Which wasn't strictly true, for beating there had been. The games had not been models of gentlemanly comportment, with the Canadians reinforcing their ugly reputation by pummeling the Swedes, and the Swedes living up to theirs with nasty stickwork and diving. Off ice, Team Canada would carry their bellicose spirit into civilian life, snarling at the Swedish media for asking dumb questions such as "Why are you so violent?" and threatening to send to Valhalla any brave barman who refused to serve the carousing players another round of drinks.

But something else happened: Team Canada began to bond. They had heard the rumours that some Canadian fans were rooting for the Swedes and the Russians, preferring their style of play to that of the maple-leaved yobs who played like storm troopers. So, "Team Ugly" closed ranks. The Soviets may have ruined the nation's party, but they hadn't yet ruined the team's party — they were just moving it along to Moscow.

Though Moscow's notion of a party, as summer turned to autumn, was a touch constrained. A joke making the rounds in the Soviet capital beautifully — and bitterly — summed up the conflict between capitalist and communist. A woman marches triumphantly into her sister's apartment and announces: "Guess what I bought today? I've finally found what I've wanted for years. My dream has come true." "What did you buy?" asks her excited sister. "A mink stole" answers the woman. "Ohhh," says the disappointed sister. "I thought you had found a meat grinder."

While mink stoles weren't even remotely within the grasp of the average Soviet citizen, neither were meat grinders, wristwatches, detergents, lightbulbs, toasters, and sometimes even cutlery in September of 1972. According to statistics cited proudly by Premier Alexei Kosygin the year before, just one Soviet family in three had a refrigerator; one in two had a washing machine; and only 124,000 cars were sold to private buyers. Yet a new Zhiguh — a Soviet-assembled Fiat — cost 5,000 rubles, at the time equivalent to $6,000 Canadian. Given that the monthly salary of factory worker and doctor alike was $132, it's easy to see why car sales to a population of 242 million people were so meagre.

The 3,000 Canadian fans who traveled with Team Canada left home confident that they had come from the greatest country in the free world, even if there was that little problem in Quebec. When the Canadians arrived in the U.S.S.R. they saw a society whose cultural identity was officially enshrined in monoliths like the Bolshoi Ballet and Red Square, but one where the consumer goods that defined the "good life" for the average Canadian were hard to find. Even if you could find one, a tough old chicken could cost one-twentieth of a teacher's monthly salary.

For Canadian fans housed with the team at the Intourist, the state-run hotel for foreigners, or for those drinking at the "dollar bars" where foreigners and their hard currency were permitted, it would have been easy enough to see the U.S.S.R. as dripping with History and Culture and a lot of men in uniform. Yet when 300 of those 3,000 Canadian fans (Maurice "Rocket" Richard among them) arrived in Moscow, they found the U.S.S.R. distinctly unwelcoming.

Though they had spent thousands of dollars to cheer on "our boys" against the Communist horde, they soon discovered they had no first-class hotel reservations, nor any hockey tickets. A meeting of the Supreme Soviet had been scheduled for the same time, so hotel rooms and hockey tickets had become scarce, even though the Canadians had paid for both. There had been a "misunderstanding."

With hastily arranged accommodation in Moscow's Minsk and Bucharest hotels, places where regular Soviet citizens were allowed to stay, the "Canadian 300" received an unsentimental lesson in what

Soviet life was really like. At the Bucharest, the Canadians had to share one toilet per floor and a shower room in the basement. Food consisted of black bread and potato soup, sometimes containing a mysterious dark meat which the suspicious correlated to a scarcity of cats.

When the impasse was finally resolved, the Canadians were once again elevated to the status of "privileged foreigners" and feted with champagne and caviar at the Intourist Hotel. They could even watch the hockey games on one of the eight colour TVs in the dining room.

If a Soviet fan could afford the 386 rubles ($463) for a black-and-white television set, and then could actually find one for sale in the state-run GUM department store, they, too, could watch hockey on the tube. "Russia's Foster Hewitt," Nikolai Ozerov, called the Summit Series' play-by-play, delivering dry and politically seasoned commentary from his rinkside seat. It was a perspective definitely more limited than Canadian Foster Hewitt's view from way up high in the gods of Luzhniki Arena.

Indeed, the symbolic value of Ozerov at ice level and Hewitt towering loftily above him would not have been lost on the Soviet viewers. Nor would they have missed the raucous, free-spirited partisanship of the Canadian fans, a display of feeling that the Canadian authorities saw no need to crush with a jackboot.

The Soviets had feelings, too, and hockey was *their* national sport, something no soft, overfed Canadian was going to take from them. Indeed, so passionate were the Soviets about hockey that the number of heart attacks rose in Moscow on the nights the Summit Series was played.

It was this mutual love of a game and the experience of watching it together that led a former Soviet ambassador to Canada, Alexander Yakolev, to claim that the 1972 series was the beginning of *glasnost* and *perestroika*. This was the first time the Soviet people had been exposed to so many foreigners who had not come to do them harm, but who had come to share in their love — even if the Canadians best thought that love would be expressed by walloping the home team.

Team Canada was still not having an easy time of it, even though their wives were along to ease the strain of the road trip. While the Soviets had to play in rinks from Montreal to Vancouver over three time zones in seven nights, the four remaining games in the U.S.S.R. would all be played in Moscow. Even with fatiguing cross-country travel out of the way, the Soviets had other ways to keep the Canadians awake.

Team Canada's specially imported steaks and beer went missing. If the players could even sleep on the hard beds, they were roused by mysterious phone calls in the middle of the night. When they answered, no one was there. It was the same kind of intimidation tactics that the Kelowna Packers had experienced 14 years earlier.

But no Team Canada official had thought to ask the Packers what to expect, and this brave new world was rattling the troops. Stalwart Boston Bruins right winger Wayne Cashman, not one to stand on ceremony, removed all the mirrors from his hotel room and put them in the corridor. It was his sign to the Soviet spies that he was wise to their dirty tricks.

There were troubles within the team. Thirty-five NHL stars had been selected to play, but coach Sinden could only dress 20 for each game. Big NHL egos were wounded, for while you might have been the brightest star at home, you were part of a galaxy here. Vic Hadfield would quit the team, as would Buffalo's Gilbert Perreault and Rick Martin, hinting at an anti-francophone bias.

Then there was the ice at Luzhniki, nearly three inches thick compared to the three-quarters of an inch perfected in Canada, ice that would become lumpy and chipped and hard the longer the game went on. If that wasn't bad enough, there was no glass behind the goal nets, but mesh netting that could ricochet a puck back out to the red line. It might has well have been a road trip to the moon.

Game 5 did not begin auspiciously. When Phil Esposito was introduced, he stepped forward onto the ice and smack onto the broken stem of a carnation given to each player. The Canadian "poet" fell flat on his back, which his countrymen in the stands — easy to distinguish from the brown-and-grey Soviet fans by their colourful clothing — greeted with hoots and applause.

Esposito raised himself onto to one knee and swept the ice with a lavish bow, punctuating it with a kiss to beetle-browed Soviet leader Leonid Brezhnev, sitting high in the stands, scowling and surrounded by grim guards. The Canadian fans cheered harder. Vladislav Tretiak would later say that Esposito's elegant, self-mocking gesture was that of "an artist."

And for two periods, the Canadians were artists indeed, going up

3–0 despite Tretiak's magnificent play, with the young goalie robbing Ron Ellis, Frank Mahovlich, and Paul Henderson. The Canadians had found their legs and their wind in this, their seventh international game, and they began to play with creativity. Their long lead passes put the Soviet defensemen off guard, and the larger ice surface now didn't seem to be an obstacle to the Canadians, but rather a friend, allowing for clever stickhandling and dekes.

Despite going off in the second period with a slight concussion after being tripped into the boards, Paul Henderson put the Canadians up 4–1 at the five-minute mark of the third. The momentum was with them; the game was theirs to lose.

And so they did. Between 9:05 and 11:41 of the third, the Soviets scored three goals to tie the game. When the Canadians gave the puck away in their own end, the Soviets took a lead they would not relinquish with just over five minutes left. Goalie Tony Esposito slammed his stick on the ice; coach Harry Sinden smashed a china coffee cup against the wall after the game. The Soviets now had a choke-hold on the eight-game series with three wins, one loss, and a tie. Canada would have to win three games straight on foreign ice to preserve the honour of the nation.

Up in the stands, 80-year-old Fred "Cyclone" Taylor looked on with dismay. Hockey's first superstar knew that the Canadians had heart— that was never in doubt. The Cyclone worried that the Canadians had become bogged down in their own roughness, drawing foolish penalties and creating in themselves a far worse opponent than the Soviets, whom he admired.

But the old hockey pioneer, along with millions of other Canadians, was looking at things realistically. The Canadians had lost two straight to the Soviets. After a loss like this one, winning a single game would be a challenge; winning three straight as likely as the Soviets renouncing Communism.

Not everyone was ready to give in. Ken Dryden wasn't called "The Thinker" for nothing. He knew he had to change his whole style of goaltending if his last two appearances in net for Team Canada were to mean what he wanted them to.

Dryden was as anomalous a hockey player as you were likely to get in the autumn of 1972, hearkening back to the scholar-athletes of a century earlier. A 25-year-old Cornell University graduate, Dryden had backstopped a Cornell team that lost only four times when he was in the nets for his three college seasons, and his goals against average was a stingy 1.60. Though the property of the Montreal Canadiens, Dryden shocked Sam Pollock in 1969 by rejecting a $50,000 offer to play pro, instead joining Canada's national team. He also turned down Harvard Law School and enrolled at McGill, where he could play goalie with the Canadiens' affiliate Montreal Voyageurs.

Dryden's big league chance came in the first round of the 1971 Stanley Cup finals against the Boston Bruins, where he kept the third-place Canadiens even with the mighty Boston Bruins after two games. When Boston drubbed the Habs in Game 5, however, conventional wisdom said Montreal had to go with their regular goalie, Rogie Vachon, if they hoped to avoid elimination.

Montreal coach Al MacNeil refused to pull Dryden, and Sam Pollock agreed saying "How can we give up on him now?" Dryden and the Habs had the answer, winning the next two games to depose the Bruins' mighty scoring machine. Boston was devastated, but Phil Esposito graciously acknowledged the unlikely victors. "The credit goes to their whole team," he said, "but if one man stood out, it was Dryden."

The Habs and Dryden would go on to win the 1971 Stanley Cup, and Dryden, for all of his scholarly mien, liked winning. There was a pleasing logic to it. Now, once again on the edge of elimination, he thought about what he could do differently against this Soviet juggernaut. When he moved out of his goal-crease to narrow the shooter's angle, Dryden saw that the Soviets would just pass the puck to come up with another angle. So he stayed put, using his size to block the net and taking away the Soviets' passing opportunities. He also stopped kicking out rebounds, as, more often than not, he was kicking the puck onto the sticks of waiting Soviet marksmen.

And if he could change, then so must his team, if they hoped to salvage everything that made them who they thought they were. Team Canada's dumping and chasing wasn't serving them well, and they would have to return to something that no amount of land training or repetitive precision drills could ever teach. They had to play as wild and free as they did when they were kids.

In Game 6, the German officials treated them like juvenile delinquents, guilty by virtue of who they were. When the Philadelphia Flyers' Bobby Clarke was knocked down and had his stick broken by

Valery Kharlamov, a shoving match followed in which Kharlamov threw a punch at Clarke. The referee, Franz Baader, gave Clarke two minutes for slashing, and, when Clarke dared to protest that the call was backward, Baader gave him a 10-minute misconduct. If the Soviets thought this a lucky break, they were wrong.

Selected a lowly seventeenth in the 1969 amateur draft, the 22-year-old Philadelphia Flyer Clarke had many battles to fight, and many things to prove. Indeed, he was scorned by some of his Team Canada mates as that toothless, diabetic kid from hardscrabble Flin Flon, Manitoba. All through Clarke's hockey career predictions of his imminent failure due to diabetes dogged him, and always he had triumphed. This series would be no different.

Clarke soon proved himself a relentless checker, penalty killer, and all-round nuisance who also managed to notch two goals and four assists in the Series. He was also the ultimate team player for whom no mission was too repulsive. When the Soviets' elegant, fearless Valery Kharlamov burned the Canadians for three goals and four assists in five games, Team Canada's enraged assistant coach John Ferguson told Clarke to do something about it.

After the Canadians' elbowing and body smashing only strengthened Kharlamov's play, Bobby Clarke had seen enough. Raising his stick like an executioner, he smote it down so hard on Kharlamov's skate that he broke the Soviet's left ankle. Though Kharlamov finished Game 6 in a state of numbed despair, he would miss Game 7 and could only go at half-throttle in Game 8, shot up with pain-killer.

While "The Slash" is not prominent when Canadians discuss the Series, it's widely remembered in Soviet hockey lore as the act that cemented the Canadians' reputation as thugs. But thuggishness persists because it works: Kharlamov would never score another point against the Canadians.

As far as the European referees were concerned, Team Canada's reputation was not up for disputation. Late in the second period of Game 6, Phil Esposito hit the ice courtesy of big Soviet defenseman Alexsandr Ragulin. Esposito got up, Ragulin knocked him down again, and the referee gave Esposito a penalty for high-sticking.

On the Canadian bench, Harry Sinden screamed at the ref, while his assistant Ferguson shouted, "You chicken-livered Kraut." Canadian towels flew onto the ice, and Team Canada crowded the referee in high-volume protest. They were heard — and received a penalty for interfering with the referee.

Despite the hostile officiating, Team Canada won the game on a second-period goal by Paul Henderson, a quick, low snap shot to cap a three-goal Canadian scoring burst in just over two minutes. Though the Soviets would come within one, the Canadians weren't backing down, fighting for their patch of the ice as if their lives would be worthless should they fail.

Sensing their new-found strength and confidence, Team Canada's 3,000 supporters began a chant that was to grow louder in the next two games: "Da, da Canada! Nyet, nyet Soviet!" Yes, yes, Canada! No, no, Soviets! With one win down and two to go, the Canadians dared to hope. They didn't yet know that hope's name was Paul Henderson.

Snow fell on Moscow on the night of Game 7, a harbinger that depressing winter would come early for the Muscovites. Paul Henderson, a 29-year-old left winger for the Leafs might have considered it a sign that unearthly powers lived in the September air, powers that would put him in the right place at the right time. He was already inclined to believe it.

Henderson was the archetypal Canadian hockey hero who had learned the game on icy roads and frozen ponds, using Eaton's catalogues for shinpads, with his father — a Canadian National Railways worker — as his coach. He owned his first real hockey equipment due to the kindness of his neighbours, the Chin family, who ran Lucknow, Ontario's only Chinese restaurant.

With linemates Ron Ellis (a fellow Leaf) and Bobby Clarke, Henderson's value lay in his hard work, which sometimes paid off in making him a very hot scorer. As a kid Henderson had dreamed of making the NHL, and that dream had come true. Now he dreamed that the Canadians would emerge in triumph over the Red Machine, and *he* was going to make that dream come true.

With nearly two minutes left in a 3–3 tie in Game 7, Henderson took a clearing pass from big Serge Savard near his own blueline. He tried to go though the Russian defense, but they squeezed him out. So he went around them, picked up the puck in the slot, and put it past the only spot Tretiak gave him: a little glimpse of paradise just above the right elbow.

The Canadians in the stands went wild, as if the team had won the whole prize. With the Series tied at three wins apiece and one tie, what had seemed impossible was now within reach: Canada could win everything with just one more victory in the final game. But so could the Soviets.

It has become a commonplace among Canadians who were sentient at the time to ask each other, "Where were you in '72?" Such was the national importance of this series that schoolchildren watched the games on televisions in their classroom, while their parents contributed to a sharp decline in the GNP for those 27 days by slipping away from work to the nearest TV. If you somehow missed the eighth and deciding game through choice, it's best not to mention this to someone who didn't.

On September 28, two passionate hockey nations shored their nerves and sucked in their collective breath as the battle of "Us vs. Them" played out its final act. The first period ended in a 2–2 tie, one marred by a penalty to Jean-Paul Parise for interference. Parise was incensed, for when his alleged interference took place, the Soviet player whom he was checking was in possession of the puck. "You can't be called for interference when the other guy has the puck," he said later, but at the time, he made his point by breaking his stick on the ice.

The West German referee, Josef Kompalla, was just as loathed as his countryman Franz Baader was by the Canadians, who nicknamed them "Badder and Worse." Team Canada had been told Kompalla would not be back to give them any more trouble in the Series, and here he was giving the Minnesota North Star a 10-minute misconduct.

Parise went berserk, skating up to the referee with his stick poised to separate the West German's head from his body. He repeated the gesture, and the official tossed him from the game. The Canadians jostled the referee, while the Canadian bench launched two chairs onto the ice. As the Canadian fans chanted "Let's go home, let's go home," an unlikely diplomat named Alan Eagleson scuttled over to the Canadian bench to calm things down.

With one period left in Game 8, the Canadians were down 5–3, and many people had now written them off as done. Canadian hockey would no longer be second to none — it would just be second. And even if they managed a tie, they would still be second.

Alan Eagleson had learned the awful news during the intermission: the Soviets were going to declare themselves victors even if Canada rallied to tie them. Under international rules, the Soviets would win on aggregate goals, despite the fact the teams would have identical records if the Canadians tied. This was not the kind of news to placate Eagleson's competitive heart, and he stormed into the Canadian dressing room to let them know the jig was up.

Nobody on Team Canada came out in that third period playing for a tie. Phil Esposito — now a cultural icon to the Soviets, who would say "Feel Esposeeto" as if describing an opposing army — started the climb to glory. At 2:27 of the third period, Esposito whacked home his own rebound. Team Canada shifted up a gear, calmly, with purpose, and 10 minutes later, Esposito shook off two Soviet players to let loose a blast at Tretiak. The rebound popped out to Yvan "The Roadrunner" Cournoyer, and with seven minutes left, the game was tied.

From where Alan Eagleson sat in the front row at centre ice, he saw neither the referee's arm signal a goal, nor the flash of the red goal light. This had happened before, when Paul Henderson scored the winner in the previous game. Eagleson was not going to let any dirty Russian trick stop his team's momentum now, so he would do what he did best: raise hell.

Leaping from his seat over a five-foot wall, Eagleson found himself in a phalanx of startled Soviet police. There was bumping, then shoving, then suddenly, Eagleson was being given the bum's rush by half a dozen military cops.

The Canadian players were still celebrating the goal, but Pete Mahovlich saw what was going on, and so did Gary Bergman. Charging to Eagleson's defense, the players soon had with them Wayne Cashman and Harry Sinden and Bill Goldsworthy fighting off the police.

Bewildered by this surreal assault by Canadians with hockey sticks, the police gave up their prisoner. Once the players had rescued Eagleson, they led him across the ice to the safety of the Canadian bench. In a gesture that summarized all the things wrong and all the things right about Team Canada, Eagleson raised his middle finger in salute to the Soviet authorities. Though it was one more nail in the diplomatic coffin, there were doubtless many Soviets watching that game who felt exactly as Eagleson did. Moments after his gesture, police reinforcements flooded the arena in case any disgruntled Soviet fans tried to repeat it.

The Soviet players, tired and rattled, were now more than willing to settle for a tie. Canada, fuming, blood in their nostrils, were not. In the third period alone, Team Canada outshot the Soviets 13–5. But they weren't finished. They wanted to win.

With less than a minute to play, Harry Sinden wanted to send out the Clarke-Henderson-Ellis line, but Esposito's line wouldn't come off. After shouting at him a biblical thrice, Henderson finally lured Mahovlich off, but Esposito and Cournoyer stayed out. Cournoyer fired a long diagonal pass just behind Henderson. With the puck loose in the Soviet corner, Phil Esposito beat three Soviet players to it, then fired it at Tretiak from 12 feet out.

There was a rebound, and now Paul Henderson, miraculously alone in front of Tretiak, could win in it all for Canada. He shot the puck, and Tretiak made a pad save going down. The puck came back to Henderson and he shot again. Thirty-four seconds later it was all over. Canada had won.

The country had gone with their team on an emotional trek of such steep valleys and sharp peaks that the national spirit was as elated as the players. And just as exhausted. Even though many Canadians were disgusted at this display of "no prisoners" hockey and chose to see the conquering heroes as men who had lost an awful lot, the rest of the country was united as if they had won a war. People packed Montreal's Dorval airport to greet the team; they lined up in the rain in Toronto's Nathan Phillips Square to cheer their heroes. Phil Esposito kept the emotional promise he made in Vancouver to apologize to the country. "You people have proved me wrong, he told the crowd. "You've proved the rest of us wrong." No one cared about his apology now. All they cared about was that everyone wearing the maple leaf had been right.

—⁓—

The legacy of the 1972 Summit Series resonates to this day. The Soviets, determined to win their ideological battles on the ice, sent even more of their best hockey players beyond the Iron Curtain. Canada learned the importance of extensive physical training and of territorial and puck control. Keeping control of the puck was more effective than dumping it and chasing, just as keeping the ball in soccer allowed a team to dictate play and increased their chances of scoring.

From the Canadians, the Soviets learned how to work the puck along the boards and in the corners, and the need for bigger defensemen to stop the likes of Phil Esposito from parking in front of their net. The Series would be a "win" for hockey.

A tradition had been established between Canada and the U.S.S.R., one that would see them compete against each other every few years in the Canada Cup, which the Soviets would finally win in 1981. Vladislav Tretiak, then 29 years old, allowed only eight goals in six games and was named the Series' most valuable player.

There had even been talk that Tretiak might come to play in the NHL, after the Red Army lieutenant volunteered that he would like to be a Montreal Canadien. The Soviet authorities were livid. "I told them I was misquoted by Western journalists," Tretiak said later. "After that I always said I belong to the Soviet people and the Red Army team. You understand I was not telling the truth. I would have loved to play in Montreal. That is my city."

Glasnost came too late for Tretiak to see his wish come true, but by the end of the 1980s, other Russian hockey players were slipping through the cracks in the Iron Curtain and into the NHL. Sergei Priakin, a big right winger seen by North American fans in the 1987 Canada Cup, was the first Russian to break into the NHL when he suited up for Calgary for two games in the 1988–89 season. The following season, Sergei Makarov joined him as a Flame, while Makarov's fabled, high-flying "KLM" linemates, Igor Larionov and Vladimir Krutov, abandoned the red and white of the U.S.S.R. for the orange, yellow, and black of the Vancouver Canucks.

From then on, Russian players became a given on NHL teams, and they have given the league some of its most exciting talents. Sergei Fedorov, Pavel Bure, and Alex Mogilny have all entered the NHL superstar class, rubbing shoulders with fellow former Soviets, as well as with their Czech, Slovak, Swedish, and Finnish contemporaries. Indeed, any NHL arena is now a place where young Canadian or American fans are just as likely to be wearing a jersey celebrating Jaromir Jagr or Teemu Selanne or Mats Sundin as they are to be sporting those of Joe Sakic or Steve Yzerman or Paul Kariya.

More than a century and a quarter after James Creighton put a roof on winter in Montreal, hockey had become an international sport that has risen (or fallen, depending on your point of view) to a level of spectacle unimaginable to Creighton, his 17 colleagues, and those 40 curious spectators who turned out to watch their revolution on March 3, 1875.

James Creighton would most certainly recognize today's game, and he might not even be all that surprised by the noise and light surrounding it. After all, Creighton lived until 1930, long enough to witness the birth of professional hockey in the United States and then in Canada; the pre-eminence of the NHL; the rise of a flashy francophone team in once stolidly Anglo Montreal; and many disputes over money and violence.

Indeed, once Creighton had roofed the game, its progress toward commercial product was swift. Less than two decades after his experiment, hockey had its greatest prize in the Stanley Cup, and teams from all corners of the vast Canadian winter wanted a piece of it, their dreams made possible by the transcontinental railway. A little more than a decade after that, pro leagues on both sides of the Canada–U.S. border were chasing the Jug with a vengeance, not only for reasons of pride, but for the money it would bring to their fancy new covered rinks.

And underneath those roofs, a star system quickly rose up, as did player salaries, and competition heated to bag the riches that Lord Stanley's silver bowl promised. Teams lived and died by the marketplace, and those born in the champagne optimism of the 1920s and who survived the dustbowl '30s soon found themselves stewards of a six-team league for more than three decades. This place underneath premier professional hockey's roof was an exclusive place indeed.

The "Golden Age of the Original Six," though in reality an iron-fisted cartel, holds a prime place in hockey's collective imagination because it is now sufficiently distant to have become romantic. Those rinks and players of yore have a majesty about them because they are sculpted by time to their most heroic dimensions, unbothered by crumbling walls or salary arbitration. Indeed, while the rinks from hockey's earliest years were either leveled by progress or eaten by flame, those that came after lasted longer, and they defined hockey for generations.

Even so, they, too, have met undignified ends at the wrecker's ball. "Tex" Rickard's Madison Square Garden, the Chicago Stadium, the Boston Garden, and the Detroit Olympia — all are gone. The Montreal

Forum and Maple Leaf Gardens now stand as museum-pieces-in-waiting, while their former tenants ply the ice of the Air Canada Centre in Toronto and the Molson Centre in Montreal, the latter jokingly nicknamed "The Keg" after its patron's beer containers, and where the once-proud Canadiens more often than not resemble a beer-league team.

NHL pragmatists would argue that the decline of a dynasty such as that of Montreal is league parity at work, and not the loss of mystique. But a loss it is. When current Maple Leafs' coach Pat Quinn was asked, upon the opening of the swank new Air Canada Centre, if he feared losing the blue-collar fan, his reply was unblinking. "We've already lost the blue-collar fan," he said, well aware of the small mortgage the average worker would have to take out in order to take his or her nuclear family to an NHL game. "I'm worried about the white-collar fan."

The white-collar fan would do well to have more such worriers, judging by the extravagant lengths to which the builders of new arenas have gone in order to attract the "corporate" fan. Since 1992, the NHL has seen more new homes built for its members than any of the other major sports leagues, with 23 of the 30 NHL teams plying the ice in swank new digs by 2001, places that make the old rinks look like what hockey players affectionately call *any* rink: "barns."

The latest zenith in the lavishness sweepstakes comes in Los Angeles, where the office-supply giant Staples paid $100 million for the right to slap its name for 20 years on L.A.'s new downtown rink, thus sharing the lustre of a $375-million privately financed "entertainment castle." Though Staples Center has a population base of 9 million people to draw on, it aimed its charms at about .004 percent of them, with 160 three-storey private seats that will set back a corporation anywhere from $197,000 to $307,500 a year, as well as the exclusive "Grand Reserve Club" for 200 members at $10,500 a head annually, a sanctuary featuring an indoor-outdoor fireplace (essential in the L.A. winter), a wine cellar, and a humidor with 36 drawers for cigars. The L.A. Kings seem to be expecting that *real* kings will show up at their games.

The force of public emotion for hockey has changed, too. The powerful sense of cultural injustice that moved Montrealers to riot in defense of their martyred hero — their Rocket — had morphed, by the time of the Habs' most recent Stanley Cup win in 1993, into a riot of drunken looting, with no principles at stake whatsoever. And the 1994

Stanley Cup Riot in Vancouver was no more than a small group of thugs feeding off the despair of a city that could almost taste Stanley Cup champagne after 80 years of waiting, and then had to watch the victorious New York Rangers toast the departure of their Curse instead. The Vancouver riot wasn't a call to arms on behalf of a symbol, but rather it was a cadre of drunken hooligans ruining the impromptu street "wake" that Vancouverites were trying to observe.

None of which is to say that the hockey pioneers should be spinning in their graves at today's climate of cynical corporate glitz, on-ice neurological mayhem, and fan discontent. The pioneer players all knew the price of a buck, they all saw horrific violence on ice, and, without the cushion of multimillion-dollar salaries, they heard all about fan discontent, because they had to hold down jobs with those same fans in the off-season.

No, they would probably say that hockey is as it ever was, except bigger and brighter and richer and louder, and its players have more consonants in their surnames as they chase pucks in places not even the team prankster would have thought possible, places like Miami and Carolina and Disneyland.

Yet when the World Cup of Hockey (now no longer the Canada Cup) comes around, and players are taken outside of their petty club concerns and thrust onto the larger world stage, hockey is reduced to its essence. Then, the emotion that James Creighton and those who followed him have generated under all those roofs of winter comes back as crisply as newly sharpened skate blades on freshly ploughed ice.

Hockey means as much now as it did to Cyclone Taylor's 1915 Vancouver Millionaires, and to dead Howie Morenz's weeping fans in 1937, and to those Team Canada players who returned in 1972 with the nation's pride battered but restored. For even though hockey fans argued then about skill versus kill, and argue now about the neutral zone trap, the game that Creighton pioneered and which generations made into a sport is one that still can bring a town or city to a standstill, with joy or with sorrow. It means the chance to escape into what is now an international drama and, with luck and skill and sweat, write an ending in which the good guys win. But most of all, it means the sheer joy of finding heat and light in the coldest, darkest season, under hockey's mighty winter roof, where the unlikely union of ice and steel and wood and rubber and heart can make magic.

INDEX